Reading and Understanding the

FINANCIAL TIMES

Updated for 2010–2011

Kevin Boakes

**Financial Times
Prentice Hall**
is an imprint of

Harlow, England • London • New York • Boston • San Francisco • Toronto
Sydney • Tokyo • Singapore • Hong Kong • Seoul • Taipei • New Delhi
Cape Town • Madrid • Mexico City • Amsterdam • Munich • Paris • Milan

Pearson Education Limited
Edinburgh Gate
Harlow
Essex CM20 2JE
England

and Associated Companies throughout the world

Visit us on the World Wide Web at:
www.pearsoned.co.uk

First published 2008
Second edition published 2010

© Pearson Education Limited 2008, 2010

ISBN 978–0–273–73181–8

British Library Cataloguing-in-Publication Data
A catalogue record for this book is available from the British Library

Library of Congress Cataloging-in-Publication Data
Boakes, Kevin.
   Reading and understanding the Financial times / Kevin Boakes. — 2nd ed.
       p. cm.
   ISBN 978-0-273-73181-8 (pbk.)
   1. Corporations—Finance. I. Financial times (London, England) II. Title.
   HG4026.B596 2010
   338.4'3—dc22

                                                              2009039558

10 9 8 7 6 5 4 3 2 1
13 12 11 10 09

Typeset in 9/13pt 2Stone Sans by 3

Printed in Great Britain by Henry Ling Ltd., at the Dorset Press, Dorchester, Dorset

The publisher's policy is to use paper manufactured from sustainable forests.

To my Mum and Dad with thanks for all their support.

Contents

Contents

Contents

Contents

About the author

 After graduating with a degree in Economics and an MSc from the London School of Economics, Kevin Boakes started his working life on the bond trading desk at Greenwell Montagu Gilt-edged, which is now part of HSBC Investment Bank. As their Chief UK Economist he was responsible for giving on the spot advice to bond traders as soon as economic stories hit the news screens. He regularly contributed articles to newspapers including *The Times*, *Observer* and *Guardian* and appeared on the BBC's *Money Programme* and the *Financial World Tonight*. In the late 1980s he decided to make a radical career change and left the City to join Kingston University, initially in the Economics Department and then at Kingston Business School where he is currently a Senior Lecturer in the School of Accounting and Finance. He teaches both undergraduate and postgraduate courses in Finance and International Financial Markets. In addition to his academic work he has run a number of economics and financial market training courses for various investment banks.

Preface

What this book does

This text incorporates a selection of articles from the *Financial Times* that relate to some of the most important issues in the world of corporate finance. The main focus of the book is to provide a brief analysis of each article, explaining how the subject matter reflects a topic which will form a key part of any corporate finance course.

The articles have been selected because:

They include substantial corporate finance content in addition to key concepts and/or specific financial market terms that need to be explained to those unfamiliar with this area of finance. They contain topical subjects and at the same time include themes that recur regularly in the *Financial Times* so that, once the reader has worked through the analysis in the book the *Financial Times* will become more accessible. The reader acquires transferable skills, which they can then use when they engage with corporate finance in any context such as television, radio reports, the internet or finance journals. Readers will learn how financial theory relates to the reality of the business world.

It provides the opportunity for self-study

This is a book that can be used by students with minimal or even no formal teaching input. As a result it is ideal as a basis for self-study ahead of normal teaching activities such as seminars, lectures and exams.

A useful classroom resource

The book is also invaluable for lecturers to use as part of their teaching programme. For each article a series of activities is included that can be set as seminar work for students to complete ahead of class. Of course it is also designed to be a useful resource for professionals working in financial markets, who will be able to utilise the book to link the practice to theory.

The main features of the book are:

Key terms

The specialised financial terms used in each article are clarified. The style of this explanation of terms is different to the standard approach of academic textbooks since practical analogies are drawn to help students from a variety of backgrounds understand the concepts.

An insider's view and self-review questions

Through a combination of practical and academic skills the author aims to bring these *Financial Times* articles to life in a user-friendly way. Linked to each article is a selection of self-review questions, which the reader can use independently to test their understanding, or they can form the basis for further discussion activities in class.

Linking this textbook to corporate finance textbooks

This book is designed to be used alongside a number of standard corporate finance textbooks. I have provided, therefore, a short guide to each topic at the start of every chapter and links to the main books that are generally used on corporate finance courses at the end of each chapter.

Research

At the end of each case I have included a section that offers the reader some useful suggestions for further reading. These references always include the relevant chapter and sometimes even particular pages from the chosen texts. Where relevant I have also suggested the topics that are best covered in this particular book.

Data exercises and web-based activities

In most cases a data exercise is also integrated which requires the reader to obtain and analyse specified data from the *Financial Times* that relate to the relevant topic. Where appropriate, students are directed to a web-based activity, which will require them to apply their newly acquired knowledge and to undertake further research or reading.

Online web content

This book is supported by a dynamic website at **www.pearsoned.co.uk/boakes**, which contains links to useful financial websites and additional topical content. It is my intention to update some of the issues discussed in this book as well as looking at some new stories as they emerge.

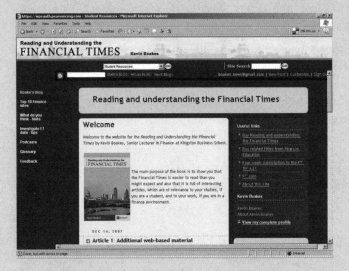

And finally some Podcasts

Finally, there will be a number of support podcasts with analysis of the key issues for a selection of the articles. This will be an alternative method for the reader to understand the analysis of the *Financial Times* articles.

This multi-strand approach within the one textbook recognises that students today are familiar with, and indeed prefer, learning through a variety of media. They no longer want to be restricted to the written word and benefit from the consolidation of material through podcasts and web resources.

The podcasts

If you go the website that supports this book you will be able to download 30 podcasts in MP3 format. Each one provides a short audio summary of the main issues relating to each article.

I recommend that you start by reading the *FT* article and my analysis. Then you should listen to the podcast to hear the key points being re-enforced. It is a good way to revise the key points in each topic.

The following podcasts are available to download at the book's website (you can also access them on iTunes):

- 1: Poor communications puts Sports Direct off track
- 2: Activist shareholders expect change at LogicaCMG
- 3: Sir Stelios spells out fears for easyJet
- 4: Bernanke to give a taste of more transparent Fed
- 5: How long can the good times last?
- 6: JPMorgan acts to reduce risk
- 7: Bank to give better guidance over rates
- 8: Surprising US job creation data rally stock markets and dollar
- 9: Bond yields spark credit concerns
- 10: Athens prepares 50-year bond issue worth €500–1bn
- 11: Convertibles stage a return to fashion
- 12: Record samurai deal by Citigroup
- 13: Flight to liquidity pushes eurozone bond yields apart
- 14: MyTravel shareholders offered 4% in £800 debt-to-equity restructuring
- 15: Blacks Leisure falls into the red
- 16: UK Investors dig in over pre-emption rights
- 17: IPO values Hargreaves at £750m
- 18: Valuing Sainsbury's
- 19: Woolies investor opposes sale
- 20: Stock splits: time to query decades of dogma
- 21: Boots provides takeover acid test
- 22: 3i chief quits following steep fall in shares
- 23: Shareholders taking a stand on handouts
- 24: De La Rue pays special dividend
- 25: Discussions unlikely to yield white knight
- 26: Poison pill's strength under analysis
- 27: Exporters curse dollar's drag on profits
- 28: Facing down the threat of tighter rules
- 29: The demise of Northern Rock
- 30: The rescue of Citigroup

A message to readers . . .

I really hope that you will enjoy your corporate finance course whether you are undergrad-uates, postgraduates, just undertaking a short course or have already started your career in the financial services industry. It is a very dynamic subject and, unlike many other courses at University, your studies can so easily be related to real-life events. The *Financial Times* is a great place to start to learn more about corporate finance in practice. You might find it difficult to read at first but it does get easier as you learn more about the subject. I hope this book will give you some guidance on how best to analyse relevant articles. Once you have done a few of the cases here, try to do your own. Look for an article on a subject that you have studied and then try to write a short review of the key points.

In addition, you should read the business sections of other newspapers, listen to the radio and watch relevant TV programmes. The BBC broadcasts an excellent early morning business programme on Radio 5, called *Wake up to money*. It looks at all the current finance stories with expert guidance from some of the top names in the city. There is no need to get up too early as you can download a podcast from the BBC's website. This is an invalu-able resource.

I hope you like the new edition of this book and I would like to wish you all the best with your studies and your future career.

Best regards
Kevin
k.boakes@kingston.ac.uk

A message to teachers . . .

An attractive feature of this subject is that it is so easy to relate the academic theory to current practice. As a starter activity I begin each lecture by spending a few minutes analysing an article that fits in with the topic that we are doing that week. The students seem to really enjoy this aspect of the course and it creates a positive working atmosphere for the rest of the session. In seminars I also try to combine some theory work with more practical exercises. Finally, in the examination paper I include extracts from *Financial Times* articles which require the students to provide relevant analysis. There is no doubt that the students find this challenging but it is a clear signal that it is a key skill which they need to acquire.

I hope you will enjoy the latest edition of the book and that you will be able to use it as part of your teaching programmes. I have added several new articles to update some of the key topics. I am sure that there are many other topics that you would have liked to see included in this edition. This is inevitable as the aim was still to keep the book fairly short, therefore I could not cover every available subject. If you see a good article that you think would be appropriate for a further edition, perhaps you could send it to me?

If you have any comments, ideas or suggestions please e-mail me at:

k.boakes@kingston.ac.uk

Thanks so much for using the book and I hope you continue to enjoy teaching corporate finance.

Best regards
Kevin

Acknowledgements

Many thanks to Andrea Dunhill, the Head of Accounting and Finance at Kingston University, for giving me her full support with this project. I would also like to thank my good friend and colleague, Brian Tan, for his assistance with the new edition.

I would also like to record my thanks to the many staff at Pearson Education who have worked on this second edition. It was a pleasure to work again with the book's editor, Ellen Morgan. She is always so approachable and enthusiastic and as a result made the whole writing process so straightforward.

To my wife Sue thanks for giving me her love and support. You are so amazing and so beautiful. And finally thanks to my daughters Katy and Rachel who have developed into wonderful young women in the blink of an eye. I am so very proud of what you have achieved so far and I look forward to seeing your many future successes.

Publisher's acknowledgements

We are grateful to the Financial Times Limited for permission to reprint the following material:

Page 5: Sports Direct warning stumps investors, *Financial Times*, 27 April 2007 (Killgren, L. and Blackwell, D.); 9: Logica's chief quits in wake of warning, *Financial Times*, 28 May 2007 (Blitz, R.); 10: Investors expecting change at LogicaCMG, *Financial Times*, 30 May 2007 (Palmer, M.); 15: Sir Stelios spells out fears for EasyJet, *Financial Times*, 24 November 2008 (Done, K.); 24: Bernanke to give a taste of more transparent Fed, *Financial Times*, 14 February 2006 (Balls, A.); 32: How long can the good times last? Bankers cautious despite bids and bumper bonuses, *Financial Times*, 27 November 2006 (Thal Larsen, P.); 36: JPMorgan to cut prop trading desk, *Financial Times*, 4 November 2008 (Guerrera, F., Baer, J. and Grant, J.); 40: Bank to give better guidance over rates, *Financial Times*, 3 May 2007 (Giles, C. and Daneshkhu, S.); 49: Surprising US job creation data rally stock markets and dollar, *Financial Times*, 2 June 2007 (FT Reporters); 54: Bond yields spark credit concerns, *Financial Times*, 8 June 2007 (Mackenzie, M., Beales, R. and Chung, J.); 55: Bond market sell-off, *Financial Times*, 8 June 2007 (Lex Column); 64: Athens prepares 50-year bond issue worth €500–€1bn, *Financial Times*, 18 January 2007 (Hope, K.); 70: Convertibles stage a return to fashion, *Financial Times*, 8 February 2007 (Turner, D.); 75: Record samurai deal by Citigroup, *Financial Times*, 6 September 2005 (Sanchanta, M.); 79: Flight to liquidity pushes eurozone bond yields apart, *Financial Times*, 27 February 2008 (Chung, J.); 90: MyTravel Shareholders offered 4% in £800m debt-to-equity restructuring, *Financial Times*, 14 October 2004 (Garrahan, M.); 94: Blacks Leisure falls into the red, *Financial Times*, 4 May 2007 (Braithwaite, T. and Urry, M.); 98: UK investors dig in over pre-emption rights, *Financial Times*, 22 October 2007 (Burgess, K.); 109: IPO values Hargreaves at £750m, *Financial Times*, 12 May 2007 (Spikes, S. and Saigol, L.); 110: Hargreaves Lansdown soars on debut, *Financial Times*, 16 May 2007 (Spikes, S.); 114: Valuing Sainsbury's, *Financial Times*, 17 May 2007 (Lex column); 118: Woolies investor opposes sale, *Financial Times*, 20 November 2008 (Braithwaite, T.); 126: Stock splits: time to query decades of dogma, *Financial Times*, 8 April 2007 (Authers, J.); 134: Boots provides takeover acid test, *Financial Times*, 21 April 2007 (Hughes, C., Braithwaite, T. and Taylor, A.); 141: 3i chief Yea quits following steep fall in shares, *Financial Times*, 29 January 2009 (Arnold, M.); 150: Shareholders taking a stand on handouts, *Financial Times*, 19 May 2007 (Hughes, C.); 155: De La Rue pays a special dividend, *Financial Times*, 23 May 2007 (Griggs, T.); 162: Discussions unlikely to yield white knight, *Financial Times*, 2 February 06 (Sanchanta, M.); 163: Mittal goes on Arcelor charm offensive, *Financial Times*, 31 January 2006 (Hollinger, P.); 167: Poison Pill's strength under analysis, *Financial Times*, 15 June 2007 (Nakamoto,

M.); 177: Exporters curse dollar's drag on profits, *Financial Times*, 14 May 2007 (Hughes, C.); 184: Facing down the threat of tighter rules, *Financial Times*, 20 June 2007 (Mackintosh, J.); 194: Fresh turmoil in equity markets, *Financial Times*, 11 August 2007 (Guha, K., Mackenzie, M. and Tett, G.); 196: Repo market little known but crucial to the system, *Financial Times*, 11 August 2007 (Mackenzie, M.); 197: Growing sense of crisis over interbank deals, *Financial Times*, 5 September 2007 (Tett, G.); 200: Bank throws Northern Rock funding lifeline, *Financial Times*, 14 September 2007 (Thal Larsen, P. and Hume, N.); 203: Brown saw no other option, *Financial Times*, 18 February 2008 (Parker, G. and Thal Larsen, P.); 205: US government agrees to take biggest stake in Citigroup, *Financial Times*, 28 February 2009 (Guerrera, F. and Beatte, A.).

We are grateful to the Financial Times Limited for permission to reprint the following figures:

Page 11: From Investors expecting change at LogicaCMG, *Financial Times*, 30 May 2007 (Palmer, M.); 34: From How long can the good times last? Bankers cautious despite bids and bumper bonuses, *Financial Times*, 27 November 2006 (Thal Larsen, P.); 71: From Convertibles stage a return to fashion, *Financial Times*, 8 February 2007 (Turner, D.); 135: From Boots provides takeover acid test, *Financial Times*, 21 April 2007 (Hughes, C., Braithwaite, T. and Taylor, A.); 151: From Shareholders taking a stand on handouts, *Financial Times*, 19 May 2007 (Hughes, C.).

In some instances we have been unable to trace the owners of copyright material, and we would appreciate any information that would enable us to do so.

Introduction to corporate finance

The Companies and Markets section of the *Financial Times* is a fantastic source of information about the trading performance of individual companies and their interaction with financial markets right across the world. If you want to learn about finance you need to be reading and understanding this part of the paper. You will find that the first few pages are devoted to companies, then the emphasis shifts increasingly to financial markets. A particularly strong section is the one titled 'Markets and Investing' which is just inside the back page. It is here that you will find clear explanations of all the new and innovative financial products that the banks have been busy developing. If you had been reading this section in 2005 and 2006 you would have seen discussion of financial market instruments such as structured investment vehicles, collaterised debt obligations and mortgage-backed securities. Shortly afterwards they became an integral part of the credit crisis that started in 2007 and soon swept through financial markets with great dramatic force.

Before we can get into the minutiae of corporate finance we should start by examining the role of finance both from within individual companies and from the perspective of the economy as a whole. For all companies the finance function is the link between them and the world's financial markets. It enables them to undertake new capital-raising initiatives both in the form of extra equity finance (this is in the form of new shares) or extra bond finance (this is borrowed money).

In corporate finance it is usual to start by examining the role of the financial manager within a company. Thie financial manager is the most senior individual manager involved in the finance function. He/she will normally be a director with a seat on the company's main board. We can split their main activities into four main areas:

1. **They will be in charge of the company's financial planning process**. This will involve the preparation of a clear financial plan to set out just how the business is expected to perform in coming years. The actual performance of the company can then be compared against what was expected.

2. **They will decide what the company should invest in**. Most companies will con-stantly be assessing new and competing investment proposals. For an energy company it might be the decision to invest in a new nuclear or a coal-fired reactor. The finance director will have a leading role in this decision making.

3. **They will set out how the company should be financed**. This will include how much money the business needs overall and what is the best mix of capital that they should be targeting. This will dictate whether they look to issue more equity finance or simply increase the company's borrowings.

4. **And lastly they will be the company's financial controllers**. The financial managers will play a key role in taking control of new investment and financing decisions. One key aspect will be managing the company's costs and expenses compared to their income. This is important because it will have a significant impact on the perform- ance and risk of the business.

When you start reading the *Financial Times* you will soon be able to pick new stories that show the role of financial managers in practice.

For example, here are three *FT* headlines from the Companies and Markets section taken from 15 September 2008:

> 'Colonial agrees euro5bn debt restructuring' – This is a good example of the financing of a business.
>
> 'Continental's profit margin squeezed' – This is a good example of the financial plan- ning process in practice.
>
> 'Aruze to open its first casino' – This is a good example of a company capital invest- ment decision.

Why not get hold of the *FT* today and do the same thing. Find some good examples of global financial managers in action. In addition if you go to the book's website you will find some current *FT* stories discussed in my latest blog. Join in with your own comments on the website.

Another common topic featured in the Companies and Markets section will be the relationship between a company's senior managers and its shareholders. One very important issue that faces all companies is defining exactly what their corporate objectives should be. This is essential to ensure that the company can decide on the best courses of action. In corporate finance it is important to understand that in a modern business there is normally a clear divide between the owners of the company (the shareholders) and the day-to-day managers (the Board of Directors). This means that it is often quite difficult for the managers to obtain a definitive idea of what the owners want the business to achieve. In corporate finance we normally assume that the primary focus of the company is in ensuring that the owners (the shareholders) are kept happy. So, while there are a number of other stakeholders (employees, suppliers, local residents, etc.) the interests of the company's shareholders are seen as the main concern of the company's senior managers. Most managers work on the principle that keeping the shareholders happy will guarantee that they will stay employed and also be very well rewarded. If they disappoint them they know that their time will soon be up.

So we assume that the goal of a company is the maximisation of shareholder value. In practice this is often simplified to be the maximisation of the company's share price. We are increasingly seeing larger shareholders becoming more active in making sure that the company's managers are acting in their interests. In reality it is true that certain shareholders may not support the objective of wealth maximisation. For example, in quoted Premier League football clubs the shareholders (and fans) may not want to see a star player sold, even if this is a good financial decision. Sadly, in reality it seems to be very difficult to apply the principles of good business practice to the running of football clubs.

What other objectives might companies have? These might include:

Reducing the company's borrowing levels In the MyTravel article (Topic 5) later in the book we will see that for a company excessive debt often leads to greater risk of business failure. So a company might have a target to reduce long-term borrowings to say 30 per cent of total capital employed.

Retained profit levels It might be important for the company to be able to finance new investments with its own internally generated profits. As a result a company might want to ensure that the payments to shareholders (dividends) do not exceed a certain level of distributable profits.

Getting a target market share There is little doubt that in practice many companies will define one major corporate goal as being the achievement of a certain share of the market in their particular sector. This might be because this gives them enhanced market power enabling them to have a strong role in setting prices in this industry.

Corporate survival For some companies when the economy is in trouble their primary focus might just be towards short-term survival. As an example, in the Autumn of 2008 we saw the bankruptcy of several airlines (including XL Leisure and Silverjet) hit by the combination of rising costs (higher oil prices) and falling demand (due to the credit crunch).

Profit maximisation If asked what the aim of a company should be many people might reply maximising profits. It should be stated that profit maximisation does not equal shareholder wealth maximisation. Maximising profits in the short term can sometimes be at the cost of damaging the business in the long term. For example, a company might reduce labour costs by sacking some key sales staff. This might raise short-term profits but as the sales start to slide due to the reduced sales force the future prospects of the company might well decline.

So we have seen that finance plays a key role for many companies. You should also understand that the financial services industry is very important to the economy more generally. The health of the national economy depends to a large extent on the financial services sector. One only has to see the grave concerns of the leading national governments worldwide during 2008 when the problems in the banking sector began to threaten the world economy to a frightening extent. So like it or not there is no doubt that we need to read and understand the financial news.

The following four articles are analysed in this section:

Article 1
Sports Direct warning stumps investors
Financial Times, 27 April 2007

Article 2
Logica's chief quits in wake of warning
Financial Times, 28 May 2007

Article 3
Investors expecting change at LogicaCMG
Financial Times, 30 May 2007

Article 4
Sir Stelios spells out fears for easyJet
Financial Times, 24 November 2008

These articles address the following issues:

- the role of shareholders in companies;
- the impact of a profit warning on the share price;
- what differences there are for a listed company;
- the importance of maintaining good investor relations;
- activist shareholders and the way they can force change within companies;
- what is meant by good corporate governance including the role of a non-executive chairman;
- conflicting corporate strategies;
- the importance of cash to a company;
- growth versus mature companies.

Poor communications puts Sports Direct off track

When reading the financial press you can sometimes get the impression that getting rich is easy. Investors should buy shares in any companies that are floating on the stock market for the first time and then just sit back and wait to see their value soar. This article shows that there is another side to the story. We look at a company called Sports Direct that floated with an initial share price of 300 p back in late February 2007. Following the difficulties highlighted in this article these shares closed on the 27 of April at just under 224 p. This shows the risks associated with buying into new share issues and also the importance of good investor relations for all companies. The City exacts a swift revenge on any company that forgets the importance of effective communication with their shareholders.

Article 1

Financial Times, 27 April 2007 **FT**

Sports Direct warning stumps investors

Lucy Killgren and David Blackwell

Sports Direct, the sports retailer that made a controversial debut on the stock market earlier this year, has suffered another blow to its credibility after warning that sales growth had slowed.

The group, run by publicity-shy billionaire Mike Ashley, expects profits to be broadly in line with latest expectations, although there have been several downgrades over the past month.

The group, owner of the Lillywhites and Sports World stores and brands including Dunlop and Lonsdale, also said: 'Sales growth in the main UK retail business is slower than earlier in the year, but remains positive'.

Analysts and investors, already puzzled by the company's decision to part company with its public relations and investor relations advisers just after the flotation, were angered by lack of access to Bob Mellors, finance director. David Richardson, chairman, said the board was 'acutely conscious of the frustration that has been expressed by analysts and the press, and we are working to close that gap – but it will take some time'.

Philip Dorgan, retail analyst with Panmure Gordon, said the statement had 'set the alarm bells ringing' and implied a dramatic slowdown in sales, given that in the last update sales were up by 22 per cent.

He said the 'total absence of numbers' was leading him to downgrade estimates by 9 per cent for the current year to £141.4 m, and by 20 per cent for the following year.

Jonathan Pritchard of Oriel Securities said making forecasts on the retailer was akin to 'pinning a tail on the donkey' as the statement had 'no numbers whatsoever'. Richard Ratner of Seymour Pierce stuck to his forecast of £143.5 m pre-tax profits. But he reminded investors that Mr Ashley was a bit of a maverick, and it did not help to have a 'no-show' finance director.

The shares, listed at 300 p less than two months ago, recovered some of their early fall to close down 12½ p at 22¾ p. The price has now fallen more than 25 per cent since listing in early March compared with a rise of 1.3 per cent for the broader market.

The analysis

Sports Direct the retailer was created by the billionaire entrepreneur Mike Ashley. He has established an impressive business based on a number of iconic sporting brand names including Lonsdale, Kangol, Slazenger, Lillywhites and Dunlop. This list takes me back to the mid-1970s when I can remember saving my weekly pocket money to buy a highly prized Dunlop Maxply tennis racquet. Armed with this new weapon, I confidently expected to take Wimbledon by storm. Sadly this was yet another sporting ambition that was never to be realised!

Let's get back to Sports Direct. At the end of February 2007 Mr Ashley floated his business on the London stock exchange with a share price of 300 p. He took advantage of the flotation to sell a large stake in the business giving him a cash bonanza of some £900 m. This no doubt provided the finance for his subsequent takeover of Newcastle United football club. Sadly, since the time of the stock market flotation, Sports Direct has been hit by a number of problems which have resulted in a severe slide in the share price.

A common factor in the company's difficulties was that it had been associated with very poor investor relations. At the time of the share issue, Mr Ashley admitted that it should have appointed a new investor relations firm well before the flotation. Since then the company has tried to improve its corporate governance and repair its damaged reputation with the City.

In this article we see that in its latest announcement 'the company was warning that its sales growth had slowed'. It is not clear whether this is a formal 'profits warning' or just a negative trading update. This results in a leading retail analyst at Panmure Gordon concluding that this statement had 'set the alarm bells ringing' as this evidence of a slowdown followed a previous announcement that sales were up by 22 per cent. As a result he made sharp profit downgrades for both 2007 and 2008.

The City likes good news about a company's prospects. It can even learn to live with some bad news if it is fully explained and there is still a well-founded confidence that things will improve. However, the one thing that the City always takes a dim view of is when a company offers a confused picture in relation to its financial performance. There are a host of highly skilled retail analysts employed by the large investment banks, and these demand good and effective communication between the company and their investors. Investors will sell the shares of any company that produces poor, confused and apparently contradictory trading statements.

On the same day as this article in the *Financial Times*, the excellent Lombard column argued that the company should not be delisted, for rather unusual reasons. The comment was: 'simply as a case study of how not to handle one's first months on the public markets,

Sports Direct has already proved to be a huge asset to the Stock Exchange'. Some might regard this as a harsh but maybe perfectly fair judgement on Sports Direct's performance. The episode underlines the importance of a company maintaining good communications with their shareholders and the financial press.

■ Key terms

Profits warning Companies are required to keep shareholders well informed about the performance of the company. As a result, if a company knows that its future profits will be significantly less than the stock market currently believes, it is required to warn the market. The result of such a warning is normally a sharp fall in the share price.

Corporate governance This is a general term used to describe the relationship between the owners of a business (the shareholders) and the managers of the business. It covers the various mechanisms by which the shareholders can try to make sure that the managers act in their interest. This should ensure that the managers are open, fair and fully accountable for all their actions.

Investor relations A key aspect of good corporate governance is the requirement that the senior managers of a company are expected to keep up a constant dialogue with the shareholders. This includes the necessity to make sure they are in touch with their opinions on a range of important issues. This should be done through such things as the annual general meeting, the sending of regular news updates and the provision of a company website. Most of these websites now include a section covering investor relations.

Delisting This is simply when a company is removed from a stock exchange. This might be done by a company that decides that it has simply become too onerous to meet all the rules and regulations set out by the stock exchange. Such companies are not necessarily bankrupt and it is quite possible that the shares will still trade in the over-the-counter market where buyers and sellers will be brought together.

■ What do you think?

1. Why is it so important for a company to maintain effective communications with its shareholders and the City in general?
2. What steps might Sports Direct take to improve its investor relations?
3. The sharp fall in Sports Direct's share price suggests that it is behaving in a way that is consistent with a semi-strongly efficient stock market. What is the evidence to support this view?

Hint: A good source for this topic is Arnold, G. (2007) *Essentials of Corporate Financial Management*, Harlow, UK: FT Prentice Hall. You should look at p. 229 to see a concise definition of the three levels of efficiency.

■ Go to the web

Go to the website for the *Financial Times* at www.FT.com.

Now go to the Quotes field at the top right and enter: UK:SPD.

a. What is the current share price for Sports Direct?

b. Look at the 52-week high and low share prices.

Using this data discuss the volatility of Sports Direct's share price in the last year.

■ Research

Arnold, G. (2007) *Essentials of Corporate Financial Management*, Harlow, UK: FT Prentice Hall. You should look at pp. 195–6 to learn more about listed companies.

Arnold, G. (2008) *Corporate Financial Management*, 4th edn, Harlow, UK: FT Prentice Hall. You should especially look at Chapter 1, pp. 15–18 to get more information about corporate governance.

Berk, J. and DeMarzo, P. (2009) *Corporate Finance*, Harlow, UK: FT Prentice Hall Financial Times. The topic of corporations is covered in Chapter 1. The corporate management team is introduced on p. 10.

Gitman, L. (2009) *Principles of Managerial Finance*, 12th edn, Pearson International Edition. There is a US-based introduction to the link between finance and business on pp. 4–21.

McLaney, E. (2009) *Business Finance Theory and Practice*, Harlow, UK: FT Prentice Hall Financial Times. You will find an introduction to the role of business finance on pp. 4–12.

Pike, R. and Neale, B. (2006) *Corporate Finance and Investment*, 6th edn, Harlow, UK: FT Prentice Hall. You should look at Chapter 1, especially pp. 5–7 to see a discussion of the role of the financial manager.

Watson, D. and Head, A. (2007) *Corporate Finance Principles and Practice*, 4th edn. Harlow, UK: FT Prentice Hall. You should look at Chapter 1. In addition the process of listing is explained on p. 96.

Activist shareholders demand change at Logica

Shareholders are the key providers of long-term finance to companies. As long as a company performs well and provides them with excellent financial returns they will leave the company to manage its business. However, if a company runs into trouble and the share price slides, the company can expect some immediate agitation, especially from its largest shareholders.

The relationship between a company and its shareholders is clear. The shareholders give up their hard-earned money to the managers of a business in the expectation that they will make good use of the funds. They will hope to see substantial returns in the form of a rising share price as well as a stream of dividends. The other long-term capital comes from the providers of debt capital. Their relationship with the company is quite different. Unless there is serious default they lend money to the company in the certain expectation of its return in the form of interest and the eventual return of the principal. The debt holders must accept lower returns reflecting the lower risk. In contrast, the shareholders expect much higher returns to compensate for the greater risks that they take.

These articles show what happens when key shareholders become unhappy with the performance of a company. The role of activist shareholders is to make it clear to managers of a business that they want to see substantial change. In this case they are demanding changes at LogicaCMG. This was to start with a new chief executive who was expected to be appointed from outside the business.

Article 2	*Financial Times*, 28 May 2007 **FT**

Logica's chief quits in wake of warning

Roger Blitz

Britain's fiercely competitive IT services market yesterday claimed the scalp of Martin Read, chief executive of LogicaCMG, who declared he was stepping down as a direct consequence of last week's profits warning from the Anglo-Dutch group.

Logica announced that it would look both inside and outside the company for a replacement. Mr Read, who has run the company for the past 14 years, will stay on until a successor is identified.

His departure came after Logica last week warned that first-half revenues and margins at its UK business would be lower than last year, and full-year revenues would be below those of 2006. The profit warning has knocked 9 per cent off the company's share price.

Mr Read said the reasons for the decline, a downturn in UK trading and a £10 m–£15 m over-run on one project, were neither 'huge' nor 'strategic' problems.

But a statement from Logica's board yesterday said that 'in the light of the unsettling speculation following the ➔

company's recent trading update, Martin Read has decided to accelerate his retirement plans'.

The company also said that its 14-strong board, which is seeking more non-executive directors, would reconsider its size and structure.

It is understood that, following the profit warning, several leading shareholders told board members that it was time for the company to look at succession.

Mr Read, who is 57, is thought to have previously broached the subject of his retirement with several board members, and decided that, with shareholders voicing their disquiet, he should accelerate his departure.

Cor Stutterheim, chairman of Logica, said that he accepted Mr Read's decision with regret, noting that he had built a UK business of 3000 staff into an international operation of 40 000 employees in 41 countries. The company was formed after the merger of UK-based Logica with CMG, the Dutch group, in 2002.

Logica is the seventh largest IT services company in Europe by revenues, and 19th in the world.

Logica, which bought French rival Unilog in 2005 for £631 m and WM Data of Sweden for £876 m last year, is competing with rivals such as Wipro, TCS and Infosys – all Indian companies – in the UK. The market, which has historically been viewed as the company's best-managed operation, generated 25 per cent of the company's £2.7 bn in revenues last year.

Logica's first quarter UK revenue was down 4.1 per cent at £174.6 m and second quarter revenues are likely to be lower than the first. First-half underlying margin in the UK was expected to be about 3 per cent lower.

The company was responding to the UK competition by accelerating the move of some staff to lower-cost offshore locations at a cost of £2 m and job losses.

It has seen growth slow in the past year when it struggled to recruit enough IT consultants in France. Mr Read was planning to focus on consolidation.

Article 3   *Financial Times*, 30 May 2007   **FT**

Investors expecting change at LogicaCMG

Maija Palmer

Investors expect sweeping changes at LogicaCMG following the departure of Martin Read as chief executive – though there is little clarity as to who will succeed him.

A successor to Mr Read is widely expected to come from outside the company although Seamus Keating, chief financial officer, and Jim McKenna, chief operating officer of the Anglo-Dutch IT services group, are obvious internal candidates.

But both are long-time LogicaCMG executives and closely associated with Mr Read, who has had a difficult relationship with the City.

Mr Read announced plans to step down from LogicaCMG this week in response to intense pressure from activist shareholders such as Morley Fund Management, who were disappointed by the company's profits warning last week.

The warning of poor performance at LogicaCMG's UK operations was the last straw for many investors, following the controversial acquisition of Sweden's WM-Data last year and a warning of poor performance at its French business in January.

'It is almost a dead certainty that the new CEO will be someone brought in externally', said Kevin Ashton, analyst at Bridgewell. 'The company has managed to keep all the executives in place for a long time, and it's quite a "cosy" board … If you are an activist investor, those guys are all tarred with the same brush'.

Another analyst, who declined to be named, said: 'The perception has been that management – not just Martin Read – have been underperforming, and so they are likely to veer towards looking outside'.

The head of European operations for a large US-based IT company would make an ideal candidate for the top job, analysts said.

LogicaCMG plans to examine the 'appropriateness' of the board's size and structure, suggesting it will be slimmed down from the current 14 members.

It has faced questions about a consulting contract worth €300 000 (£203 732) a year the company had given

Gerard Philippot, non-executive director and former president of Unilog, the French business LogicaCMG acquired in 2005.

Investors have questioned the independence of Cor Stutterheim, the non-executive chairman and former chairman of CMG, which merged with Logica to form the group in 2002. His close ties with the group mean he is not considered independent under the combined code on corporate governance.

LogicaCMG yesterday said Mr Stutterheim did not plan to step down in the immediate future. But many believe he may go shortly after the new CEO is installed.

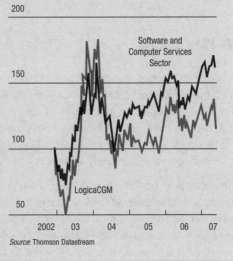

LogicaCGM
Total return indices (rebased since merger)

Source: Thomson Datastream

■ The analysis

LogicaCMG is a leading information technology outsourcing and services group which employs some 41 000 people worldwide. The chief executive officer (CEO), Martin Read, spent some 14 years establishing the business in this sector. During May 2007 the company announced a profits warning with the news that first half revenues and margins at its UK's business would be lower than the previous year and full year revenues would be below those of 2006. This announcement had the immediate impact of wiping 9 per cent off the company's share price. The first article reports that the reasons for the decline include a sharp deterioration in its trading performance in the UK and a large overspend on an individual project. In response to this announcement, the CEO decided to bring forward his retirement plans. The second article reports that his successor was widely expected to come from outside the company despite two possible internal candidates.

One of the key activist shareholders, Morley Fund Management, was clearly expressing a strong desire for change. An analyst at Bridgewell Securities is quoted as saying that 'the company has managed to keep all the executives in place for a long time, and it's quite a "cosy" board ... If you are an activist investor, those guys are all tarred with the same brush'. As a result, the activist shareholders will want to see someone new who can come in and shake up the business.

Some key aspects of the way that the business was being run were being called into question. This includes the need to reduce the board of directors down from 14. The *Financial Times* also reports that there were concerns about the consultancy position enjoyed by Gerard Philippot, a non-executive director and former president of a French business that LogicaCMG acquired in 2005. Finally there were doubts about the level of independence of Cor Stutterheim the non executive chairman and former chairman of CMG which merged with Logica to form the combined group in 2005. His association with the group undermined his independence 'under the combined code on corporate governance'. He was expected to leave after a new CEO was in place.

■ Key terms

Long-term finance In most companies this is the key finance that underpins its business activities. It is made up of a combination of equity finance (provided by the shareholders) and debt finance normally issued in the form of new bond issues. This long-term finance will allow the company to make new investments and it could also fund mergers and acquisitions.

See Article 16 for more discussion of long-term finance. You should look at the capital structure section in the 'Key terms' section.

Shareholders (activist) In most companies the shareholders provide the bulk of the long-term finance. This makes them the key stakeholders in the business. They are the owners of the business and the managers must always remember that they are merely acting as agents working on behalf of the shareholders who are the principals. We normally assume that the primary objective of a company is to maximise the wealth of its shareholders. In practice this is simplified to maximising the company's share price.

The shareholders range from private investors with small stakes in the business right up to the large financial institutions that often own a significant percentage of the equity of a business. It is normally among these larger shareholders that we find the activist shareholders. These are the shareholders who believe that the managers are not doing a good job and as a result they will attempt to alter company policy and even possibly seek to replace existing senior managers with new people who they think will do a better job.

Chief executive officer (CEO) This is the top person in the company who will have the main responsibility for implementing the policies of the board of directors on a daily basis. Put simply, they are running the business.

Non-executive chairman This is supposed to be a person who is independent of the core management team. They will normally be employed on a part-time basis and will chair the main board of directors. In addition the CEO can look to them for advice and guidance. You will also see the term NED, which stands for non-executive director. Most public companies will employ a number of part-time NEDs to give independent advice on the running of the company's operations.

Default This is where a borrower takes out a loan but fails to keep to the original agreed schedule of interest payments and final capital repayments. See Article 7 on p. 36 for a full definition.

■ What do you think?

1. Discuss how company shareholders can encourage their managers to act in a way which is consistent with the objective of shareholder wealth maximisation.

2. In what situations might we expect there to be a significant increase in the number of activist shareholders in a company?

    Hint: Think about the performance of the company's share price.

3. Using the Logica articles above, discuss the role of a non-executive chairman in a company.

■ Investigate FT data

You will need the Companies and Markets section of the *Financial Times*. In addition, go to the website for Tesco plc at www.tescoplc.com.

Go to the section entitled 'Investor Centre'.

1. Find the current share price for Tesco plc.

2. Look at the London share price service in the *Financial Times* and find the high/low for this share in the last 52 weeks. How does the current share price compare to this high/low?

3. Go back to the Tesco website (Investor Centre section).

    Identify the main shareholders in Tesco plc.

4. You are now required to prepare a PowerPoint presentation:

    Go to the latest summary and annual review.

    Now find the chief executive's statement. Using this information, you are required to prepare six PowerPoint slides.

    Slide 1: provide a short profile of the company (nature of business, market capitalisation, etc.).

    Slide 2: what are the corporate goals (financial and non-financial)?

    Slide 3: what does the company say about total shareholder return and/or dividend policy?

    Slide 4: discuss some current *FT* stories about this company.

Slides 5–6: review the company's financial management – look at any new issues of bonds and shares and the role of its treasury department, including any risk-management activities.

■ Research

Arnold, G. (2007) *Essentials of Corporate Financial Management*, Harlow, UK: FT Prentice Hall. You should look at pp. 28–29 for a very clear discussion of the problems of corporate governance in practice.

Arnold, G. (2008) *Corporate Financial Management*, 4th edn. Harlow, UK: FT Prentice Hall Financial Times. You should especially look at Chapter 1. The topic of corporate governance is well explained on pp. 15–18.

Atrill, P. (2007) *Financial Management for Decision Makers*, 5th edn, Harlow, UK: FT Prentice Hall. You should look at chapter 1, pp. 6–20 set out 'why businesses exist'.

Berk, J. and DeMarzo, P. (2009) *Corporate Finance*, Harlow, UK: FT Prentice Hall Financial Times. The topic of corporate governance is covered in Chapter 29.

Gitman, L. (2009) *Principles of Managerial Finance*, 12th edn, Harlow, UK: Pearson International Edition. There is a US-based introduction to corporate governance on pp. 16–17.

McLaney, E. (2009) *Business Finance Theory and Practice*, 8th edn, Harlow, UK: FT Prentice Hall Financial Times. You will find an introduction to corporate governance on pages 9–12.

Pike, R. and Neale, B. (2006) *Corporate Finance and Investment*, 6th edn. Harlow, UK: FT Prentice Hall. You will find a discussion of the problems of corporate governance on pp. 14–16.

Watson, D. and Head, A. (2007) *Corporate Finance Principles and Practice*, 4th edn, Harlow, UK: FT Prentice Hall. You should look at pp. 18–21 for an introduction to the topic of corporate governance.

Not so easy for Sir Stelios!

The corporate profile of easyJet and its flamboyant founder, Sir Stelios Haji-Ioannou, was much enhanced by the 'fly on the wall' documentary series *Airline* which was first shown on the ITV network in 1999. It went on to become one of the defining docusoaps that came to dominate our screens in the new millennium. Many of the weekly episodes of *Airline* focused on the interaction between easyJet's staff and their eclectic mix of passengers during some pivotal moments in their lives. These included weddings, births, crucial international football matches as well as the more mundane holidays. The highlight of many episodes was the inevitable tears that resulted from passengers missing their flight check-in times by a few minutes. Such tension made perfect watching for the millions of viewers.

At the time of this article the world's airlines were facing up to the realities of the impact of a worldwide recession on their businesses. These issues were brought into sharp focus in late 2008 when Sir Stelios fought a bitter battle with the rest of the senior management team at easyJet. He wanted the company to restrict its growth plans and instead focus on generating cash which would be needed to fund the acquisition of new A320 short-haul aircraft over the next four years.

Article 4   *Financial Times*, 24 November 2008 **FT**

Sir Stelios spells out fears for easyJet

Kevin Done

Sir Stelios Haji-Ioannou, the founder and largest shareholder in easyJet, dug in his heels on Sunday in his public disagreement with the rest of the airline's board over its growth strategy in the midst of the deepening recession.

In an interview with the *Financial Times*, he said he was engaging with other shareholders and with financial analysts to explain his concern that the group was not sufficiently focused on conserving cash and on limiting its big capital expenditure commitments. The group's leading institutional investors include Standard Life, Wellington, Fidelity and Schroders.

'The real issue is the Airbus contract', he said, under which easyJet is committed to taking delivery of 109 new A320 family short-haul jets during the next four years

with a total value of $5.1 bn (£3.4 bn) at list prices before heavy discounts.

'I am keen to focus the debate on how much they cost, and how they are to be paid for, rather than on passenger numbers', he said.

Sir Stelios, who founded easyJet in 1995, has been a pioneer, alongside Ireland's Ryanair, of the low-cost business model in Europe. It has been built on capturing large chunks of market share from established carriers as well as on stimulating growth by offering much lower fares and by having a lower cost base than other airlines.

The rapidly expanding low-cost carriers have been given a valuation premium as growth stocks, but Sir Stelios said he believed this era was over. 'At the heart

→

15

the question is are we a growth company or a mature company. I think it [easyJet] is a mature company.'

EasyJet's management, backed by the rest of the board, said last week it was taking a cautious approach, but Sir Stelios, a non-executive director, told investors he believed that the group's approach was 'based on optimistic assumptions about future revenues'.

EasyJet's shares are down 5 per cent since the row emerged a week ago.

Yesterday Sir Stelios expressed the concern that low-cost airlines were not recession-proof like low-cost food stores such as Wal-Mart, Aldi or Lidl.

He feared the customers would not be there to fill all the 'aluminium tubes' on order from Airbus. 'Anyone just unemployed must still go to Aldi to buy the cheapest food to survive', he said, 'but he does not need to go for a stag party to Prague with his mates.'

■ The analysis

When companies perform well and their share prices behave in a robust manner it is quite possible for their senior managers to remain in the background driving the business forward and enjoying substantial personal financial rewards. However, when economic activity slides and share prices go into reverse these same managers start to hit the headlines. This case is slightly unusual, as the person involved was Sir Stelios Haji-Ioannou who is the founder and largest shareholder in easyJet. It would be hard to describe him as a shy and retiring individual. On the contrary, whenever the media wanted a savvy business person to comment on a news story, he would be high on the list, perhaps coming just below Sir Alan Sugar or one of the members of the BBC's *Dragon's Den*.

This particular *FT* story related to a rather embarrassing public spat that developed at the end of 2008 as Sir Stelios vented his displeasure at the corporate strategy being employed by the other board members at easyJet. It was a particularly interesting article as it must have mirrored a number of similar debates that were taking place in boardrooms up and down the country at that time. The important question was just how a company should be run against the background of a rapidly ailing economy where sales were shrinking and sources of business finance were very scarce.

In the case of easyJet Sir Stelios was pushing the company to operate a far more cautious strategy with a strong emphasis on the company holding on to as much cash as possible and limiting any capital investment projects to the bare minimum required. He was particularly concerned that the company should preserve as much cash as possible to fund the new Airbus aircraft which easyJet was committed to purchase. Sir Stelios made a direct appeal to the company's main institutional investors, Standard Life, Wellington, Fidelity and Schroder's, to lend their support to his viewpoint. This was very different from his previous more flamboyant approach which had seen the business enjoy rapid growth with its low fares substantially boosting the market for air travel particularly in the European market. He argued that by late 2008 easyJet should no longer consider itself to be a growth company, but instead should position itself as a more mature business which should operate a cautious strategy in this economic downturn. The *FT* article quotes him as saying low-cost airlines were not recession-proof companies like low-cost food stores such as Wal-Mart, Aldi and Lidl. While we all need to eat food no matter what, we do not need to fly to Bilbao, Catania or Dortmund!

The other board members at easyJet would not have regarded themselves as being particularly rash or irresponsible in their running of the business. At this time they included individuals like Sir Colin Chapman (former Chief Executive of Rolls-Royce), Sir David Michels (Deputy Chairman of M&S) and Dawn Airey (from Channel Five). They would surely be just as sensitive to the worrying decline in business confidence and just as likely to have set the correct course for easyJet against this changed economic background.

Sir Stelios, a non-executive director, also challenged the company's dividend policy. Since its birth as a business easyJet had never paid any dividends to its shareholders. Instead it sought to reward its shareholders through share price gains in the same way as other similar high-growth companies. Some critics at the time wondered if Sir Stelios's desire to see the business rebranded as a mature company that paid dividends had something to do with his need to get some income from his own shareholding. With easyJet's share price falling so sharply during 2008 it could be seen as one way of protecting his primary financial asset during a period of declining economic activity.

■ Key terms

Growth strategy This refers to the strategy employed by a company aimed at increasing its market share. It is possible that in the short term a company might set out to chase additional sales even at the cost of reducing short-term earnings. The tactics used to increase market share might include the development of new products or services and diversification into new international markets.

Capital expenditure This term is used to cover any money that is invested in a business to buy new fixed assets like machinery, technology or industrial buildings. The aim of this expenditure is to enable the company to increase production of goods or services and generate higher income in future years. Economists see this type of investment as being vital in terms of securing higher rates of economic growth in the future.

Valuation premium In corporate finance we use many different techniques to arrive at the correct valuation for the shares in a company. These are normally based on important factors like the company's future dividends or earning streams. It is normally the case that we place a higher value on companies that are expected to achieve significantly higher growth rates than other companies in similar business sectors.

Growth/mature company It is important to be able to distinguish between a growth company and a more mature one. A growth company is one that has a rate of growth that is significantly higher than is the norm. They will generally be characterised by heavy investment programmes and low dividend payments to their shareholders. In contrast, a mature company has already done its growing and it has now reached the stage where future expansion plans are limited by the size of their market. These companies will be characterised by much less ambitious business investments but rather more generous dividend payments to shareholders.

Non-executive director (NED) You will often see the term NED, which stands for non-executive director. Most public companies will employ a number of part-time NEDs to give independent advice on the running of the company's operations.

■ What do you think?

1. What were the main concerns of Sir Stelios Haji-Ioannou, the founder and largest shareholder in easyJet, in terms of the airline's future business strategy?

2. Why might it have been particularly important for easyJet to hoard cash at this time?

3. What is the difference between a growth company and a mature company? Discuss the likely dividend policy of these different types of companies.

4. Why are the profits of airlines particularly susceptible to economic slowdowns?

Hint: Consider the likely impact on demand for air travel and their main costs like oil and the nature of their capital expenditure on new aircraft.

■ Investigate FT data

You will need the Companies and Markets section of the *Financial Times*. Go to the London Share Price Service. This is normally 2–3 pages inside from the back page of the Companies and Markets section. You will find here lots of useful share price data for the companies that have their shares quoted on the London Stock Market. You will see that the companies are allocated to a range of different sectors ranging from **Aerospace and Defence** to the **Utilities**. The shares shown in **bold** are the ones currently included in the main UK stock market index, called the FTSE 100.

1. You are now required to identify five companies that could be regarded as being 'mature companies'. Explain why each one matches this definition.

2. You are now required to identify five companies that could be regarded as being 'growth companies'. Explain why each one matches this definition.

■ Research

Arnold, G. (2007) *Essentials of Corporate Financial Management*, Harlow, UK: FT Prentice Hall. Chapter 1 sets out the objectives for a business.

Arnold, G. (2008) *Corporate Financial Management*, 4th edn, Harlow, UK: FT Prentice Hall Financial Times. You should look especially at Chapter 1. On pp. 3–15 you will see a good discussion of the objectives of companies. In addition you will see a discussion of the dividend policies of companies in Chapter 22.

Atrill, P. (2007) *Financial Management for Decision Makers*, 5th edn, Harlow, UK: FT Prentice Hall. There is a useful discussion on the subject of shareholder activism on pp. 19–23.

Berk, J. and DeMarzo, P. (2009) *Corporate Finance*, Harlow, UK: FT Prentice Hall Financial Times. The topic of corporations is covered in Chapter 1. Ownership versus control of corporations is on pp. 9–12.

Gitman, L. (2009) *Principles of Managerial Finance*, 12th edn, Harlow, UK: Pearson International Edition. There is a US-based introduction to the goal of a firm on pp. 13–21.

McLaney, E. (2009) *Business Finance Theory and Practice*, 8th edn, Harlow, UK: FT Prentice Hall Financial Times. There is a discussion of the organisation of businesses on pp. 6–7.

Pike, R. and Neale, B. (2006) *Corporate Finance and Investment*, 6th edn, Harlow, UK: FT Prentice Hall. You should look at Chapter 1. There is a good section on 'Cash – the lifeblood of the business' on p. 7.

Watson, D. and Head, A. (2007) *Corporate Finance Principles and Practice*, 4th edn, Harlow, UK: FT Prentice Hall. You should look at Chapter 1.

Go to **www.pearsoned.co.uk/boakes** to access Kevin's blog for additional analysis of recent topical news articles and to post your comments. Download podcasts containing short audio summaries of the main issues relating to each article and check your understanding of in-text questions with the handy hints provided.

1

INTRODUCTION TO CORPORATE FINANCE

Financial institutions featuring investment banks

In contrast to Companies and Markets, the main section of the *Financial Times* focuses much more on economic issues, especially the way they impact on the most important financial institutions. We can define a financial institution as an agent that provides a range of important financial services for its various clients. Its primary purpose is to bring together the economic players with spare money (the lenders) and those with a financial deficit (the borrowers). Financial institutions facilitate the transfer of resources between them. Let us look at a simple example.

A company may need to raise extra capital to finance a new investment opportunity. It needs to raise £1bn, with half of it coming from extra share finance (equity) and the other half from additional borrowing (debt). It might well go to a large investment bank (for example Goldman Sachs) which will make this capital raising much easier. The bank's equity team will organise a new share issue allowing large pension funds to buy shares in a new stock market issue. The bank's debt team will launch a new bond issue on behalf of the company. If these new issues are successful, the company will soon have the finance that it requires to move ahead with the new investment project.

The investment bank is important because:

a. It will manage the **return** on the new issues. This means that it will help the two parties arrive at a reasonable price for the new shares and a fair interest rate on the new debt securities.

b. It will manage the **risk** on the new investments. This means that it will organise the new financial instruments in such a way as to ensure that both parties (the borrower and the lender) do not end up with more risk than they can deal with.

c. It will combine **amounts** of capital from various lenders to ensure that the company can borrow the full amount that it requires.

d. It will manage the **liquidity** on the new investment. It is possible that the company will want to raise very long-term finance in order to fund the new investment opportunity. The lenders might be reluctant to make their finance available for such a long period. The investment bank can structure the new financial market securities in such a way that both sides get what they want. For example, with a new 20-year bond issue the company gets long-term funding. At the same time the buyers of these bonds can sell them long before their maturity if they need to cash in their investments.

The most common financial institutions include the retail banks, building societies, investment banks and the central banks. We should start this section by setting out what these all do.

1. **Retail banks**. These are the well-known high street banks like HSBC, NatWest and Barclays. They take deposits from their retail clients and then lend this money out to their individual and commercial customers. The banks also offer a range of other services including foreign exchange facilities, investment advice and secure deposit facilities.

2. **Building societies**. These days it is increasingly difficult to differentiate between the role of banks and the role of building societies. In the past the main difference was that building societies were mutual organisations owned by their members who held savings accounts with them. In addition, the main role of a building society used to be the provision of mortgages to enable people to buy their homes. In recent years we have seen many building societies turn themselves into public companies through share issues. Furthermore, building societies have now diversified the range of their activities to include many new services.

3. **Investment banks**. Whenever a large company needs to raise finance, the first port of call will be an investment bank. As classic examples of financial intermediaries, these banks act as go-betweens to the issuers of capital (governments and companies) and the investors in capital (pension funds and insurance companies). Most investment banks are split into two main divisions. The first helps companies with the issue of new equity market securities. The second offers companies the chance to issue new bond market securities.

4. **Central banks**. Just about all countries now have a national central bank and it is normally their most important financial institution. National banks have two primary functions. The first is to oversee the workings of the financial system and to ensure that all other financial institutions are operating securely. The second key role of the central banks in most countries is to determine the correct stance of monetary policy. In practice, this means that they set the level of short-term interest rates in the economy. In so doing, they must achieve the economic goals that are set by the national government. The central bank in the United States is called the Fed. The central bank for the Eurozone is called the European Central Bank. Finally, in the UK the central bank is called the Bank of England. It is not clear where this leaves Scotland, Northern Ireland and Wales!

In this section you will see articles that examine the role of central banks, as their actions have a major impact on the stock markets, the currency markets and the bond markets. I have also included two articles on investment banks, which are at the centre of a number of corporate finance activities, and I have tried to give an insider's view of their main functions.

The following four articles are analysed in this section:

Article 5
Bernanke to give a taste of more transparent Fed
Financial Times, 14 February 2006

Article 6
How long can the good times last? Bankers cautious despite bids and bumper bonuses
Financial Times, 27 November 2006

Article 7
JP Morgan to cut prop trading desk
Financial Times, 4 November 2008

Article 8
Bank to give better guidance over rates
Financial Times, 3 May 2007

These articles address the following issues:

- the role of central banks;
- some of the key official interest rates – Fed funds rate (used by the Fed) and the repo rate (used by the European Central Bank and the Bank of England);
- the Federal Open Market Committee and the Monetary Policy Committee;
- role of yield curves;
- US Treasury bond market;
- getting an inside view of an investment bank;
- looking at the key activities of an investment bank;
- what is meant by an initial public offer?
- explaining a company default;
- primary and secondary markets;
- principal and proprietary trading explained;
- the impact of the credit crunch on investment banks.

Financial markets watch the new Fed chairman

When you start reading the *Financial Times* regularly, you will quickly see how important central banks are in terms of their impact on financial markets. This theme is a recurrent one in the financial pages, as the actions of these banks have a massive impact on the stock markets, the currency markets and the bond markets. They are normally in sole charge of setting the level of short-term interest rates in each country. For example, in the United States they are set the task of ensuring that the US economy operates at a level of activity that is compatible with sustainable non-inflationary economic growth. In order to achieve this target, the Fed meets most months to set the target level for the Fed funds rate. It is really important that you understand the role of central banks in practice.

In this article we will see how closely financial markets follow the actions and statements made by the people who run the main international central banks. There is no doubt the main focus is on the chairman of the US Federal Reserve who is currently Ben Bernanke.

Article 5   *Financial Times*, 14 February 2006   **FT**

Bernanke to give a taste of more transparent Fed

Andrew Balls

Ben Bernanke's debut on Capitol Hill this week will provide the first glimpse of the more transparent approach he intends to take as chairman of the Federal Reserve.

A host of Fed watchers expects more plain language from the new Fed chairman, in contrast to the Delphic approach of his predecessor, Alan Greenspan.

Reflecting his belief that the Fed should provide more quantitative guidance to market participants, Mr Bernanke is also expected to place much greater emphasis on the consensus forecasts of the Federal Open Market Committee Members. Mr Greenspan, who did not participate in the forecast round, often avoided mentioning them in testimony.

But it is unlikely Mr Bernanke will provide much more detail on the likely course for the federal funds rate. He will be speaking on behalf of the whole committee, and although the need for further rate increases is a matter of debate among members, the view that decisions will be data-dependent is unanimous.

The FOMC said after its January meeting, at which it raised rates in the 14th consecutive step to 4.5 per cent, that 'some further policy firming may be needed' to keep the risks to growth and inflation in balance. Futures markets are pricing in another increase at Mr Bernanke's first meeting as chair, in March, to 5 per cent, and a good chance of another increase in May.

John Lipsky, chief economist at JPMorgan, said he hoped that Mr Bernanke's commitment to greater transparency meant he would provide more detail on how the central bank would judge when to end the campaign of interest rate increases, to help guide expectations. 'To date, the Fed has been singularly opaque on the criteria that will be used to determine when the tightening is sufficient', Mr Lipsky said.

It is only when presenting the twice-yearly testimony on the monetary policy report that the Fed chairman speaks for the whole of the FOMC rather than in a personal capacity. Mr Bernanke will appear before the House financial services committee tomorrow and on Thursday before the Senate banking committee.

Over time, Mr Bernanke is likely to want to be more specific about the committee's outlook for interest rates and the assumptions used in making its forecasts. A leading advocate of inflation targeting, he is expected to introduce a more formal inflation objective over time, but has said this will require the FOMC's support.

'He can't really focus on the innovations he wants in this testimony, since he has just arrived and he will be speaking on behalf of the whole committee', said Larry Meyer, a former Fed governor and founder of the consultancy Macroeconomic Advisers.

The consensus of FOMC forecasts is likely to show the economy growing slightly faster than its trend rate, commonly put at 3–3.5 per cent, this year and slowing to trend growth in 2007. Core inflation this year is likely to be in the top part of the 1–2 per cent comfort range, popularised by Mr Bernanke when he was a Fed governor before joining the White House staff last year.

In one of a number of steps towards greater transparency during Mr Greenspan's tenure, the Fed last February started providing two-year forecasts in the first monetary policy report of the year. Over such a period, monetary policy would be expected to influence the outcomes, meaning that the committee's inflation forecast for 2007 can be seen as an objective as well as a forecast.

A number of Fed watchers expect a slightly hawkish tone from the new chairman to help bolster his inflation-fighting credibility. Fed policymakers were not troubled by the slowdown in the economy in the fourth quarter and expect strong growth in the first half of this year.

Lawmakers are also likely to quiz Mr Bernanke on the flat yield curve and the implications for the Fed's deliberations. At 4.5 per cent, the federal funds rate is little different to the yield on the 10-year Treasury note.

Some economists see this as foreshadowing a slowdown in the economy. However, the view at the Fed is that low long-term rates are stimulating growth, a point Mr Greenspan is reported to have made at a meeting with hedge fund managers, organised by Lehman Brothers, in New York last week.

Mr Bernanke has in the past stressed that the Fed must take into account broad financial conditions in setting the federal funds rate, including long-term interest rates, currencies and the stock market.

'I would like him to come out and say that the reason they are still raising rates is because financial conditions – long-term rates, the dollar and equities – remain accommodative. They are tightening the fed funds rate to keep financial accommodation where it is', Mr Meyer said.

■ The analysis

The focus is on the first appearance of the new chairman of the Federal Open Market Committee (FOMC) in front of the politicians on Capitol Hill. The FOMC is the body that is in charge of setting the level of short-term interest rates in the United States. It meets eight times per year and it can organise emergency conference calls if immediate action is necessary. The Committee is chaired by Ben Bernanke who took over from Alan Greenspan, the Fed's best-known chairman, who held office from 1987 to 2006.

This *Financial Times* article argues that in comparison to his predecessor the statements of the new Fed chairman should be easier to understand. Mr Bernanke was expected to pay far more attention to the formal economic forecasts produced for the FOMC. The key event discussed here is the so called 'Humphrey Hawkins Testimony' which is a biannual statement made by the Fed chairman, first to House Financial Services Committee and then to the Senate Banking Committee. Every word spoken on these occasions is closely followed by the so-called 'Fed Watchers' who try to predict future changes in US interest rates. Getting these forecasts correct can be worth a fortune to the money and bond market traders inside the investment banks.

At its last meeting the FOMC had raised the target for the key Fed funds rate for the fourteenth consecutive time to reach 4.5 per cent. Financial markets were looking for any clues about when this period of Fed tightening would finally be over. Fed watchers were hoping that policy-making would now become far more transparent. A key part of this change in strategy was the expectation that Mr Bernanke would advocate a more formal inflation target just like the ones used by the Bank of England and the European Central Bank. It was also possible that at least initially he would adopt a more hawkish tone to demonstrate his tough anti-inflation stance.

One key issue that economists have latched onto was the presence of an almost flat yield curve. In simple terms this means that the level of interest rates is virtually the same all the way from overnight money market rates right through to long-term US Treasury bonds. There were two alternative explanations offered for this development. They had sharply different implications for the economic outlook in the United States.

The first view was that the flat yield curve simply reflected the high level of short-term interest rates that had effectively killed off any fears of rising inflation. This favourable back-ground caused long-term bond yields to fall back in line with short-term interest rates. There was some concern that this highly restrictive monetary policy would eventually lead to a significant slowdown in the economy. The alternative view voiced by Alan Greenspan was that the flat yield curve, was actually due to the presence of very low long-term bond yields and this was a key factor behind the resilience of the US economy. Whichever view best described the shape of the yield curve, there is no doubt that financial markets would be watching closely Mr Bernanke's every move in the coming months.

■ Key terms

Fed watching This refers to the various economists who spend their time studying every market movement or speech from a key official of the Federal Reserve Bank in order to try and predict the next move in US interest rates. Getting these predictions right is worth a great deal to the large investment banks as their traders can use these forecasts to make massive profits in their bond, share and money market trading operations.

Fed funds rate This is the most important short-term interest rate in the United States. It refers to the overnight inter-bank lending that takes places in the United States money markets. The money that one bank lends to another comes from any excess reserves held at the Fed. All banks have to hold a certain level of money at their local Federal Reserve District Bank. These deposits are called *required reserves*.

The Fed funds rate – A simple example

Bank 1

Required reserves = $100 m

Actual held = $0 m

So it has a deficit = $100 m

Bank 2

Required reserves = $200 m

Actual held = $300 m

So it has an excess = $100 m

Bank 2 can lend the excess reserves to Bank 1.

The rate for this type of short-term loan is the Fed funds rate.

The Federal Open Market Committee (FOMC) This is the committee that decides on changes in US monetary policy. It is made up of twelve individuals. The core seven come from the Central Federal Reserve Bank (based in Washington) and the other five represent the various Federal District Reserve Banks. One of these, New York, has a permanent place on the FOMC. The other eleven banks share the remainder of the votes on a complex rotation system.

The FOMC reviews the outlook for the economy before deciding on the next move in interest rates. At the end of the meeting a vote from the twelve members decides on the correct target level for the Fed funds rate in the immediate future.

Transparency This is one of the key criteria used to assess a Central Bank's performance. The level of transparency at a central bank tells us how open it is in terms of any major decisions that it makes. As a result we judge a central bank to be highly transparent if these actions are clear and easy to understand.

Hint: For more information see Article 8 which has a much more detailed discussion of this term in the 'key terms' section.

Yield curves The yield curve is a very important tool in financial markets. It is vital that you understand this concept very well because it is often discussed in the *Financial Times* and it is a key determinant of future economic growth.

So what is a yield curve? It is a graph that shows the current structure of interest rates or yields right across the full range of maturities.

What do we mean by the 'range of maturities'? Maturity simply means the length of time that we are borrowing money for. So a company might take out a bank loan with a maturity period of just three months. This means that in three months time they must repay this loan.

The 'range of maturities' refers to the different time periods which might run from very short-term borrowing in the money markets (starting with overnight loans) all the way to extremely long-term borrowing in the bond markets extending all the way to 40 years plus.

2

FINANCIAL INSTITUTIONS FEATURING INVESTMENT BANKS

What do we mean by interest rates/yields? When an individual or a company borrows money there is a cost that they have to pay in order to obtain the funds. If it is a short-term loan (up to one year) this is normally referred to as an interest rate. So we might take out a one month bank loan with an annual interest rate of say 8.5 per cent. This is the interest rate, or the cost of obtaining the funds.

If a company needs to borrow funds for a longer time period this will normally be through the issue of a bond market security which is usually repaid at a fixed rate of annual interest (this is called the 'coupon') until it is finally repaid on the date that it redeems or matures. The yield on the bond issue is the cost to the issuer or the return to investor who buys the bond.

The yield curve always shows the interest rate or yield plotted vertically with the maturity plotted horizontally. The yield curve is described as being *upward sloping* (Figure 2.1) when the level of interest rates/yields increases in line with maturity. This is the normal shape of the yield curve. This is not surprising. You should expect the rate of return on your money to increase the longer you invest your money. So you would expect a 5-year bond to pay a better rate of return than a one-month deposit account. In addition the higher return on longer-term maturities also reflects the risk that rising inflation will reduce the real return to the bond holder. This risk of rising inflation will be greater on longer-dated bonds.

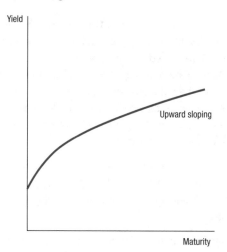

Figure 2.1 Normal or upward sloping yield curve

Sometimes the yield curve will take on a very different shape. For example, it can become inverted or *downward sloping* (Figure 2.2). This tends to happen when the central bank tightens monetary policy aggressively, resulting in a very high level of short-term interest rates. Consequently, there is an expectation that the economy will slow down with very little threat of rising inflation. As a result, the level of long-term bond yields will be relatively low reflecting the expectation of low inflation rates.

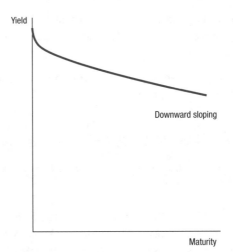

Figure 2.2 Inverted or downward-sloping yield curve

Finally, there are times when the yield curve will become relatively *flat* (Figure 2.3). Indeed this is the case with the US bond market at the time of this *Financial Times* article. There were two alternative explanations for this development. First, the high level of short-term interest rates, caused by the Fed's aggressive tightening of monetary policy, had killed off any risk of higher inflation. This resulted in long-term bond yields and short-term interest rates hitting similar levels. The second explanation is that the presence of low long-term bond yields was resulting in a very resilient economic background in the United States. This caused short-term interest rates to be kept at a high level.

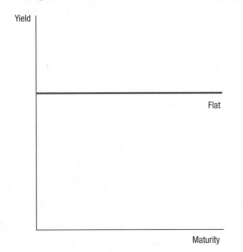

Figure 2.3 Flat yield curve

10-year Treasury notes This refers to the US Treasury bond market. The US government issues a range of 'I owe you' (IOU) certificates sold internationally to finance its budget deficit (the difference between its revenue and spending). The level of returns on shorter-dated US Treasury bonds is influenced by the outlook for the economy which will determine the level of short-term interest rates. The level of bond yields on longer-dated issues will be primarily determined by the outlook for inflation in the United States. In the US all Treasury bonds are referred to as Treasury notes until they go past maturities of 10 years. (See Article 9 for more details of the US bond market.)

Tightening monetary policy When you see the term 'monetary policy' in the context of central banks it refers to interest rate policy.

Central banks tighten monetary policy when they raise interest rates.

Central banks ease monetary policy when they cut interest rates.

In this article the Fed is coming to the end of a period of significant tightening in monetary policy as they have raised interest rates in the last 14 consecutive FOMC meetings. This restrictive monetary policy is designed to counter the other financial conditions that remain accommodative. These include low long-term interest rates (which stimulates lending), the buoyant level of share prices (which stimulates spending as people feel wealthy) and the weaker dollar (which boosts US exports).

Hawkish In the context of central banks, commentators often use the terms 'hawkish' and 'dovish' to describe members of the Central Bank Committees who set interest rates. For example, a hawkish member of the FOMC tends to be very concerned about maintaining a clear anti-inflation policy and so is more likely to vote for an increase in interest rates. In contrast, a dovish member of the FOMC tends to be more relaxed about the inflation outlook and as a consequence is less likely to vote for any increase in interest rates.

■ What do you think?

1. In the context of central banks what is meant by the term 'transparency'?

2. The article suggests that the new Fed chairman might want to introduce a more formal inflation objective over time. What do you think would be the advantages and disadvantages of such a move?

   Hint: You might like to compare the Fed's policy with the more formal inflation targets that are used by the Bank of England and the European Central Bank.

3. Why has the FOMC raised the Fed funds rate at the last 14 consecutive meetings?

4. What are the two alternative explanations for the flat shape of the yield curve? What are the implications of these views for the outlook for economic activity in the US?

5. What would the likely impact be of this slowdown on the US stock markets, bond markets and money markets?

■ Investigate FT data

You will need the Companies and Markets section of the *Financial Times*.

Go to the Market Data section and look at the top right-hand side of the page.

In this section you will see various data on interest rates. You need to examine the section that looks at the level of official rates.

Now answer these questions:

1. What is the current level of the Fed funds rate?
2. When it was last changed?
3. What was it a year ago?
4. How does the level of US official interest rates compare to the other major world economies?

■ Go to the web

Go the Federal Reserve's official website: www.federalreserve.gov.

Find the section on the Fed's monetary policy. Locate the latest minutes of the FOMC.

Look at the last few pages where the decision on interest rates is being discussed.

a. What were the main economic factors discussed by the FOMC at this meeting?
b. What was the target rate for the Fed funds rate set by the FOMC?
c. Can you identify any particularly hawkish or dovish members of the FOMC?

■ Research

The best place to learn more about central banks are the official websites from the major central banks. They all have a great deal of material on monetary policy and the key roles of the central banks.

For reference you will find these at:

www.federalreserve.gov

www.ecb.int/home/html/index.en.html

www.bankofengland.co.uk

In addition you might find these references helpful:

Howell, P. and Bain, K. (2008) *The Economics of Money, Banking and Finance*, 3rd edn, Harlow, UK: FT Prentice Hall. You should focus on Chapter 4, especially pp. 103–6.

Mishkin, F. and Eakins, S. (2008) *Financial Markets and Institutions*, 6th edn, Pearson Addison Wesley. You should look at Chapter 6 on the Federal Reserve.

Valdez, S. (2007) *An Introduction to Global Financial Markets*, 5th edn, Basingstoke: Palgrave Macmillan. You should look at Chapter 3. This provides a good general introduction to the role of central banks.

2

FINANCIAL INSTITUTIONS FEATURING INVESTMENT BANKS

The roller-coaster life of an investment banker

The gap between these two articles was almost exactly two years. However, during this period the state of the investment banking industry had gone from boom to bust. In the wake of the credit crunch we had seen the demise of some of the premium names in this sector including Lehman Brothers and Bear Stearns, and the rest had been forced to write off billions of dollars due to the much reduced value of a wide range of their financial assets. At the time of the second article the investment banking industry was in a perilous state. However, these financial institutions are remarkably resilient and very skilled in changing the nature of their businesses. They have a tradition of being able to reorganise their operations and finding a series of new activities that will once again prove to be profitable in time.

So, despite the difficulties that faced the industry, investment banking remains a very attractive career combining real influence with enormous wealth. Certainly a significant number of students decide to embark on the difficult search for a place on a graduate training scheme with one of these prestigious institutions. With a starting salary as high as £50 000 soon growing to six figures and the ultimate lure of seven figure bonuses, the attraction is obvious. However, be warned, this is no easy ride. The hours can be horrendously long, and as a new graduate you are required to make a significant commitment to the company. For example, you will be expected to stay and work on projects long into the evening, sometimes through the night and at weekends. It is an extreme environment which you will quickly grow to either love or hate.

Article 6   *Financial Times*, 27 November 2006   **FT**

How long can the good times last? Bankers cautious despite bids and bumper bonuses

Peter Thal Larsen

At a private dinner in the City of London early last week, the top brass at one of the Square Mile's leading investment banks were reflecting on the tumultuous events of the past few days.

In 24 hours, takeovers with an aggregate value of $75 bn (£38.8 bn) had been unveiled. These included the largest private equity deal on record – Blackstone's $36 bn offer for Equity Office Properties, the commercial real estate group, as well as Nasdaq's $5.1 bn bid for the London Stock Exchange.

The flurry of deals capped what could be a record year. Powered by cheap debt and buoyant equity markets, most investment banking businesses expect to hit new highs in profitability, surpassing records set in 2000, at the peak of the dotcom bubble.

This will fuel a new round of bumper bonuses in the City and on Wall Street, as bankers whose earning power has been eclipsed by traders in recent years once again climb up the compensation league tables.

Yet the mood round the dinner table last week was cautious, even bordering on the pessimistic. Bankers marvelled at the aggressive takeover bids, shook their heads at the amount of leverage some companies were willing to take on, and warned that it could not last.

Whether in New York, London or Hong Kong, dealmakers acknowledge they are operating in a near perfect environment. Low long-term interest rates, combined with the globalisation of capital flows and booming demand for raw materials and energy have created the ideal incubator for deals.

Despite the rise in short-term interest rates this year, investors searching for additional yield are still piling into the leveraged finance market, allowing private equity groups and companies to finance large acquisitions with cheap debt.

Volatility in the equity markets has declined, making it easier to launch initial public offerings. 'The stars are still incredibly well aligned and there's rightly a fear that this can't last', says Franck Petitgas, head of European investment banking at Morgan Stanley. 'But my sense is we are in an environment that still is very good for our business.'

By their very nature, investment bankers tend to be optimists. But in private, many agree conditions can only get worse. Default rates on the most speculative grades of corporate debt, now at lows, will rise. Equity markets will become more volatile and corporate executives less confident.

'We just have to carry on making hay while the sun shines', says one London-based dealmaker.

The cautious mood is in striking contrast with the peak of the last cycle in 2000. At the time, many bankers argued that the buoyant market could continue indefinitely, and that the impact of new technology had made traditional business

cycles less relevant. Memories of the painful downturn in 2001 and 2002, when investment banks slashed costs as activity dried up, are still vivid.

That said, there is little to suggest an impending downturn. Long-term interest rates are still low and economic growth prospects relatively benign. Surplus savings built up in Asia and the Middle East are still being recycled in the capital markets.

The market has also proved remarkably resilient to shocks: the collapse of Amaranth, the hedge fund that lost $6 bn betting on US gas prices, barely registered.

Barring a large-scale terrorist attack, a widespread outbreak of avian flu, or another war in the Middle East, few can see what will cause the cycle to turn.

That said, there are signs of excess. Bankers point to the competing bids for Corus, the Anglo-Dutch steelmaker, and the offer for Qantas, the Australian airline, by a consortium of private equity and infrastructure groups as signs that lenders are now willing to apply financial leverage to industries that were traditionally not seen as sufficiently stable to service large amounts of debt.

Shareholders in companies that are on the receiving end of takeover bids have also become more demanding: despite concerns about competition and the absence of any credible rival buyers, investors in the London Stock Exchange responded to Nasdaq's bid by pushing the shares well above the US exchange's 'final' offer.

But some are becoming more cautious. Merrill Lynch's monthly survey of fund managers for November showed cash balances had increased from 3.8 per cent in the previous month to 4.1 per cent, while one in five fund managers had an overweight position in cash.

Last week, more than 100 of Lazard's top investment bankers cashed in shares worth about $300 m; their first opportunity to sell shares since Lazard's IPO last year. Shares in the independent

→

investment bank, which is heavily geared to the M&A cycle, are up 80 per cent since joining the market.

Investment banks are also hedging their bets by preparing for a downturn. Goldman Sachs has hired several bankers who specialise in bankruptcies and restructuring work while one of the bank's funds has handed $685 m to Wilbur Ross, the leading distressed debt investor.

Perella Weinberg, the newly created investment banking boutique, recently recruited a top Wall Street bankruptcy adviser.

Despite their willingness to underwrite debt offerings for leveraged buy-outs, banks also appear to be pulling in their horns. Simon Maughan, an analyst at Blue Oak Capital, points out that asset growth in the UK banking industry has slowed sharply this year after reaching a peak of more than 20 per cent.

Previous slowdowns have been associated with slowing revenues. 'Our thesis is that excess liquidity in the global economy has allowed banks to create more and more derivative products from a stock of debt and equity. This is banking alchemy, the ability to turn a given asset into new money-making opportunities several times over', he says. 'The current boom in banking revenues is thus a liquidity bubble, like many others throughout history, and the major question is when it will end. That is, if it hasn't already.'

Few bankers are willing to call the top of the cycle. Some point out that regulators and credit ratings agencies have been warning about a possible turn for several years. Besides, if there is a slowdown this does not mean the market will collapse. One senior investment banking executive argues expectations of a downturn make it less likely to occur.

'It's only when everyone begins to believe that this will go on for ever that we really need to start worrying.'

M&A volumes
Annual total ($'000bn)

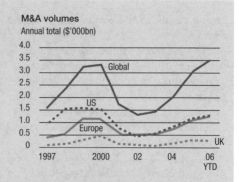
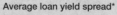

Average loan yield spread*
Over Euribor, basis points

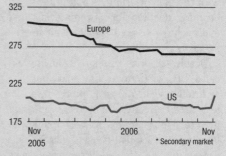

UK resident banks' asset growth
Per cent

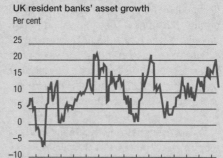
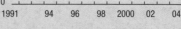

Equity volatility
VIX index

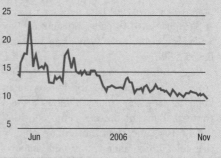

■ The analysis

Investment banks are very powerful financial institutions that are right at the heart of most corporate finance activities reported in the *Financial Times*. It is useful to split them into two parts. The Investment Banking Division (IBD) will work with the issuers of new capital. So they will advise on new primary market issues of debt or equity. The clients of the IBD will be mainly companies and governments. At the same time the Markets Division focuses on the trading of existing issues in the secondary market. The clients of the Markets Division will be the main investors in capital market products. This will primarily be the pension funds and the insurance companies.

This *Financial Times* article clearly sets out the conditions that have created the 'near perfect environment. Low long-term interest rates, combined with the globalisation of capital flows and booming demand for raw materials and energy have created the ideal incubator for deals.' Investment banks rely on new deals to keep them busy and to justify their enormous fee income. This has led to a record level of bonuses being paid to the directors in the Investment Banking Division.

However, faced by this boom period, there is not surprisingly a mood of some caution creeping in, since many insiders believe we are reaching the top of the cycle. There are signs of excesses appearing, and the article cites the increasing willingness of the banks to lend large amounts to industries like steel and the airlines which have been traditionally seen as too risky to service large amounts of debt finance. In addition, the investment bankers at Lazard Brothers recently sold some $300 m of shares in their firm following the initial public offer (IPO) in 2005. Other investment banks are beginning to ready themselves for a downturn by hiring staff specialising in bankruptcies and corporate restructuring.

As usual there are mixed views on the exact timing of the top of the market, and the catalyst for this reversal of fortunes is never clear until it happens. However, the one thing we know is this business is highly cyclical and a wise investment banker is always planning for the downturn. We might soon see the following advert in the classifieds section of the *Financial Times*:

Second hand Ferrari for sale.
£50 000 ono.
One careful investment banking owner.
Only 5000 miles on the clock.
He was too busy to get to drive it!

| Article 7 | *Financial Times*, 4 November 2008 | FT |

JPMorgan to cut prop trading desk

Francesco Guerrera, Justin Baer and Jeremy Grant

JPMorgan Chase is to scrap its standalone proprietary trading desk, highlighting how the dearth of investment opportunities is prompting banks to retreat from in-house hedge funds that had thrived before the turmoil.

People close to the situation said the decision to fold the 80-strong global proprietary trading unit into JPMorgan's other trading operations could result in job losses. The bank is believed to be looking at other areas where operations overlap and could announce further reorganisations and job cuts in months to come. JPMorgan, which has acquired the investment bank Bear Stearns and the regional lender Washington Mutual, has already announced 4100 job cuts, according to Bloomberg data.

JPMorgan's move, announced in an internal memorandum, is a sign of financial groups' reluctance to deploy their own capital on large trading positions amid uncertain market conditions.

'Our business and industry have changed dramatically this year and within this new market paradigm, the advantages of aligning our proprietary trading activities with the core business are clear', Steve Black and Bill Winters, co-heads of JPMorgan's investment bank, said in the memo, which was obtained by the *Financial Times*.

The disappearance of JPMorgan's separate proprietary trading desk, which mirrors similar moves by rivals, is a reversal of the strategy followed by many financial groups in the recent past.

During the years that preceded the current turmoil, most large banks rushed to create in-house hedge funds to put their own capital to work and exploit favourable market conditions.

Proprietary trading became an important source of profit for Wall Street companies such as Goldman Sachs and Morgan Stanley, as well as their European counterparts.

Banks do not publish results of their proprietary trading units, but analysts estimate that many of them suffered significant losses on mortgage securities and other toxic assets when the financial boom turned to bust last year.

A senior official at a US brokerage house based in London said: 'I think a lot of people are taking a step back and looking at their risk matrices from top to bottom, and working out whether they have good risk models in place.'

JPMorgan declined to comment, but people close to the company said that merging the unit that used the group's own capital with the operations that trade equities, fixed income, commodities and other assets on behalf of clients would reduce duplication and increase efficiencies.

Until the expected completion of the merger of the two groups at the end of the month, the proprietary unit will not be allowed to place any new trades, according to people close to the situation.

People close to JPMorgan said the move would not necessarily mean that the bank would reduce its proprietary trading activities but added that, in the short term, that was likely. They argued that the markets' convulsions of the past few months made it difficult and riskier for any bank to place proprietary trades with its own capital.

■ The analysis

At the end of the analysis of Article 6 I suggested that, despite the boom times for investment bankers in the autumn of 2006, they might soon find conditions much tougher. That was one prediction that came right very soon. This article focuses on the impact of these more challenging times on the US investment bank JPMorgan Chase. Earlier in the year they had hit the headlines when they played a pivotal role in rescuing the cash-strapped investment bank Bear Stearns from the brink of collapse. JPMorgan Chase bought out the assets of Wall Street's fifth-largest investment bank for a fraction of its previous value. They paid just $236 m for a financial institution that had been valued at over $140 bn before the credit crunch had undermined confidence in the bank.

A few months on from this deal JPMorgan Chase was back in the news, this time acting to reduce its own risk within their trading teams. An internal memo written by Steve Black and Bill Winters, the co-heads of JPMorgan's investment bank, confirmed that they were acting to close an 80-strong global proprietary trading team. It is important to explain the significance of this development. Proprietary trading is where the investment bank uses its own capital to take a trading position in the hope of making a significant financial gain.

For example we might have an equity proprietary trader who thinks that the share price of Barclays Bank has fallen too far. They buy 1 million shares in Barclays for, say, £2.50 each. If they are right and the share price rises to £3.50 in the next week or so, they will make:

1 m x £1 = £1 m for the bank.

However, if instead the share price falls, this trade will run up huge losses.

You should see that proprietary trading is just about the most risky thing that an investment bank does! So at a time of huge financial market uncertainty we should not be too surprised to see the investment banks curtailing these activities.

However, the decision to cut back on the activities of proprietary trading teams was quite a departure for the banks. Prior to the credit crunch these investment banks had spent large amounts of money developing in-house investment funds which aimed to use the bank's own capital to make money from these types of trading activities. However, it was clear that in the new world where the focus was on risk reduction this was one type of activity that would be on the back burner at least for a while.

■ Key terms

Investment banks An investment bank acts as an intermediary between the issuers of capital (governments and companies) and the investors in capital (pension funds and insurance companies). They are normally split into four divisions:

Bonds – new issues
Equities – new issues
Merger and acquisitions (M&A)
Real estate (property).

Their staff will work either in the investment banking division (IBD) which deals with the new issues of debt and equity capital or the markets division which deals with the investors in new bond and equity deals.

The people who work in the IBD division will typically work on several projects. As an example this might involve meeting a company to suggest that they should take advantage of favourable market conditions to launch a new international bond issue. This will involve the senior staff making a presentation to the finance director/CEO of the company involved.

Proprietary trading This is where the investment bank uses its own capital to fund trading strategies that are designed to earn them significant profits. This form of trading can be in a wide range of financial markets.

Real Estate Group This is a key division within an investment bank that deals with any aspects of commercial property deals.

Primary and secondary market The IBD will work with companies with their initial issue of new shares. This is called the 'primary' market. The markets division will then work in the secondary market which is where new buyers can purchase these shares from existing holders. This is normally a standard marketplace like the Stock Exchange's official list.

Hedge fund These are specialised funds that use large amounts of borrowed money to invest in bonds, equities, currencies or various derivative products. They take more risk than a traditional investment fund in the hope of making much higher returns.

Leveraged This refers to the capital structure of the new company being formed. The term 'leveraged' suggests that the company will be financed largely by borrowed money.

Default This is where a borrower takes out a loan but fails to keep to the original agreed schedule of interest payments and final capital repayments. A bond issued by the United States or United Kingdom government is generally regarded to be free of default risk. In contrast, a bond issued by a company might well have significant risk of default. For example, a company might not be able to keep up with the interest payments on the loan as a result of a downturn in its profitability.

Initial public offer (IPO) In the primary capital market this is where a company makes its first issue of shares. These IPO's are organised by investment banks who charge substantial fees to their clients for this service.

Mortgage-backed securities This is where a large amount of mortgage debt is pooled together and then sold to a different set of investors in the form of a securitised financial market instrument. During the credit crisis the existence of these securities was at the heart of the multi-billion dollar write-offs required at many of the banks.

■ What do you think?

1. Describe the main functions of an investment bank.

2. Explain the various factors that have contributed to the 'near perfect environment' for the investment banking industry during 2006.

3. How did the investment banks react during the last downturn between 2001 and 2002?

4. What were the main risks that threatened the outlook for the investment banking industry at this time?

5. What is meant by the term 'proprietary trading'?

6. Why did many investment banks suffer large losses on proprietary trading in mortgage-backed securities and other toxic assets?

7. What are the main risks that investment banks face?

8. It has been argued that in the search for extra profitability retail banks had made a grave mistake in allowing their investment banking arms to take on excessive risks. To what extent does this show that there is a fundamental problem in trying to combine retail and investment banks in one business?

■ Go to the web

Go to the website for Barclays Capital Investment Bank at www.barcap.com.

Take a look at the main sections (on the left-hand side)

Financing
Risk Management
Investment Banking
Distribution, etc.

You are now required to write a short note (500 words max) explaining what each of these key areas does in practice.

■ Research plus careers advice:

Gitman, L. (2009) *Principles of Managerial Finance*, 12th edn, Harlow, UK: Pearson International Edition. The role of investment banks is briefly mentioned on p. 340.

Valdez, S. (2007) *An Introduction to Global Financial Markets*, Basingstoke: Palgrave Macmillan. You should look at Chapter 5. This contains a very good introduction to the role of investment banks.

In addition, most of the large investment banks have excellent websites. You will often get some outline of some recent corporate activities that the banks have worked on.

These sites also include advice on careers in most areas of the bank. This might include details of useful internships that the investment banks run. They are an excellent way to gain an insight into a career in this sector. Be warned: if you want to apply to an investment bank, they have very early closing dates normally in the January before their next graduate training scheme starts.

A few examples of these investment bank websites are:

www.nomura.com/europe (Nomura)

www2.goldmansachs.com/uk (Goldman Sachs)

www.jpmorgan.com/pages/jpmorgan/investbk (JP Morgan)

2

FINANCIAL INSTITUTIONS FEATURING INVESTMENT BANKS

More transparency needed at the Bank of England

Whenever I write about the Bank of England it always makes me feel slightly uneasy. This is because back in 1997, when I was combining an academic career with consultancy work in the City, I happened to be talking to an audience of fund managers on the day the new Labour government came to power. I was asked if I thought the new government would make the Bank of England independent and allow it to set UK interest rates free of interference from the politicians. My answer was confident and short. I said: 'There is no chance of that happening; who waits 18 years to gain political office and then gives up a major instrument of economic power?' The next day I opened my *Financial Times* and saw with horror the headline 'Chancellor Brown to make Bank of England independent'.

Article 8   *Financial Times*, 3 May 2007   **FT**

Bank to give better guidance over rates

Chris Giles and Scheherazade Daneshkhu

The Bank of England has pledged to give financial markets a better idea of the circumstances that are likely to trigger interest rate changes.

The undertaking follows mounting criticism of the bank's communications policy as it celebrates the 10th anniversary of its independence to set interest rates.

Mervyn King, governor, told the *Financial Times* that the central bank was 'clearly' failing to explain properly to markets how it was likely to respond to economic data.

Futures markets have bounced erratically this year as investors struggled to understand the Bank's thinking in raising interest rates by a quarter-point to 5.25 per cent in January.

A Reuters poll of 49 City economists yesterday found 25 saying that the Bank had become less effective in communicating policy over the past year.

In a speech last night, Mr King rejected the idea of publishing a forecast for interest rates. Speaking to the FT, he insisted the Bank would not 'do monetary policy by code word', the practice by which the Federal Reserve and the European Central Bank use particular phrases to signal future rates decisions.

But he added that he viewed favourably the demand from City economists for 'something to guide them how to interpret the future data as they come out, as they want to know how we are likely to interpret that data'.

'It will require quite a lot of hard work on our part in thinking it through, but I think we should do it', he said, telling the FT the Bank was 'clearly not doing enough of it now – which is to give people this feel for how we are likely to react to data'.

Looking back over the past decade, Mr King said he was convinced that the Bank's independence had improved Britain's economy. From being the lowest ranked Group of Seven economy before 1997, the UK had moved towards the top.

While other factors were also at work, the governor insisted that the strong belief among the public that inflation would remain low 'has been fundamental'.

Mr King repeated earlier comments that bank officials 'weren't terribly enthusiastic' about the 2003 change in the inflation target to the consumer price index, partly because this measure excluded housing costs.

He also said that current efforts by Eurostat, the European statistical agency, to include housing were late and unsatisfactory.

'I must say that the experiments they've been carrying out have not been with measures of housing costs that I would find the most attractive', he said.

On the topic of appointments to the Monetary Policy Committee, Mr King said he did not think there was 'anything basically wrong with the process'.

An FT survey of 13 of the committee's 14 past members, however, found a majority suggesting that the process should be overhauled.

Professor Willem Buiter, who served between 1997 and 2000, argued: 'The process for internal members is completely non-transparent. For external members it is both completely non-transparent and a shambles'.

■ The analysis

The key activity of the Bank of England's Monetary Policy Committee (MPC) is to set the level of the repo rate which is consistent with the government's 2 per cent target for consumer price inflation in the UK. The MPC meets at the start of every month and it has a detailed discussion of the current state of the economy before deciding on the right level of interest rates. It comprises five members appointed from within the Bank of England and four external members. The latter members normally come from academia, industry or the trade unions.

Financial markets watch the MPC meetings very closely, trying to predict any future moves in interest rates. In January 2007 the MPC surprised virtually every City economist with the decision to raise the repo rate by 25 basis points to 5.25 per cent. One reason for the shock was that the previous meeting had reached a unanimous decision to hold rates at 5 per cent and the markets did not expect any increase in interest rates at least until the inflation report was published in February 2007. After this move the markets became concerned that the Bank of England either had an early sight of some bad economic news or that it was radically changing the way that it was reacting to published economic data. Either way the markets were confused and sought immediate clarification.

One sign of these worries is well stated in this *Financial Times* article. As it says 'the futures markets have bounced erratically this year as investors struggled to understand the Bank's thinking in raising interest rates by a quarter point in January'. Normally these markets are an excellent guide to future interest rate policy. If you want to get a good indication of how official interest rates will move in the next twelve months, you just look at 'one-year' sterling Libor rates in the money markets. However, in recent times these futures rates have become very volatile, reflecting the uncertainty about what drives official interest rate policy in the UK.

In this latest speech by the Governor of the Bank of England, Mervyn King rejected the formal publication of an interest rate forecast. This policy might be considered too inflexible and in addition he was not keen to follow the Fed or the European Central Bank in using various 'code words' to signal future interest-rate decisions. However, the markets would like to be given more insight into the relative importance of various economic data releases and to see how the Bank of England interprets this data. For example, in terms of the inflation outlook what is the relative importance of wage costs versus other important inflationary factors such as raw materials or housing costs?

The Governor also confirmed that the Bank of England was not keen on the decision in 2003 to change the measure of inflation being tracked by the government. The move then was to abandon the Retail Price Index (RPI) in favour of the Consumer Price Index (CPI). This was a significant change designed to bring UK inflation measures more into line with other European countries. However, there are severe problems with the CPI as it does not include council taxes and mortgage interest payments. These factors have both been partly responsible for the sharp rise in the RPI which has led to calls for compensating pay rises especially in the public sector.

Finally, the Governor turns to the controversial area of the appointment of members of the MPC. A previous member of the MPC, Willem Buiter, said 'the process for internal members is completely non transparent. For external members it is both completely non-transparent and a shambles'. Some of this criticism followed the appointment of David Blanchflower who teaches at Dartmouth College in the US. It has been argued it is fundamentally wrong to appoint someone who lives outside of the UK as an external member of the MPC. I am not sure that I agree with this view. However, I might be somewhat biased. This is because back in 1977 Mr Blanchflower had the misfortune to have to teach A-level economics to one less than brilliant pupil. However, as an inspirational teacher he helped this pupil to achieve a good A-level grade and he even persuaded him to go onto university to study Economics further. Perhaps, it is a little late now but I would just like to record my sincere thanks to him!

■ Key terms

Monetary Policy Committee The Bank of England's Monetary Policy Committee (MPC) is in charge of setting UK interest rates. It is made up of nine members:

    The Governor
    Two Deputy-Governors
    Two Bank of England Executive Directors
    Four independent members.

They are required by the government to ensure that the UK economy enjoys price stability. This is defined by the government's set inflation target of 2 per cent.

Repo rate This is the UK's official interest rate which is used to supply funds to the money markets through sterling money market operations. On the Bank of England's website it states that the Bank of England's first objective in the money market is that 'overnight market interest rates [are] in line with the Bank's official rate, so that there is a flat money market yield curve, consistent with the official policy rate, with very limited day-to-day or intra-day volatility in market interest rates at maturities out to that horizon'. Put simply, this means that they try to impose their repo rate target on the UK's money markets.

Retail Price Index/Consumer Price Index Until 2003 the UK government's target for inflation was set in terms of the percentage annual increase in the average prices of goods and services as measured by the Retail Price Index (RPI). There was some controversy in 2003 when the relevant inflation measure was changed to the Consumer Price Index (CPI) which excludes certain important costs such as council tax and mortgage interest payments. If you want much more information on this go to the National Statistics website at www.statistics.gov.uk.

Futures markets In the money markets there is a well-established futures market that allows banks to deal at a set interest rate for a transaction on a specified future date. For example, a bank could arrange to lend £10 m to another bank at a set interest rate on a specific date in the future. The attraction of this deal is that both parties know now what the interest rate is going to be. There is no uncertainty as this transaction will not be affected by any subsequent rise or fall in money market interest rates.

London Interbank Offered Rate (Libor) If you look at the Market Data (in the Companies and Markets section of the *Financial Times*) you will see a column marked 'Interest Rates'. In this column you will see interest rates for US$, € Libor and £ Libor. Libor stands for the London Interbank Offered Rate. This is the rate used for loans made to low-risk banks in the London money markets. You can get a Libor rate for a wide range of money market maturities. It starts with overnight money and then goes to one month, three months, six months and one year.

The Libor for sterling is set each day by 16 banks including Abbey National, Barclays Bank, Citibank, JPMorgan Chase and the Royal Bank of Canada. On the day I wrote this case study (18 June 2007) the one-year rate was 6.11 per cent compared to 5.61 per cent for overnight money. This suggests that the money market traders were expecting a further 50 basis points increase in official interest rates in the next year.

During the first part of September 2007 there were dramatic events in the UK money markets in the wake of the US sub-prime loan crisis. There were concerns that some banks had a significant exposure to the resulting bad loans in the US. As a result the banks became reluctant to lend money to each other. This had a significant impact on the UK interbank money markets with three-month Libor rising to a nine-year high of 6.8 per cent.

Transparency This refers to the methods used by the central bank to make information available about the process of setting interest rates. The term 'transparency' refers to how open this is in practice.

We could, for example, rank the Bank of England out of a score of five on the basis of three measures of transparency:

1. Publication of minutes of the MPC: Score = 4.5/5

    They are very clearly written and they state the range of factors used to decide on the correct level of short-term interest rates.

2. Timing of publication of minutes: Score = 5/5

    The minutes are published about two weeks after the meetings take place.

3. Inflation target: Score = 4/5

    The inflation rate that the Bank of England targets is set by the UK government.

Total score = 13.5/15 which makes it highly transparent.

However, there is one aspect of the MPC that is possibly less than transparent. This is discussed at the end of this article where there is a suggestion the current policy of selecting internal (from within the Bank of England) and external (from outside the Bank of England) members of the MPC is non-transparent. This means that to any outsider the selection procedure and criteria are unclear.

Group of Seven This refers to some of the most influential economies in the World including the United States, Germany, Japan, France, UK, Canada and Italy. They meet regularly to discuss economic policy. These days their meetings often involve Russia (so it is really a G-8 now).

■ What do you think?

1. What are the disadvantages in the Bank of England publishing a formal interest rate forecast?
2. Explain what is meant by the Bank of England's repo rate.
3. What is the main role of the Bank of England's Monetary Policy Committee?
4. Explain the difference between the Retail Price Index and the Consumer Price Index.
5. Why have there been calls for greater transparency in terms of the way that the Monetary Policy Committee works?
6. In September 2007 we saw the three-month sterling Libor rate hit a nine-year high at 6.8 per cent. Give reasons for this sharp rise in Libor and discuss the possible implications for both savers and borrowers.

■ Investigate FT data

You will need the Companies and Markets section of the *Financial Times*. Go to the Market Data section and look at the middle right-hand side of the page. In this section you will see various data on interest rates. You need to examine the section that looks at the level of market rates.

Answer these questions:

1. What is the current level of £ Libor overnight?
2. What is the current level of £ Libor three months?
3. What is the current level of £ Libor six months?
4. What is the current level of £ Libor one year?

On the basis of these answers give a clear explanation of the market's view of the Bank of England's interest rate policy in the next year.

■ Go to the web

Go the Bank of England's official website at www.bankofengland.co.uk.

Find the section on monetary policy. Locate the latest minutes of the MPC. Read these minutes and take some brief notes.

a. What were the possible interest rate options that were discussed by the MPC?

b. What was their final decision?

c. Were there any members of the MPC who dissented?

■ Research

The best places to learn more about central banks are the official websites of the major central banks. They are all fantastic learning resources with a great deal of material on monetary policy and the key roles of the central banks. You will also see a wide range of current data on inflation and interest rates.

For reference you will find these at:

www.federalreserve.gov

www.ecb.int/home/html/index.en.html

www.bankofengland.co.uk

It is also essential to read the *Financial Times* just after the major meetings of the central banks. These articles appear in the main section of the paper.

Hint: Look in the headlines for references to the FOMC, MPC or the key interest rates.

Go to **www.pearsoned.co.uk/boakes** to access Kevin's blog for additional analysis of recent topical news articles and to post your comments. Download podcasts containing short audio summaries of the main issues relating to each article and check your understanding of in-text questions with the handy hints provided.

Financial markets

If you are going to read the *Financial Times* successfully on a regular basis you must get to grips with the daily movements in the world's main financial markets. If there is a major new story, you will normally find it on the front page of the main section of the paper with more analysis in the Lex column on the back page. The feature article included here looks at the impact that rising bond yields might have on the outlook for share prices around the world.

Financial markets exist to facilitate the transfer of funds from people who have excess funds (the lenders) to those who have a deficit of funds (the borrowers). The lenders include individuals, banks, pension funds and insurance companies. The borrowers include individuals, companies and governments. If we examine the individuals, the concepts of excess and deficit funds should become much clearer. If you are at the stage of studying at university or just starting out on a career, it is very likely that you have a financial deficit. Your spending will be greater than your earnings. This is only to be expected. You are investing time and money partly in the hope of securing a well-paid job after graduation. When this happens, you can start to repay your loans and eventually when your income rises you might even get into a position of having a financial surplus. At this stage you will invest your surplus money in a bank or in some shares. This cash will find its way to one of the individual or corporate lenders probably via a financial intermediary like a bank.

The way that cash moves from lenders to borrowers is normally through one of the financial markets that have been created for this purpose. The various financial markets are there to meet the specific requirements of its participants. We can see this by briefly introducing each of the existing major markets:

1. **The money market**. This allows banks with surplus cash to lend these funds to banks with a financial deficit. The key characteristic of this market is its short-term nature. Money market securities are defined as having a maturity of anything up to one year. The key interest rate that is traded in this market is called the London Interbank Offered Rate (Libor). This is the rate used for loans made to low-risk banks in the London money markets. You can get a Libor rate for a wide range of money-market maturities. It starts with overnight money and then goes to one month, three months, six months and one year. This is the market that saw a sharp reduction in liquidity in the wake of the credit crunch.

2. **The bond markets**. Many of the borrowers need to obtain funding for much more than one year. This will include governments, companies and banks that can all access the bond markets to issue longer-term securities.

3. **The equity markets**. These markets allow the lenders to contribute risk capital to a

range of different businesses. They lend their money to these companies without a guarantee of any capital repayment or dividend income in the future. This makes it a risky form of investment but with the possibility of securing very high rates of return at a later stage.

4. **The foreign exchange markets**. These allow people to convert one currency into another. For example, a Japanese investor can exchange Yen for US dollars and use the proceeds to buy some government bonds issued by the United States Treasury. You will see this discussed in detail in Topic 12, which covers international economics.

5. **The derivative markets**. These are the financial instruments which have been developed to allow investors to manage and exploit risk. The name derivative is used because they derive from the fundamental financial products outlined above. The most common examples are futures, options and swaps.

It is likely that as you study finance you will start to develop a keen interest in the trading and performance of these financial markets. I often find that my own students become keen to try their hand at real trading by forming small investment clubs. This is a good way to start to establish a feel for the factors that drive the prices of financial market securities. My advice would be to at least start by not playing with real money but rather just create fictional portfolios and then measure your performance over time. You will quickly see whether you have the right skills needed to become a successful market guru.

The following three articles are analysed in this section:

Article 9
Surprising US job creation data rally stock markets and dollar
Financial Times, 2–3 June 2007

Article 10
Bond yields spark credit concerns
Financial Times, 8 June 2007

Article 11
Bond market sell-off
Financial Times, 8 June 2007

These articles address the following issues:

- the US unemployment and non-farm payroll data;
- key stock market indices;
- the impact of economic releases on financial markets;
- what is meant by benign credit conditions;
- relationship between bond yields and economic activity.

At 1.30 p.m. in London all eyes are on the screens

Every day financial market traders sit at their desks surrounded by a vast array of electronic news services. They wait nervously for the latest economic data to hit their screens and send the financial markets into a trading frenzy. Even though it is many years ago since I sat with them, I can still remember the intense feeling of anticipation ahead of these occasions. My role back then was to sit with the government bond traders and give my instant reaction as the new data was published.

The banks take huge trading positions ahead of these economic releases. The resulting market movements determine whether the traders make serious profits or losses. Their future employment and lucrative bonuses are determined by these outcomes. Moments of joy can be fleeting as they are replaced by anguish as a market goes into freefall.

In terms of economic releases the absolute highlight is the employment data from the United States. It is always published at 1.30 p.m. London time on the first Friday of each new month. This release often sets the tone for the later releases and it can cause major shifts in market expectations.

| Article 9 | *Financial Times*, 2–3 June 2007 **FT** |

Surprising US job creation data rally stock markets and dollar

FT reporters

The US economy appeared to be pulling out of a stall yesterday as figures showing surprisingly strong job creation and factory expansion pushed stocks into record territory.

With inflation also slightly softer, there is little immediate pressure on the Federal Reserve to change interest rates in either direction.

Alan Ruskin, a currency strategist at RBS, said the figures 'should send another dagger in the heart' of those investors betting that the Fed would cut rates.

Employers added 157 000 staff to their payrolls last month following an increase of 80 000 the previous month, while the unemployment rate held steady, near to five-year lows at 4.5 per cent, the government said.

Surprisingly, no net loss of construction jobs was reported, in spite of the severe weakness in the housing market.

The service industries accounted for the overwhelming majority of new jobs with an increase of 176 000 in sectors such as banking and restaurants.

Peter Kretzmer, an economist at Bank of America, said: 'The resilience of the labour market will reassure policymakers and market participants that job demand remains relatively healthy'. He added that the figures would allow 'the central bank to maintain its focus on core inflation'.

The demand for staff was seen as a sign that the economy was snapping back from

→

its anaemic performance in the first quarter. It sparked a rally in the dollar.

Labour income also grew at a healthy rate, offering support for consumer spending in spite of the higher petrol price drag.

Bond prices fell as the yield on the benchmark 10-year Treasury note rose 5.3 basis points to 4.945 per cent.

The dollar rose to its highest level against the yen in nearly four months and to a seven-week high against the euro. It was 0.1 per cent higher against the euro at $1.3430 and 0.3 per cent up against the yen at 122.09.

In early trading, the S&P 500 index was 0.6 per cent higher at 1,539.69, while the Nasdaq Composite was up 0.7 per cent at 2,623.11. The Dow Jones Industrial Average was 0.4 per cent firmer at 13,687.77.

Note: reporting by Eoin Callan and Krishna Guha in Washington, Neil Dennis in London and Richard Beales in New York.

■ The analysis

There are many different economic releases published each month. So how can we assess the expected financial market impact of each bit of data? One way to do this is to put them through a three-step screen test to judge their relative importance.

Test 1

What impact do the data have on economic policy making in a particular country? This is important because economic releases become significant if they force changes in economic policy-making.

Test 2

How reliable are the data in this economic release? What does this mean in practice? A good analogy would be if you went to your optician for an eyesight test and he used equipment that gives an initial reading that will be revised to a more accurate level at a later stage. If the initial reading shows that your eyesight is nearly perfect but this is later revised to show that you are in fact seriously short-sighted, you would rightly conclude that the first test was totally unreliable. In the same way we should not regard any economic release that is likely to be heavily revised later to be sufficiently reliable to impact on financial markets. So any economic release must first be considered to be accurate before it can have an impact on financial markets.

Test 3

How soon in a particular month is this data release published? Financial markets are all about finding out information sooner rather than later. So not surprisingly they pay most attention to the indicators that are published first each month.

Let us apply this test to the US employment release

1. *Policy impact.* This is a key factor in US economic policy-making. Just look at any set of Federal Open Market Committee minutes. You will see several references to the state of the labour market in the United States. The employment data do have a significant impact on the direction of the Fed's interest rate policy.

We will score it 9 out of 10.

2. *Reliability.* These employment data are very reliable. Sure, they will get revised, but this does not seriously undermine the initial release.

   We score it 8 out of 10.

3. *Relative timing.* This is the first important economic release each month.

   We score it a maximum 10 out of 10. This gives it a total score of 27 out of 30 making it the number 1 data release in the United States.

The influence of this release goes far wider as traders in all markets watch this release for clues about the state of the world's most important economy and the next move in the Fed's interest rate policy.

This *Financial Times* article reports on the latest employment situation report for May 2007 published on Friday 1 June 2007. It shows a surprisingly strong economic picture with employers adding 157 000 jobs to their payrolls. This followed an 80 000 increase in the previous month. The headline unemployment figure remained at 4.5 per cent. There was further good news in the breakdown of the data with construction employment holding steady, and employment in the services sectors such as banking and restaurants remaining buoyant.

Economists were very upbeat after this release. The article reports one economist at the Bank of America as saying 'the resilience of the labour market will reassure policymakers and market participants that job demand remains relatively healthy'. He goes on to suggest that the resilience of the economy means that the Fed can stay focused on the need to keep inflation under control.

Not surprisingly, the US equity markets reacted positively to the data. These strong economic data are good news for equity prices as long as there are no signs that the economy is overheating. The faster economic data will translate into more profits, more dividends and higher share values. With little fear of the Fed raising interest rates, the markets can just focus on the positive aspects of the employment report. However, it does remove any prospect of an imminent cut in interest rates. The relatively high level of short-term interest rates continues to attract funds into the US money markets which can explain the dollar's rise against the yen and the euro.

The only market to react negatively to the employment data was the US bond market. The *Financial Times* reports that prices fell for the benchmark 10-year Treasury note with the yield rising 5.3 basis points to 4.945 per cent. This is because the risk of higher inflation caused investors to demand a higher rate of return on bonds. This applies especially to long-term investors, as the uncertainty of their purchasing power is even greater.

■ Key terms

Unemployment and non-farm payroll employment release This economic release is made up of three parts. The first figure is the percentage rate of unemployment, which is based on a random survey of people. The second part tells us the change in thousands each month in the number of people on companies' payrolls. It excludes various special categories such as farm workers (hence the non-farm), the self-employed, unpaid family workers and the armed forces.

The final measure looks at the current trends in employee wage costs. It can provide early evidence of any rising cost-push inflation.

Benchmark 10-year Treasury note The United States has the world's largest government bond market. The Treasury market is backed by the US government and as a result is seen as having no default risk. It sets the standard for all other dollar denominated bonds. As a result other dollar issues will see their yields set in relation to the equivalent US Treasury issue. The market can be split into three divisions:

a. *Treasury bills*: This covers three months to 1-year maturity issues.

b. *Treasury notes*: This covers 2–10 year maturity and coupon bonds.

c. *Treasury bonds*: This covers bonds with a maturity of 10 years plus. The key long-term bond is the 30-year benchmark issue.

Standard and Poor's (S&P) The S&P composite index is based on the market movements of 500 companies that are listed on the New York Stock Exchange. This index is one of the most widely used measures of US equity performance.

NASDAQ Composite This is a rival stock market exchange based in the United States. It is run by the National Association of Securities Dealers and their automated quotation system gives us the NASDAQ Index which began in 1971 with a value of 100. It now includes nearly 5000 companies with each one assigned to one of the eight sub-indices – banks, biotechnology, computer, industrial, insurance, other finance, telecom and transportation. In general the NASDAQ index is seen to focus on newer and emerging companies.

Dow Jones Industrial Average (DJIA) The DJIA is the main US stock market index. It is based on the market movements of 30 of the largest blue-chip industrial companies that trade on the New York Stock Exchange. The selection of these companies is revised regularly. It includes companies like American Express, Boeing, Disney, General Electric, Honeywell, Intel, JP Morgan Bank, Procter and Gamble.

■ What do you think?

1. Why does the US employment release have such a significant impact on financial markets?

2. What are the main features of the US employment report released on the first Friday of each month?

3. The latest US employment data shows that economic activity is surprisingly sluggish in the final quarter of the year. There is a sharp fall of 160 000 in employer payrolls compared to an expected rise of some 50 000. In addition there were downward revisions of 40 000 to the previous two months' numbers.

Discuss the likely reaction to this data of:

a. the US stock market

b. the US dollar

c. US government Treasury bonds

d. US short-term interest rates.

■ Investigate FT data

You will need to look at the *Financial Times* on the first weekend edition in any month. Go to the Markets section on the back page of Companies and Markets.

Answer these questions:

1. What impact did the latest US employment data release have on the world's financial markets?

2. What was the impact on the three main US stock market indices?

Hint: Look at the World Markets data on the front page.

■ Go to the web

Go the Bureau of Labor's official website at www.bls.gov/ces.

a. Go to CES News Releases. Read the Employment Situation summary. Take some notes for future reference.

b. You are now required to write a short essay on the latest report from the Bureau of Labor. This should be approximately 300 words.

■ Research

Vaitilingam, R. (2006) *The Financial Times Guide To Using The Financial Pages*, 5th edn, Harlow, UK: FT Prentice Hall, Financial Times. You should especially look at Chapter 7 to get more information on US stock market indices.

In addition www.bloomberg.com often gives excellent coverage of these economic releases.

Financial markets standing at a crossroads

When you first start reading the *Financial Times* there is no doubt that one of the hardest tasks is trying to understand the complex range of factors that cause major market movements. It is similar to trying to find your way around a new capital city. At first the whole process looks like a challenge that you will never master. However, with a little patience you gradually get a feel for the place and you start to see the way the streets fit together. In the same way the technical jargon associated with financial markets can be daunting. But with practice it does get easier and you soon develop an understanding of what drives the major movements in the world's financial markets.

These articles were published at a crucial time. World markets were seen to be at a crossroads. On the one hand there was a rising tide of bearish sentiment expressing the view that interest rates were on a clear rising trend and that this would lead to a severe correction in share prices. At the same time other analysts still remained very bullish. They argued that the rise in interest rates would soon run out of steam and that the fundamental background remained positive for the stock market. The front-page story from the *Financial Times* broadly sets out the prevailing bearish view while the Lex column argues that for now the increase in bond yields was unlikely to cause any serious damage to world markets.

Article 10

Financial Times, 8 June 2007 **FT**

Bond yields spark credit concerns

Michael Mackenzie, Richard Beales and Joanna Chung

The benign credit conditions that have helped fuel the global buyout boom came under threat yesterday as the yield on 10-year US government bonds registered its biggest daily jump in years.

Some analysts suggested the dramatic rise in yields could herald a sustained period of higher interest rates, increasing the cost of borrowing for companies, deflating borrower-friendly credit markets and eventually crimping the outlook for equity markets.

The S&P 500 index fell 1 per cent by midday in New York while the German DAX dropped 1.4 per cent.

'Stocks need to reflect what bond yields are saying', said Michael Kastner, portfolio manager at Sterling Stamos. 'Rate cuts have been taken away and, if yields start to reflect that rate hikes are likely this year, then it will get pretty ugly for stocks.'

The yield on the 10-year US government note hit 5.14 per cent in New York trading, marking the biggest one-day advance in several years, before settling back to 5.10 per cent. That brought 10-year yields above those on shorter-term Treasuries, restoring a more normal – that is, 'steeper' – yield curve.

For much of the past year and a half, longer-dated notes have offered lower yields than shorter-duration bills, creating a 'conundrum', as Alan Greenspan, then chairman of the Federal Reserve, put it in 2005.

But yields on US, European and Japanese government bonds have been climbing for a month, fuelled by strong economic data and, in places, fear of inflation.

Government bond yields soared yesterday in the eurozone and the UK, pushing the 10-year Bund yield to a four-and-half-year high and the 10-year gilt yield to its highest for nine years.

The moves come a day after the European Central Bank raised its main interest rate to 4 per cent. Many investors fear the ECB will continue raising rates this year to counter inflationary pressures. The Bank of England yesterday kept its main interest rate on hold at 5.5 per cent, amid investor worries that rates

could rise next month or in August. Predictions of a Fed rate cut have largely been abandoned.

The sharp rise in the US 10-year bond yield was particularly disturbing to technical analysts who monitor the pattern of Treasury interest rates, which have been broadly on the decline since the late 1980s. Over this period, each peak in rates has been progressively lower. Yesterday's advance created a higher peak, breaking the trend and potentially signalling a longer-term advance in rates.

'A lot of people are scared of that 20-year trend line and rightfully so', said Gerald Lucas, senior investment adviser at Deutsche Bank. 'A close above that level at the end of this week would likely target a further rise to 5.25 per cent.'

The 10-year Treasury is widely used to hedge risk associated with fixed income securities.

Financial Times, 8 June 2007 **FT**

Bond market sell-off

Lex column

The Treasury market has long acted as an automatic stabiliser for the US economy. When the growth outlook looked poor, yields would fall, stimulating activity. The opposite would happen when growth prospects were strong. That did a lot of the Federal Reserve's work for it. Meanwhile, bond yields were kept lower than might have been expected by flows from overseas buyers.

Does the sudden run-up in yields now risk acting as an automatic destabiliser? The obvious weak points are housing and credit markets. Residential real estate remains weak and could be hit further by the half point rise in 15-year mortgage

rates during the past six months. Meanwhile, credit investors who have taken risky positions based on low volatility and low yields in the Treasury market could get a shock.

A lot depends on the reasons behind the surge, which has taken 10-year yields from 4.5 per cent to 5.08 per cent in two months, and how far it goes. Much of the jump is down to a reassessment of US economic prospects. Fears of a housing meltdown have subsided, labour market statistics are still strong and manufacturing data have improved. Investors have stopped factoring in interest rate cuts and started betting on a stronger economy.

→

If the bond market stays weak, however, investors will worry that the international effects that have helped keep yields low are unwinding. There is already a fear that Asian central banks will diversify their huge foreign exchange holdings away from US Treasuries.

Meanwhile, strong global growth and rising international yields could pull US yields higher.

For now, the change in yields is unlikely to cause too much pain. If they repeat their performance of the past two months, however, it could really start to matter.

■ The analysis

Article 10 suggests that a sharp rise in US government bond yields could signal the end of a period when low interest rates have acted as a catalyst for booming stock markets worldwide. The first signs of this unease were clear from the sharp fall in both the US S&P index and the German DAX index. So what caused the rise in bond yields?

First, one major factor was stronger economic data. This rebound in economic activity raised fears of a return to inflationary pressures both in the US and Europe. Bond markets always take fright when faced by this combination of higher economic activity and rising consumer prices. There were rises in yields right across the maturity spectrum. In the shorter-dated bonds there were rises in yields reflecting the increase in short-term interest rates in the US, the Eurozone and the UK. Remember short-term bonds must compete with the money markets for the funds of investors. So if short-term interest rates increase, so must the returns on shorter-dated bonds otherwise investors will not buy them.

As for longer-term bonds, yields also rose to protect investors against any threat of rising inflation. Do not forget that most bonds are fixed-rate investments. So if inflation rises it is only natural that investors will demand higher yields to maintain their real level of return.

Take a simple example . . .

A US 10-year Government bond:
It has a nominal yield of 6.5%
With inflation at 2.5%
Real return = 4.0%

If inflation rises to 3.5% . . .

The nominal yield must rise to 7.5% to maintain the same real return.

A US 10-year Government bond:
It has a nominal yield of 7.5%
With inflation at 3.5%
Real return = 4.0%

One consequence of these movements in the US bond market was that the yield curve returned to a more normal shape with long-term bond yields once again above those of shorter-term Treasuries. This upward move in bond yields was matched in the Eurozone and UK bond markets as investors reacted to increased interest rates from the European Central Bank and the fear of another increase from the Bank of England soon. In addition there was a clear realisation that there was no prospect of the Fed cutting interest rates in the near future.

The role of the Lex column is to pick out the key financial stories each day and provide a clear commentary putting some perspective on the short-term market reaction. It starts here by suggesting the bond market has been acting as a 'stabiliser for the US economy'. So, when the economy takes a downturn we see a fall in bond yields that acts as a stimulant to economic activity; and when the economy picks up we see a rise in bond yields which acts to suppress economic activity.

However, there is now a worry that this latest rise in bond yields could act to destabilise the US economy. There are three main factors that have caused the surge in 10-year bond yields. First, the economic outlook in the United States has shown a marked improvement. The labour market is strong, the housing market looks less vulnerable and manufacturing activity is recovering. This all means that investors can no longer look to the Fed to cut interest rates. A second factor that might explain the rise in bond yields could be the foreign selling of US Treasuries as the Asian central banks start to diversify their massive foreign exchange reserves into non-dollar currencies. As they sell US Treasury bonds their yields must increase. Finally, there is the strength of the global economy and the consequent rise in international yields which could pull US yields higher as well.

At this stage the Lex writers appeared to be fairly relaxed. They see the small rise in bonds yields so far as being 'unlikely to cause too much pain'. However, there remains the threat that any further spike in bond yields could signal a much more serious correction in stock prices.

■ Key terms

Benign credit conditions This simply refers to the cost of borrowing money. It might be a government borrowing (in the government bond market), a company borrowing (in the corporate bond market), a house owner (with a mortgage) or a consumer (with a credit card). We have 'benign credit conditions' when the cost of borrowing is considered to be low by historic standards. So low bond yields are seen as supporting the stock market. How does this work?

Well, in the first place, if bond yields are low then investors will look to buy shares instead in the search for a better return. Second, a low cost of borrowing will encourage a stronger level of economic activity which will fuel demand for goods and services which leads to higher corporate profits. This ultimately feeds through into higher dividend payments which are the key to higher share prices. Finally, a low cost of borrowing will make it cheaper for companies to borrow money, which will make investments more profitable.

German DAX index The DAX index is the most important German stock market index. It is considered to be the standard benchmark for shares quoted on the Frankfurt Stock Exchange. It started in 1984 with an initial value of 1000.

3

FINANCIAL MARKETS

10-year bunds Bunds are simply German government bonds. These are used to fund the difference between Federal government spending and revenue. As normal the benchmark long-term government bond is the 10-year maturity.

European Central Bank (ECB) and key interest rate The ECB is the Eurozone's most important financial institution. It is in control of a single monetary policy for all the countries that have adopted the euro. The main policy objective of the ECB is to maintain price stability in the medium term. This is defined as a 0–2 per cent target range for consumer price inflation. The key part of the ECB is the Governing Council that meets every fortnight on a Thursday. However, interest rate changes can only be made in the first meeting each month.

The key interest rate is the ECB's repo rate. This is the main tool used by the ECB in providing refinancing operations in the money markets. Under a repo operation commercial banks bid for funds from the ECB at a fixed interest rate. The ECB will purchase various high-quality financial market securities from theses banks to act as security for the loans. Then after a set period (usually 14 days) the banks must repurchase their securities back from the ECB and pay interest on the borrowed funds at the agreed repo rate.

Yield curve The yield curve is a graph that shows the relationship between interest rates or yields and the level of maturity. You should see the key terms for Article 5 for a more detailed discussion of yield curve shapes.

The relationship between bond yields and economic activity A key aspect of economic activity is the borrowing and lending of money which causes a set of interest rates to be established. Economic activity is a key influence on short-term interest rates which ranges from overnight to one-year borrowing. In practice other economic factors tend to dominate in the setting of the longer-term bond market yields.

Short-term loans are set by the demand from companies for loans and the rates of return they think they can expect to earn on these funds.

In good times there are opportunities for high profits.
Companies borrow more money at high interest rates.

In bad times these opportunitites diminish.
Companies are less willing to borrow money at high interest rates.

The interest rates derived from economic activity tend to be very short term.

But most bonds are in practice much longer term. As a result a range of other factors come into the picture when setting long-term interest rates. The key factor for long-term interest rates is the rate of inflation. As inflation rises investors will demand a higher rate of return on bonds. This especially applies to long-term investors as the uncertainty of their purchasing power is greater. Inflation is very important in setting long-term bond prices.

The level of a country's fiscal deficit can also be of some relevance in setting longer-term bond yields. A larger deficit will require higher yields to attract new investors. At some stage increased borrowing can also impact on the level of credit risk. If a country is perceived as being a lower credit risk, the level of its bond yields must rise to compensate for this higher risk. Argentina is a good example of a country that has often had a bad credit rating because it has frequently defaulted on its bond issues in the past.

To conclude, there is a very complex set of factors that determines the level of interest rates. Most short-term interest rates and short-term bond yields are determined by the level of economic activity and the resulting activities of the central bank. In contrast, longer-term bond yields are primarily set by the inflation outlook.

■ What do you think?

1. Clearly define what is meant by the term 'benign credit conditions'.

2. Why is there a strong link between the level of bond yields and the world's stock markets?

3. What reasons does the Lex column article suggest can explain the 'surge' in US Treasury yields?

■ Investigate FT data

You will need a copy of the *Financial Times*. Go to the front page of the main section and look at the World Markets data on the bottom of the front page.

1. What is the current level of the S&P 500 index?

2. What is the current level of the Xetra Dax index?

3. What is the yield on 10-year US government bond yields?

4. What is the yield on 10-year German government bond yields?

■ Go to the web

Go the ECB's official website: www.ecb.int/home/html/index.en.html.

Find the current level of the ECB's main refinancing operation minimum bid. Now go to the section on monetary policy.

a. What are the main aims of monetary policy?

b. What are the benefits of price stability?

■ Research

For a good understanding of what moves the financial markets on a daily basis there is no short-cut. You need to read the *Financial Times* regularly, particularly after days when there have been significant movements in the main financial markets. Read the articles regularly (look at the Lex column as well) and you will soon get a feel for what drives the financial markets.

Go to **www.pearsoned.co.uk/boakes** to access Kevin's blog for additional analysis of recent topical news articles and to post your comments. Download podcasts containing short audio summaries of the main issues relating to each article and check your understanding of in-text questions with the handy hints provided.

Debt finance

We should begin this topic by explaining what is meant by the term 'debt'. This is actually quite a straightforward concept as it simply represents something that must be repaid in the future. It could be a favour that a friend has granted you in the expectation that you will return the compliment in the years ahead. In financial markets we define debt in relation to financial commitments that often stretch far ahead in the future.

These arrangements are formalised in terms of a bond which is a contract where the holder lends money to another party in return for annual interest payments and the eventual repayment of the loan. On almost any day a quick review of the *Financial Times* will show that the international bond markets are a very important area in terms of their impact on financial markets. You will see many examples of new bond issues from companies, governments and a wide range of other large organisations. There are three main definitions for these new bond issues:

1. **Domestic bonds** where the issuer launches a bond in its local currency and home country. For example, a UK company might launch a new £500 m bond issue in London.

2. **Foreign bonds** where an issuer goes to another country to issue a bond in a foreign currency. For example, a German company might launch a new $500 m bond issue in the United States. This type of foreign bond issue is called a 'Yankee bond'.

3. **Eurobonds** where the issue takes place outside the country of the currency in which the bond is denominated. For example, a German company might launch a new $500 m bond issue in France. This type of bond is called a Eurobond because the issue is in US dollars and it takes place outside of the United States. You should be aware the term 'Eurobond' does not mean that the issue has to take place within the European financial markets.

In the context of corporate finance, the term 'debt finance' refers to the money that a business has to borrow in order to fund its various activities. In practice, we normally divide this debt finance into short-term and long-term borrowing. We also differentiate between the different degrees of risk attached to various types of corporate debt issues. The main types are:

1. **Secured debt** (commonly known as a *debenture*). This is the highest grade of debt issued by a company. The issuing company gives the debt holders a secured claim on various assets that are owned by the business. So, if the company cannot meet interest or redemption commitments, the holders are entitled to receive these assets in exchange. The assets in question might be financial (various types of securities), property or other physical goods owned by the company.

When this form of debt is secured on property assets it is called a *mortgage debenture*.

2. **Senior unsecured debt**. This comes next in terms of the debt capital hierarchy. In the case of a company liquidation the holders have claim on the assets left after the secured debt providers have been fully paid.

3. **Subordinated or junior debt**. The holders of these debt securities accept a lower rank than the first two levels of debt in the case of a corporate default. In return, they will be normally compensated in the form of higher interest to offset this additional risk. In terms of risk they are often little better off than the preference shareholders. The only providers of capital below them are the ordinary shareholders, who always take the biggest financial loss if a company fails.

There are a number of other key terms associated with debt products that you should understand before we start to analyse the articles in this section:

1. **Fixed-income securities**. You might see the debt markets referred to as fixed-income securities. This is simply because most bonds carry a fixed interest rate (called the *coupon*) and a fixed maturity date (called the *redemption date*). You should be aware that, although this is the most common form of debt issue, there are many other types with variable interest rates and redemption dates.

2. **Convertible bonds**. These are bonds issued by companies that give the holder the right to exchange their debt market products for shares in the issuing company at some stage in the future. We will learn more about them in the articles that follow.

3. **Warrants**. These are financial instruments that give the holder the right to purchase financial market securities from the issuer at a set price within a certain time period. They are commonly attached to certain new bond issues giving the holder the right to buy some shares in the issuing company.

4. **Zero-coupon bonds**. These are bonds that do not have any interest payable but will instead be offered at a significant discount to the par value. This results in a large capital gain at redemption.

5. **Commercial paper**. This is a form of very short-term financing instrument used by companies. The normal maturity of commercial paper is 270 days. They are usually only made available to those companies with the best credit-rating.

6. **Bond yield**. When an individual or a company borrows money, there is a cost that they have to pay in order to obtain the funds. If it is a short-term loan (up to one year), this is normally referred to as an *interest rate*. So we might take out a one month bank loan with an annual interest rate of say 8.5 per cent. This is the interest rate, or the cost of obtaining the funds. If a company needs to borrow funds for a longer time period, this will normally be through the issue of a bond market security, which is usually repaid at a fixed rate of annual interest (this is called the *coupon*) until it is finally repaid on the date that it redeems or matures. The yield on the bond issue is the cost to the issuer or the return to the investor who buys the bond.

Every day there are many new bond issues from companies, governments and a wide range of large organisations. The first article in this topic looks at the process of launching a new bond issue. In the second and third articles we discuss some of the more innovative products that now feature in the bond markets. The last article shows how in the wake of the credit crunch bond investors were looking towards the premium eurozone countries that offer greater security.

The following four articles are analysed in this section:

Article 12
Athens prepares 50-year bond issue worth €500 m–€1 bn
Financial Times, 18 January 2007

Article 13
Convertibles stage a return to fashion
Financial Times, 8 February 2007

Article 14
Record samurai deal by Citigroup
Financial Times, 6 September 2005

Article 15
Flight to liquidity pushes Eurozone bond yields apart
Financial Times, 27 February 2008

These articles address the following issues:

- different types of bonds defined;
- liquidity in bond markets;
- bond auctions;
- bond yield spreads and credit-rating;
- budget deficits;
- the convertible bond market;
- exotic products;
- book runners;
- arbitrage;
- liquid yield option notes;
- divergence in bond yields (European bond markets);
- sovereign entities.

Greek government launches new bond issue

The international bond markets are an increasingly important area in terms of financial market activity. Every day we see many new bond issues from companies, governments and a wide range of large organisations. This article examines the process of a government looking to issue a very long-term debt security. It shows clearly the relationship between a countries' credit-rating and the expected yield on the new bond issue.

Article 12

Financial Times, 18 January 2007 **FT**

Athens prepares 50-year bond issue worth €500 m–€1 bn

Kerin Hope

Greece is planning to issue a 50-year bond in the first half of this year to take advantage of strong liquidity in international markets and a flat yield curve, Petros Doukas, the deputy finance minister, said yesterday.

Mr Doukas put the size of the issue at €500 m–€1 bn. The funds would be raised through an auction process rather than a syndication. Greece has already received several offers from banks to make private placements for a 50-year bond.

'With the yield curve flat, the cost of the 50-year bond will not be above that of 30-year paper', Mr Doukas said. Greece is already popular with the market as the eurozone's high-yield borrower, with spreads of 30–35 basis points above the bund on its 30-year paper. Greece, which would be following in the footsteps of France and the UK last year, would be the smallest country to date to launch a 50-year bond.

While Greece's credit rating is still the lowest in the eurozone, Moody's last week changed the outlook on its single A rating from 'stable' to 'positive', indicating an upgrade may be on the way. Market-watchers said they expected the 50-year issue to take place at the end of the first quarter or beginning of the second. It would follow 15- and 30-year issues that are already planned under this year's €33.5 bn borrowing programme. 'It's prudent for an issuer to borrow at the long end, and there's definitely appetite in the market for a Greek bond of this tenor', said George Kofinakos, managing director of Citigroup Greece.

Greek prospects are picking up, with GDP growth this year projected at about 4 per cent for the fifth successive year.

The country is poised to emerge from the European Union's excessive budget deficit procedure, after reducing the 2006 deficit below the 3 per cent of GDP eurozone ceiling.

The analysis

In this article the focus is on a prospective new international bond issue from Greece which was planning to launch a 50-year bond in the first half of 2007. The move was announced by their deputy finance minister Petros Doukas. The new bond issue was timed to take advantage of strong liquidity in financial markets and the presence of a relatively flat yield curve. Greater liquidity in financial markets suggests that there would be plenty of demand for a new large bond issue. Also, the flat yield curve suggests that the costs of issuing a longer-dated bond would be relatively cheap compared to shorter-term maturities. The article quotes Mr Doukas as saying 'the cost of the 50-year bond will not be above that of a 30-year paper'. We would normally expect to see an upward-sloping yield curve where longer-term bond yields would be significantly higher than short-term bond yields.

In the context of the European government bond market, Greece stands out as the market with the highest level of yields among the Eurozone economies. Their bonds have a positive yield spread of some 30–35 basis points above the equivalent German 30-year bonds. This reflects the fact that Greece's credit rating is the lowest in the Eurozone. One rating agency, Moody's, rated Greece's credit risk at a single A with the outlook recently upgraded from stable to positive. Against the background of a favourable economic outlook, the article concludes with a glowing assessment from the managing director of Citigroup Greece. Economic growth is expected to hit an annual rate of 4 per cent for the fifth successive year and the budget deficit has been reduced to below the European Union's ceiling of 3 per cent of GDP.

■ Key terms

Flat yield curve A flat yield curve shows the level of yields being broadly similar across the maturity spectrum. (See Article 5 for a detailed explanation of yield curves.)

Liquidity In financial markets this normally refers to how easily an asset can be converted into cash. Therefore, notes and coins are the most liquid financial asset. In general, the more liquid an asset, the lower is its return. In this article it is used to indicate there is a great deal of cash available to invest in new government bonds.

Bond auction process Most new government bond issues are sold through a system of auctions. Normally the country's Treasury is in charge of new issues. It will give an early warning of the maturity of the issue, and then a week or so before it will firm up details of the size of the issue, the total amount being raised, the maturity and the bond's annual coupon.

This very simple example might show how the bidding works

A government invites bids for a new bond auction. The new issue is a £3 bn 6 per cent bond issue due to mature in 2035.

The following bids come in:	Price bid	How much accepted?
£100 m at	£98.65	100% = £100 m
£125 m at	£98.60	100% = £125 m
£135 m at	£98.50	100% = £135 m
£140 m at	£98.45	100% = £140 m
£160 m at	£98.40	100% = £160 m

| £2200 m at | £98.35 | 100% = £2200 m |
| £1400 m at | £98.30 | 10% = £140 m |

This gets us to the £3 bn available.

Any bids below £98.30 will be rejected. This is a competitive bidding process so you pay the price you bid if it is accepted.

Bond yield spreads This refers to the yield on a particular bond issue minus the yield on the nearest comparable government bond issue. So in this case we are comparing 30-year bonds from Greece with those from Germany (bunds).

German 30-year bunds yield = 4.17%

The spread equals +30–35 basis points

So the Greek 30-year bond yield = 4.47–52%

Note: 100 basis points = an extra 1 percentage point on the yield.
50 basis points = an extra 0.5 percentage point on the yield, etc.

The spread is determined by a combination of the bond's credit rating, liquidity and the market's perception of its risk relative to the other bond.

Bond credit rating Most new bond issuers are assigned credit ratings by the various companies that are involved in this activity. They include Standard and Poor's and Moody's. The highest credit rating allocated by Moody's is a triple A. For example, this is awarded to the German government's bond issues. In this article we learn that Greece has a rating of a single A. And this is under review with a 'positive' outlook favoured.

Short summary of Moody's credit ratings

AAA = Capacity to pay interest and principal extremely strong
AA = Differs only in a small degree
A = More susceptible to adverse changes in circumstances
BBB = Adequate capacity
BB, B = Speculative
C = No interest being paid
D = In default

Budget deficit A country's budget deficit refers to the difference between its spending and its revenue. It is normal for any government to spend more money on health services, education, defence, etc. than it can raise revenue from income taxes, sales taxes, etc. The result is a fiscal deficit or a budget deficit. We normally like to compare a country's budget deficit by expressing it as a percentage of the country's gross domestic product or income.

This would be just the same for an individual. It is fine for a Premiership footballer with an income of £5 m per year to run a deficit of £1000 in a particular year. This amounts to a tiny percentage of his annual income. So he can repay this debt very easily in the next year. It is quite another matter for a student running up a deficit of £1000 in a particular year when her income is only £5000 per year. Her deficit is 20 per cent of her annual income and it will be much harder for her to repay this debt until her income rises significantly when she lands that lucrative job with an investment bank after graduation!

▓ What do you think?

1. What are the main factors that will determine the sovereign risk on a new international bond issue?

   Hint: Sovereign refers to the risk of a particular country.

2. Are the following bonds:

   Eurobonds (E)

   Foreign Bonds (F)

   Domestic Bonds (D)?

      (i) The Swiss government issues a euro-denominated bond in Germany.

      (ii) Microsoft issues a US dollar bond in the United States.

      (iii) Deutsche Telecom issues a yen bond in Japan.

      (iv) The French government issues a Swiss franc bond in London.

      (v) The World Bank (based in New York) issues a euro-denominated bond in Paris.

3. Why is the Greek deputy finance minister expecting to be able to issue this new long-term bond issue at a particularly low cost at the time of the article? What are the potential financial market risks that could result in a much higher yield on this new bond issue in reality?

4. What are the advantages for Greece in raising these funds through a bond auction compared to a placement process?

5. There is a very positive view on the prospects of the Greek economy expressed here by the managing director of a large investment bank's Greek office. Why should we read these comments with a degree of caution?

6. Undertake some research and set out a balanced view of the current prospects for the Greek economy.

▓ Investigate FT data

You will need the Companies and Markets section of the *Financial Times*. Go to the Market Data section and look at the bottom left-hand side of the page. In this section you will see a section called Benchmark Government Bonds.

Answer these questions:

1. What is the current level of 30-year bond yields for Germany?

2. What were they a year ago?

3. By looking at the four US government bond issues describe the current shape of the US bond yield curve.

4. Which country has the highest 10-year bond yield?

5. What has happened to the level of 10-year Greek government bond yields in the last day, week, month and year?

Now look to the right of this column and examine the High-Yield and Emerging Market Bonds section.

Answer these questions:

1. Choose any four bonds in the emerging US$ section. Discuss the link between their spreads versus US Treasuries (see the last column) and their credit-rating.

2. In the high-yield € section which bond has the largest spread compared to US Treasuries?

■ Go to the web

Go to the official website of the *Financial Times*: www.ft.com.

Go to the Markets section and select Market Data from the drop-down menu.

Go to the Bond and Rates section. Select FT Bonds Tables.

On the drop-down menu select the International Bond Issues section. You will be able to access details of recent new international bond issues.

a. Find a recent example of a new bond issue from a sovereign nation.

b. Compare the yield on this bond to a bond issue from a more risky corporate issuer in the same currency and with a similar maturity.

c. Calculate the yield spread between these two issues.

d. Explain the rationale for the size of this spread.

e. Which large international banks tend to be the bookrunners on most of the new issues?

■ Research

Arnold, G. (2008) *Corporate Financial Management*, 4th edn, Harlow, UK: Prentice Hall Financial Times. You should especially look at Chapter 11, pp. 449–56 to get more information about international bond issues.

Berk, J. and DeMarzo, P. (2009) *Corporate Finance*, Harlow, UK: FT Prentice Hall Financial Times. The topic of corporate bonds is covered in Chapter 8. You should look at pp. 228–33.

Gitman, L. (2009) *Principles of Managerial Finance*, 12th edn, Harlow, UK: Pearson International Edition. There is a US-based introduction to the corporate bonds in Chapter 6 on pp. 291–8.

McLaney, E. (2009) *Business Finance Theory and Practice*, 8th edn, Harlow, UK: FT Prentice Hall Financial Times. There is an introduction to loan notes and debentures in Chapter 8.

Pilbeam, K. (2006) *International Finance,* 3rd edn, Basingstoke: Palgrave Macmillan. Chapter 12 provides a very good overview of the Eurobond market. The main features of Eurobonds are set out on pp. 315–16.

Valdez, S. (2007) *An Introduction to Global Financial Markets*, 5th edn, Basingstoke: Palgrave Macmillan. You should look at Chapter 6, especially pp. 137–53. This provides a good general introduction to bond markets.

Watson, D. and Head, A. (2007) *Corporate Finance Principles and Practice*, 4th edn, Harlow, UK: Prentice Hall Financial Times. You should look at Chapter 5, especially pp. 126–28.

4

DEBT FINANCE

Japanese convertibles back in fashion

The fundamental financial market products are shares, bonds, foreign exchange and also cash traded in the money markets. However, over time the banks have created a range of more complex products with each one designed for a specific purpose. One new type of bond might reduce the debt issue costs for a particular company. Others might have a tax advantage for the issuer, at least until the tax authorities clamp down on this practice.

This article examines one of the first innovative financial market products to be created. These are convertible bonds which are a delightfully simple instrument. A convertible is a debt issue that allows the holder to convert the bond into shares in the issuing company at a set price at some stage in the future. This article looks at the strong rebound in the convertible bond market in Japan during 2006.

Article 13   *Financial Times*, 8 February 2007   **FT**

Convertibles stage a return to fashion

David Turner

A couple of years ago, Japan's convertible bond market looked on the brink of extinction. Annual issuance by Japanese companies was running at just $2.7 bn – less than a sixth of the level of issuance in 2004 and the lowest amount since 1998.

But in recent months, the sector has started to make a spectacular return, spurred by higher share-price volatility, the hunger of hedge funds and a continuing stream of new and exotic products.

Last year total issuance bounced back to $12.6 bn through more than 50 deals. Investment bankers say it could be even higher this year if share prices remain volatile.

The biggest reason why convertible issuance has risen so fast is exactly the same reason why it fell so far in 2005: share price volatility. This allows issuers to gain a good price for their convertibles on the grounds there is a strong chance that the underlying shares will reach the price at which investors can convert the bonds into equity.

Because of low volatility in 2005 'the condition of the market was terrible', says Takashi Masuda, a senior official in the syndicate department of Nomura, Japan's biggest book runner of convertibles last year in both value and number of deals. Some investment banking departments responded pessimistically by trimming the number of convertibles staff in Japan.

Among bankers there were fears this was more than a mere temporary blip caused by market conditions. In particular, they feared structural changes might be afoot – most notably because Japanese companies are increasingly scared of hostile takeovers and afraid convertibles could be used a weapon to storm the ramparts.

The wary could point to the example of Sumitomo Warehouse. In 2005 activist shareholder Yoshiaki Murakami became the leading shareholder in the company by using convertibles.

But other investment bankers thought these fears of a permanent souring against convertibles were excessively pessimistic. And these days the optimists are starting to look right.

Higher volatility was not the only blessing that restored the market. Gareth Lake, managing director of equity capital markets at Nikko Citigroup, one of Japan's biggest convertible book runners, says 'the dearth of issuance' in 2005 encouraged funds to start 'looking for new paper'. The biggest investors are the global convertible arbitrage hedge funds, which often follow a strategy of buying an issuer's convertible bonds while shorting its shares (or betting that its share price will fall). Japanese pension funds have also shown interest.

The market has been further boosted by the spectre of rate rises from the Bank of Japan. The bank has lifted rates only once in the current cycle, back in July, but is expected to start raising them again soon – albeit rather slowly.

Alex Woodthorpe, Tokyo-based chairman of Pacific Rim equity capital markets at Merrill Lynch, says: 'The ability to fund at zero coupon ahead of the interest rate curve is appealing to issuers'.

For those investors reluctant to buy zero-rate products because they think the bank may raise rates more rapidly than the market expects, there is a solution: liquid yield option notes, or 'lyons'.

These are convertibles that are issued at sub-par, thus generating a yield despite the zero coupon. Merrill Lynch arranged Japan's first ever lyon, a 1.022 bn deal for leasing company Orix, in 2002.

The range of styles of convertible that is being offered in Japan is mind-boggling and is used by different underwriters to jockey for competitive position. This creates a relentless quest for further innovation to find something new for Japan to offer issuers, though Japanese issuers are reluctant to experiment with outright 'firsts' for the world. This innovation cycle means, according to Mr Woodthorpe, that 'whatever you did yesterday becomes plain vanilla today'.

But one factor that could help the market even more than innovation is something more prosaic: regulation. One investment banker who arranges the small and mid-size convertible deals sold into the domestic rather than international market says issuance is hampered by the seven-day rule that applies to all deals sold to retail investors.

After announcing a convertible issue, issuers have to wait a week before setting the conversion price. But in the week that has elapsed, the share price may have fallen sharply, leaving issuers with a much lower conversion price than they first expected.

Japanese equities
Nikkei 225 Average ('000)

Source: Thomson Datastream

The analysis

2006 saw the Japanese convertible bond market very much back in favour with 50 new corporate issues raising over $12.5 bn. This article looks at the main reasons behind this strong rebound in the market. It argues that it was due to three principal factors.

1. **Higher share price volatility**. This was the single most important factor. When investors buy a convertible they have the right to convert their bond into shares in the issuing company at a set price which is set at a premium to the current market share price.

   We can work this out from the **conversion ratio** which is the number of shares into which a convertible bond can be converted. For example, if the conversion ratio is 40 then an investor will be able to convert every $100 nominal value of the bond issue into 40 shares in the issuing company. This would mean that the **conversion price** would be $2.50 ($100/40). This conversion price is normally set at a premium to the company's current market share price. So in this case the market price might be $2.00, which means that the **conversion premium** is 25 per cent.

$$\frac{2.50 - 2.00}{2.00} = 0.25 \text{ or } 25\%.$$

   A final important term associated with a convertible bond is the **conversion value of the bond**. This is the value of the bond assuming it was converted into shares at the current market share price.

   In this case the conversion value of the bond would be $2.00 \times 40 = \$80$.

   A company clearly wants to be sure that the bond will convert into equity finance which will only happen when the share price at least rises to the conversion price level. When share prices are static or, even worse, falling, any conversion is much less likely. This brings the potential risk to the issuing company that they might have to redeem a bond which they had assumed would convert into equity finance. So, we need to see rising share prices to encourage issuers to launch new convertible bonds and for investors to be willing to buy them.

2. **Demand from hedge funds**. Hedge funds have become big players in the fund management industry. The *Financial Times* reported that they were using complex arbitrage operations that involved buying a company's convertible bond and at the same time shorting (selling) its shares. It seems that the hedge funds' traders had identified a price anomaly in the market which created this opportunity for them to make profits through these arbitrage trades.

3. **An ever-growing stream of new innovative products**. We have also seen the clever 'financial engineers' employed by the investment banks designing new and innovative products. One such instrument is the 'liquid yield option note' (lyon). The *Financial Times* article provides a clear description of them. 'These are convertibles that are issued at sub-par thus generating a yield despite the zero coupon.' Put simply, this means that you buy the bond at a discount to its redemption price so that the resulting capital gain compensates for the lack of any **coupons**. The great attraction of these new products is that they were issued at a time when Japanese money-market interest rates were at last starting to increase. With these new products companies have been able to issue their **zero coupon bonds** to meet their funding requirements before any sharp increase in bond yields which would inevitably follow the tightening in Japanese monetary policy.

The article ends by claiming that a final boost to the market would come from reduced regulation. There is one particular rule that investment bankers argue has held back this market. This is the so called 'seven day rule', which means that a convertible issuer has to wait seven days before setting the conversion price. It represents a significant risk for the issuer since if the share price falls during this period the final conversion price might be much lower than expected.

■ Key terms

Convertible bond These are bonds which provide the holders with the right to convert their bonds into shares in the issuing company. This conversion option will be at an agreed price at a set date in the future. Initially this will not be a worthwhile transaction as the conversion share price will be set well above the current market share price. However, as the market share price rises in value over time, so the conversion will soon be a valuable option for the bond holder.

Convertibles are a classic debt equity hybrid product. One way to explain their attraction is to compare them to swimming in the sea. Most people would love to dive straight into a warm ocean for a relaxing swim. However, if they are told that there are sometimes sharks around in the sea they will become much more cautious. So, instead, they may prefer to paddle in the breaking waves until they feel more confident that the risk of sharks is over. Only then will they be willing to swim further out into the ocean. In the same way buying convertible bonds is a way for risk-averse investors to start with a relatively safe bond investment. Then when they feel more confident about the prospects for the company, they can convert the bonds into the more risky shares.

Hedge funds This refers to a particular type of investment management where the fund manager will employ a range of different investment tools in an attempt to maximise the returns or try to make gains even in a falling market.

Exotic products This is a term to cover new innovative financial markets products. The use of the term 'exotic' denotes that these are different to the normal version of this product. You will see it used in several contexts such as exotic bonds, exotic swaps, exotic options, etc.

Book runner This is the lead manager who is in charge of the whole process in a new bond issue. They will be jointly responsible with the issuer for inviting other banks to work on the new issue in activities such as syndication and underwriting.

Arbitrage This is a very common practice amongst financial market traders. They will simultaneously sell (or buy) a financial instrument (for example a share or a bond) and at the same time take an equal and opposite position in a similar instrument. This transaction will give them a financial profit. This is possible where there is a clear price anomaly that has been identified between the markets involved. In theory such arbitrage trading is considered risk free. This makes it particularly attractive.

Shorting its shares This is used to refer to traders who sell a financial market security that they do not yet own. In other words, they have not yet made an offsetting purchase. This is a very risky activity since, if the price of the financial market security rises, the trader will have to pay an ever higher price to secure the stock.

The reverse process is when a trader goes long. This means that they have bought some financial market securities which they have not yet sold.

Liquid yield option notes (lyons) These are defined well in the article. They are zero-coupon bonds that are issued below their par value. This guarantees the holder a return despite the zero coupon.

Plain vanilla This denotes the simplest version of any type of financial market instrument. It alludes to ice cream varieties. A plain vanilla ice cream is the simplest type you can buy. It has no chocolate flake or any sauces!

Apparently the same term is used for DVDs. So a vanilla DVD is one that has no extras such as commentaries or special features. I have to thank Mark Kermode (Radio 5's film critic) for that information!

■ What do you think?

1. What are the advantages for companies in issuing convertible bonds?
2. What factors determine the correct level of the premium between the conversion share price and the current market share price?
3. What financial market conditions are necessary to ensure that a new convertible bond issue will be converted in good time?
4. Explain what is meant when a trader is described as engaging in 'short selling'.
5. What is meant by a plain vanilla financial market security?

■ Research

Arnold, G. (2008) *Corporate Financial Management*, 4th edn, Harlow, UK: FT Prentice Hall. You should especially look at Chapter 11. There is a superb section on convertible bonds from pp. 441 to 443.

Berk, J. and DeMarzo, P. (2009) Corporate Finance, Harlow, UK: FT Prentice Hall Financial Times. The topic of convertibles is covered in Chapter 24 (see p. 794).

Gitman, L. (2009) *Principles of Managerial Finance*, 12th edn, Harlow, UK: Pearson International Edition. There is an excellent section on convertibles on pp. 732–7.

McLaney, E. (2009) *Business Finance Theory and Practice*, 8th edn, Harlow, UK: FT Prentice Hall Financial Times. There is a useful introduction to convertibles on p. 240.

Pike, R. and Neale, B. (2006) *Corporate Finance and Investment*, 6th edn, Harlow, UK: FT Prentice Hall. You should look at Chapter 5, pp. 128–36 to see convertible bonds well explained.

Pilbeam, K. (2006) *International Finance*, 3rd edn, Basingstoke: Palgrave Macmillan. Chapter 12 has a brief section on convertible bonds on p. 316.

Watson, D. and Head, A. (2007) *Corporate Finance Principles and Practice*, 4th edn, Harlow, UK: FT Prentice Hall. You should look at Chapter 5.

Bulldog, Yankee and samurai bonds . . .

When you start reading the *Financial Times*, you might come across a term that will both intrigue and confuse you. In this article there is a classic example with the discussion of 'samurai bonds'. It might make you wonder what possible link can there be between medieval Japanese warriors and the modern world of international finance. The answer is simple. A samurai bond is the term given to identify a Japanese foreign bond. Other foreign bonds have been given equally unusual names. So we also have bulldogs (sterling foreign bonds), Yankees (dollar foreign bonds) and matildas (Australian dollar foreign bonds). Once you know what they are, the rest of this article is much easier to understand.

Article 14   *Financial Times*, 6 September 2005   **FT**

Record samurai deal by Citigroup

Mariko Sanchanta

Citigroup, the world's largest financial institution, yesterday sold ¥230 bn in samurai bonds, marking the largest such issuance ever.

The figure surpasses the record-high ¥220 bn in samurais issued in 2000 by DaimlerChrysler. Samurai bonds are yen-denominated bonds issued in Japan by foreign governments and companies.

Citigroup sold six tranches of samurais with maturities ranging from five to 30 years. The issuance of 30-year samurai bonds is also the first in the market, indicating demand is growing for longer-dated maturities. Citigroup Japan said it had not yet decided how to use the proceeds from the samurai issuance.

'We've seen a pick-up from financial institutions offering samurais', said Jason Rogers, banks analyst at Barclays Capital in Tokyo. 'It highlights the strong demand for samurais, which is due to low interest rates and tight credit spreads.'

Japan's benchmark 10-year government bond yielded an average of 1.37 per cent in the past year, sending institutions and individuals searching for investments with better returns. In comparison, the coupon on Citigroup's 10-year samurai bond is 1.58 per cent.

Nikko Citigroup, a joint venture of Nikko Cordial and Citigroup, lead managed the sale.

Citigroup Japan said the Japanese market remained 'very important' to the US financial services giant, and it would continue to expand its presence in the market.

Citigroup last year was ordered by Japan's financial regulator to shut its private banking operations in Japan for breaking banking laws. Its Japanese private banking business will close by the end of this month.

■ The analysis

The US banking giant, Citigroup, has just sold the largest ever issue of samurai bonds. These Japanese foreign bonds are yen-denominated bonds issued by non-Japanese companies but sold primarily to Japanese investors. The dual incentive for Citigroup to make such an issue comes in part from the low level of Japanese interest rates right across all maturities, but the article also points to the presence of 'tight credit spreads'. This means that the cost of issuing higher risk bonds has fallen to very low levels. As a result, they were able to sell a huge amount of bonds at a low cost of finance.

At the same time demand would have been strong from a wide range of Japanese investors, including banks, insurance companies and pension funds. These firms were awash with spare investment cash and a samurai bond enables them to obtain some diversification in their bond portfolio with this international exposure. However, at the same time they have none of the currency risk that would apply if they simply purchased bonds issued in other countries.

The article explains that this new issue will be split into six tranches with some issues, for the first time, having a very long-term maturity of up to 30 years. This issue confirmed that Citigroup would be likely to expand their activities in the Japanese financial services market.

The *Financial Times* reports that Citigroup has so far had mixed fortunes in the Japanese finance sector. Back in 2004 the Japanese financial services authorities forced it to shut all its private banking operations 'for breaking banking laws'. It is expected that its Japanese private banking business would be closed by the end of September.

■ Key terms

Bonds A bond is a security issued by a government or a corporation which represents a debt that must be repaid normally at a set date in the future. Most bonds pay a set interest rate each year.

Foreign bonds are bonds issued by a foreign borrower in another country's domestic market. For example, we might have yen-denominated bonds issued by a foreign borrower in the domestic Japanese market. They are called **samurai bonds**.

These foreign bonds are often given strange names:

Name	Country
Samurai	Japan
Yankee	United States
Bulldog	United Kingdom
Matildas	Australia

Tight credit spreads This is a measure of the relative cost of issuing more risky bonds. It is best seen with an example:

Let us assume that the United States government has close to zero risk of default. As a result a 10-year US Treasury bond might have a yield of 4.5 per cent.

In contrast a 10-year issue from Ford Motor Company which has significantly more risk of default might have a yield of 6.5 per cent.

This gives us a credit yield spread of 6.5 per cent minus 4.5 per cent = 200 basis points difference.

If investors now start to buy lots of the higher yielding (more risky) bonds, this could result in 'tighter credit spreads' as the relative cost of these bonds falls.

In this case the yield on the 10-year issue from Ford might fall back to 5.5 per cent. This would reduce the yield spread to just 100 basis points. This would be a 'tighter credit spread'.

In this article this term is used to explain why there had been a spate of new samurai bonds. The relative cost of issuing more risky bonds in yen-denominated markets had fallen sharply. In this case Japan's benchmark, 10-year government bond yield had fallen to an average of 1.37 per cent in the past year. This had forced Japanese investors to look elsewhere for better returns. For example, the coupon on the new Citigroup issue was 1.58 per cent which was more attractive to investors but also shows the impact of 'tight credit spreads' in terms of reducing the cost of the bond finance for Citigroup.

Tranches This term is derived from the French word 'tranche' which means a slice. In this context a tranche simply refers to the individual parts of a new bond issue. You might also see the terms 'tap' or 'mini-taplet' used.

Private banking This refers to banks that manage the financial affairs for 'high net worth' individuals.

Banks analyst This is the person employed at an investment bank (in this case Barclays Capital) whose job it is to advise the bank's clients on the major financial institutions operating within the financial services industry. They will be required to value these businesses and offer comparisons between their own and the market's valuations as reflected in the current share prices.

■ What do you think?

1. Explain what is meant by the term a 'samurai' bond.

2. Why might a Japanese investor prefer to buy a samurai bond rather than a simple domestic bond issue?

3. Why might a foreign company prefer to issue a samurai bond rather than a simple domestic bond issue?

■ Investigate FT data

You will need a copy of the Companies and Markets section of the *Financial Times*. Go to the Market Data section.

Hint: This is normally one page before the London Share Price Service.

Locate the Global Investment Grade section. Look at this table and select any five major corporate bond issues.

1. You should calculate the spread on these bond issues compared to the benchmark government bond.

2. Comment on the reasons for this additional yield.

Hint: Focus on the credit rating of the bond issuer.

■ Research

Arnold, G. (2008) *Corporate Financial Management*, 4th edn, Harlow, UK: FT Prentice Hall. You should especially look at Chapter 11.

Berk, J. and DeMarzo, P. (2009) *Corporate Finance*, Harlow, UK: FT Prentice Hall Financial Times. The topic of Eurobonds (including samurai bonds) is on p. 784.

Gitman, L. (2009) *Principles of Managerial Finance*, 12th edn, Harlow, UK: Pearson International Edition. There is a short introduction to Eurobonds on p. 297.

McLaney, E. (2009) *Business Finance Theory and Practice*, 8th edn, Harlow, UK: FT Prentice Hall Financial Times. The definition of a Eurobond issue is on p. 239.

Pike, R. and Neale, B. (2006) *Corporate Finance and Investment*, 6th edn, Harlow, UK: FT Prentice Hall. You should look at Chapter 16, p. 442 for a brief introduction to foreign bonds.

Pilbeam, K. (2006) *International Finance,* 3rd edn, Baringstoke: Palgrave Macmillan. There is a good introduction to foreign bonds on p. 314.

Valdez, S. (2007) *An Introduction to Global Financial Markets,* 5th edn, Basingstoke: Palgrave Macmillan. You should look at Chapter 6.

Watson, D. and Head, A. (2007) *Corporate Finance Principles and Practice*, 4th edn, Harlow, UK: FT Prentice Hall. You should look at Chapter 5 (pp. 127–8).

European bond markets start to diverge

There are some advantages of watching the financial markets from a safe distance these days. Sometimes I feel that I am able to see things more clearly now than when I was right in the heat of the action. I used to spend all my working day staring at the various news screens struggling to find anything original to say to my Head of Trading and Head of Sales who were the key players in the bond market-making desk that I serviced as an economist for some four years. Ironically these days being far removed from the action I feel that I am able to gain a much clearer insight into the financial markets than ever before.

It was like that with European government bonds prior to the introduction of the euro in 1999. At that time I was mainly occupied teaching Economics to new classes of investment bank graduates. I can clearly remember thinking that there was a tremendous trading opportunity available. Surely if all these markets would soon be denominated in the same currency, there could not possibly be any justification for the continued level of divergence between their government bond yields. So, a financial killing could be made by buying the high-risk bonds (Italy, Greece and Spain) and selling the less risky bond markets (Germany and France). Then, as the markets converged, there would be sizeable profits for the bond market traders. Sadly, as good as this idea was I never acted on it. I am probably too cautious by nature!

Article 15   *Financial Times*, 27 February 2008 FT

Flight to liquidity pushes Eurozone bond yields apart

Joanna Chung

For almost a decade, yields on bonds issued by different governments in the eurozone have moved closer together. Investors who bet on the story of continued convergence profited handsomely.

But that trend has reversed in recent months. As the credit global crisis gathered in intensity last year, yields started to diverge. Investors became more selective, and started demanding higher rates for some government debt.

Now, spreads diverge more widely than they have done since the creation of the euro nearly a decade ago, with Germany at the top of the pecking order and Italy and Greece at the bottom. Even bonds issued by AAA-rated countries such as France and Spain are being shunned – relatively speaking – by investors.

For example, the risk premium of 10-year Italian government bonds has risen 12 basis points to 43 bp over comparable German Bunds since the beginning of the year, while that of 10-year Greek government bonds rose 14 bp to 44.5 bp over Bunds. Meanwhile, the spread of Spanish 10-year bonds over Bunds has added 8bp during the same period.

The phenomenon highlights the degree to which the global credit turmoil is causing strains in markets that are traditionally seen as safe, and raises questions over how long spreads will continue to widen.

→

'The unfolding credit crunch is a catalyst, but spreads between Europe's sovereigns [have been] set to widen for the past few years', says Louis-Vincent Gave, who runs GaveKal, a money management and research firm based in Hong Kong.

'Why should Italy borrow at the same rate as Germany. Why should Greece borrow at the same rate as Ireland? That shouldn't happen.' In other words, he says, investors should be demanding higher premiums for bonds from governments that are seen as fiscally lax, such as Italy and Greece.

Mr Gave says one reason why rates converged in recent years was the fairly indiscriminate buying of Eurozone government debt by central banks and other sovereign entities in Asia and elsewhere as they rebalanced their reserves away from dollars.

Now these governments have indicated that they have enough bonds and are looking at other investment targets, in part through sovereign wealth funds, he says. So the fundamental differences among eurozone issuers have begun to reassert themselves.

Together with Corriente Capital, which reaped millions from correctly calling the fallout in the US subprime market, GaveKal launched its European Divergence Fund in November. The fund, which closed to new investors after raising $450 m, rose 20 per cent between November and end January, says Mr Gave, who expects divergence in the eurozone to continue.

But the causes of the divergence are many, experts say. One reason for the spread widening is the existence of a liquid futures market in Germany, which traders use to hedge investments and which has created a natural demand for German Bunds over other eurozone debt, particularly during recent months of market uncertainty.

'The high volatility and uncertainty in the market is prompting investors to cover their exposures', says one French debt management official. 'The Bund futures contract is the most liquid debt instrument in Europe and that is causing a natural demand for Bunds on the cash side.'

The so-called liquidity premium has become just as important as credit risk premium in setting the spread between the most popular and least popular European government bonds.

'It is more a liquidity story than a credit story', says Erik Wilders, head of the Dutch State Treasury Agency. 'Germany is the biggest and most liquid market, and that is what investors want right now.'

Meanwhile, some countries, including Belgium and Italy, have suffered political uncertainty, while other specific factors, such as housing market worries in Spain, have also affected sentiment for particular bonds.

But Stan Malek, analyst at Bank of America, says 'there is no reason why countries like Austria should trade 10 bp over Germany or why Belgium should trade about 20 bp over Germany'.

'We are in a very, very risk-averse mode', he says. 'The consensus belief is that spreads will stay elevated for some time but if there is a positive event for bonds, like a rate cut, yields could converge again.'

Ciaran O'Hagan, head of Paris fixed income strategy, at Société Générale, says: 'Many investors are asking if Italy and Greece are seriously sick, or if the recent asset price moves are just driven by global risk aversion.'

'The answer for us is firmly the latter … both Greece and Italy will be around in 30 years' time and will probably be much more prosperous than what is reflected in today's repricing of sovereign risk.'

But movements in credit default swaps markets indicate investors' perception of risk is rising. For example, the five-year CDS on Greek sovereign debt has risen 28.8 per cent to 56.7 basis points in the past month, according to Markit prices. That means it costs investors €560,700 annually to protect €10 m worth of debt against default over a five-year period.

'It is a difficult environment in which to put on a contrarian trade because there is so much risk aversion right now', says Sean Maloney, strategist at Nomura International.

Mr Wilders of the DSTA says: 'It took a while for spreads to converge after the euro was launched, and it might take a few years for them to reconverge because a lot of people got burnt in the last few months. Basically the question is, how long will it take people to forget?'

■ The analysis

This *FT* article focuses on an interesting story that had been developing in the European bond markets over the previous few weeks. When the euro was introduced in the late 1990s the yields on government bonds right across the whole eurozone saw a very rapid convergence. In simple terms this means that they all fell to the level of the lowest yield that existed at this time. As a result, the yields on offer from the traditionally much more risky countries like Spain and Greece became virtually the same as those on offer from much safer countries like Germany and France. The view was that, if the bonds were now issued in the same currency, they should enjoy the same level of risk and therefore have identical yields. The yield differential between Italian and German government bonds which had been as high as 600 basis points fell back to just a few basis points.

You should remember that we use the term 'basis points' to show the credit spread that exists between bond issues. Every percentage point of yield in a bond equates to 100 basis points so that a yield of 6 per cent is 100 basis points more than a yield of 5 per cent.

However, in the wake of the worldwide credit crisis investors became more reluctant to take on any unnecessary risk. So, they now placed a premium on buying German government bonds rather than the more risky options available in the Greek and Spanish markets.

As the *FT* article reported:

> [T]he risk premium of 10-year Italian government bonds has risen 12 basis points to 43bp over comparable German bunds since the beginning of the year, while that of 10-year Greek government bonds rose 14 bp to 44.5 bp over Bunds.

The article suggests that the search for better credit risk only partly explains this development. The additional factor is the search for greater liquidity attached to certain eurozone government bond markets. One attraction of the German Bund market is that it has a highly liquid futures contract attached to the market. This gave bond traders the ability to utilise these instruments to manage their trading strategies.

The *FT* article quotes Erik Wilders, head of the Dutch State Treasury Agency: 'Germany is the biggest and most liquid market, and that is what investors want right now'.

These movements in the European bond market were matched in the credit swaps market (CDS). The figure quoted in the *FT* article show that the five-year CDS Greek sovereign debt had risen 28.8 per cent to 56.6 basis points in the past month. The result is that it now cost investors €56 700 each year to protect €10 m worth of debt against a default over a 5-year period.

■ Key terms

Eurozone This simply refers to all the countries that use the euro as their common currency.

Bond yields When an individual or a company borrows money there is a cost that they have to pay in order to obtain the funds. If it is a short-term loan (up to one year) this is normally referred to as an 'interest rate'. So, we might take out a one-month bank loan with an annual interest rate of say 8.5 per cent. This is the interest rate, or the cost of obtaining the funds. If a company needs to borrow funds for a longer time period, this will normally be through the issue of a bond market security which is usually repaid at a fixed rate of annual interest (this is called the 'coupon') until it is finally repaid on the date that it redeems or matures. The yield on the bond issue is the cost to the issuer or the return to investor who buys the bond.

Convergence This refers to the process that took place in the late 1990s whereby all the prospective Eurozone countries saw their government bond yields fall to the level of the lowest yield that existed at this time. This meant that the yields on offer from the traditionally much more risky countries like Spain and Greece were virtually the same as those on offer from the much safer countries like Germany and France. The view was that if the bonds were now issued in the same currency they should enjoy the same level of risk and therefore identical yields.

Global credit crisis This refers to the crisis that affected financial markets in the summer of 2007. This was caused by the subprime crisis that started in the US. As a result banks became very reluctant to lend to each other and the interbank markets saw their liquidity dry up.

Government debt These are simply bonds issued by governments to fund the difference between their spending and revenue.

Spreads This is a measure of the relative cost of issuing more risky bonds. It is best seen with an example.

Let us assume that the German government has close to zero risk of default. As a result a 10-year German bund might have a yield of 3.5 per cent. In contrast, a 10-year issue from the Greek government which has more risk of default might have a yield of 4.5 per cent. This gives us a credit yield spread of 4.5 per cent minus 3.5 per cent = 100 basis points difference. The spread is determined by a combination of the bond's credit rating, liquidity and the market's perception of its risk relative to the other bond.

AAA rated Most new bond issuers are assigned credit ratings by the various companies that are involved in this activity. They include Standard and Poor's and Moody's. The highest credit rating allocated by Moody's is a triple A. For example, this is awarded to the German government's bond issues.

Short summary of Moody's credit ratings

AAA = Capacity to pay interest and principal extremely strong.
AA = Differs only in a small degree.
A = More susceptible to adverse changes in circumstances.
BBB = Adequate capacity.
BB, B = Speculative.
C = No interest being paid.
D = In default.

Risk premium This is simply the extra financial reward that will be required to convince an investor to hold an asset that has a risk of returning a capital sum that is less than the original amount paid for it. For example, you will only buy shares in a company if there is a good prospect of achieving a financial return well in excess of the interest rate that is available for a 'risk-free' bank account.

Bunds Bunds are simply German government bonds. These are used to fund the difference between Federal government spending and revenue. As normal the benchmark, long-term government bond is the 10-year maturity.

Sovereign entities This simply refers to a country or a supranational body like the World Bank or the European Bank for Reconstruction and Development that are both regular issuers of bonds.

Liquidity premium This term refers to how easily an asset can be converted into cash. Therefore, notes and coins are the most liquid financial asset. In general, the more liquid an asset, the lower is its return. Investors will pay a higher price in order to secure a liquid financial asset. This is what is known as the liquidity premium.

Futures market (liquid futures market) In the financial markets a well-established futures market will allow traders to deal in a financial market asset at a set price on a specified future date. For example, a trader could arrange to buy £10 m of a government bond issue from another bank at a set price on a specific date in the future. The attraction of this deal is that both parties know now what the price is going to be. There is no uncertainty as this transaction will not be affected by any subsequent rise or fall in bond prices. A liquid futures market is simply one where there is a high degree of trading activity which will allow investors to trade easily.

Credit risk premium This is the higher return that a bond investor will require to compensate for the possible financial loss due to the bond issuer being unable to make timely payments of interest or the principal.

Credit default swaps (CDS) This is a financial market instrument that is designed to offer a bond investor complete protection against the risk of default. Essentially, the seller of the swap takes over the risk of default on the bond issuer for a one-off payment. In the event of any default the seller of the swap will be fully liable to pay the par value of the bond and any due interest payments to the credit swap buyer.

Risk aversion Most rational people will always prefer to buy investments that carry the lowest possible risk. So, if faced with the choice of a perfectly safe government bond (AAA–rated) or a bond issue from another country with a poor credit history, the rational person will always select the low-risk option.

■ What do you think?

1. In the context of the European government bond market explain what is meant by the term 'convergence'.

2. According to the *FT* article what factors have resulted in the recent divergence in government bond yields across the Eurozone?

3. What is meant by the following terms?

   ■ liquidity premium

   ■ credit risk premium.

4. How do bond holders use credit default swaps to minimise the risk on their bond investments?

■ Investigate FT data

You will need the Companies and Markets section of the *Financial Times*.

Go to the Market Data section. Now go to the Benchmark Government Bond section.

Highlight all the 10-year government bonds from the countries that make up the Eurozone. Start with the German 10-year bund yield. Now calculate the spread between this benchmark bond and all the other eurozone government bonds.

Write a short commentary on the current level of convergence between the government bond yields in the Eurozone.

■ Research

Arnold, G. (2008) *Corporate Financial Management*, 4th edn, Harlow, UK: Prentice Hall Financial Times. You should especially look at Chapter 11 to get more information about the bond markets.

Berk, J. and DeMarzo, P. (2009) *Corporate Finance*, Harlow, UK: FT Prentice Hall Financial Times. The topic of Eurobonds is on p. 784.

Gitman, L. (2009) *Principles of Managerial Finance*, 12th edn, Harlow, UK: Pearson International Edition. There is a short introduction to Eurobonds on p. 297.

McLaney, E. (2009) *Business Finance Theory and Practice*, 8th edn, Harlow, UK: FT Prentice Hall Financial Times. The definition of a Eurobond issue is on p. 239.

Pike, R. and Neale, B. (2006) *Corporate Finance and Investment*, 6th edn, Harlow, UK: FT Prentice Hall. You should look at Chapter 3, pp. 64–7 for a brief introduction to bond pricing.

Pilbeam, K. (2006) *International Finance*, 3rd edn, Basingstoke: Palgrave Macmillan. There is a useful chapter on Eurobonds starting on p. 304.

Valdez, S. (2007) *An Introduction to Global Financial Markets*, 5th edn, Basingstoke: Palgrave Macmillan. You should look at Chapter 6.

Watson, D. and Head, A. (2007) *Corporate Finance Principles and Practice*, 4th edn, Harlow, UK: FT Prentice Hall. You should look at Chapter 5 (pp. 127–8).

Go to **www.pearsoned.co.uk/boakes** to access Kevin's blog for additional analysis of recent topical news articles and to post your comments. Download podcasts containing short audio summaries of the main issues relating to each article and check your understanding of in-text questions with the handy hints provided.

4

DEBT FINANCE

Capital structure

In corporate finance the term 'capital structure' refers to the long-term finance that a business needs to have in order to fund new investment projects and to maintain its growth and success. This includes debt issues, ordinary shares, preference shares and retained earnings. It is regarded as a key topic in corporate finance as companies must decide in particular on the appropriate balance between equity and debt finance. Before we examine that debate we must answer three key questions:

1. **How much capital does a company need?** A company needs enough capital to pay for its fixed assets (any asset designed to be used for the long term, including buildings or new office equipment) and to ensure that there is enough working capital (the part of capital used to allow the business to trade from day to day, including stock or cash). The correct level of long-term financing will allow the company to trade, produce the goods and offer the services that it is involved in.

2. **What happens when the company has too much capital?** Some companies can get themselves in a position where they have more long-term finance than they actually need. This is easily solved. The company should first repay any loans that it does not require. This can be followed by the payment of special dividends to the shareholders or a programme of share buybacks.

3. **What happens when a company has too little capital?** This can be a serious problem and it is much harder for a company to solve. At a minimum it might prevent it from taking advantage of some excellent investment opportunities. Even more seriously it might threaten the whole future of the company if the lack of capital begins to concern their customers, suppliers or financial backers. In this situation they need to undertake a series of new capital issues with some urgency. The problem is that the investors in either new debt or equity issues might be reluctant to invest more money in a business that is seen to be in financial difficulties. The message is that a well-run business must anticipate its capital needs well in advance. This is rather like a successful soccer team where a good manager always adds a new quality player before he is actually needed. In the same way a well-run business will be looking to raise extra finance well before it becomes an urgent requirement.

In corporate finance it is essential to understand the important role that a company's capital structure plays in all its business activities. When a company looks to raise new finance, the choice is between equity finance and debt finance. You can read much more about both types of finance in Topics 4 and 6. At this stage it is important to understand what is meant by the terms 'gearing' or 'leverage'. If a company has any level of debt in their capital structure we say in the UK that they are using gearing. In the US we would say that they are employing financial leverage. In either case the use of these terms suggests that the company is employing a financial strategy that will amplify the returns to its shareholders. The use of debt finance can lead to higher rewards for the owners of a business, but this is normally at the cost of greater risk.

This means that the best choice for companies will depend on their relative risk and cost profiles. These are set out in the box below. This shows that for companies the issue of debt capital is considered to be more risky because they must make financial commitments to the investors in these securities. If they do not meet their obligations to pay interest or the principal, they risk being forced into liquidation. In contrast, they make no such promises to the investors in equity finance. These know that they will be well rewarded in good years, but they must accept any losses in income or capital in the bad years.

Point of view of the issuing company
Debt capital   High risk but lower cost
Equity capital   Low risk but higher cost

Before we get into the articles chosen for this section of the book, we should focus on one more issue: the costs of financial distress and insolvency for companies. One consequence of a company issuing ever-increasing amounts of cheaper debt capital is that the resulting increase in gearing (the ratio of debt to equity capital) will reduce the company's chances of being able to meet the demands of its bond investors. Failure to make the required payments of interest or principal is likely to result in the company being forced into a period of financial distress that will ultimately lead to its becoming insolvent. There are significant direct administrative costs associated with this whole process. In addition the risks of corporate failure will lead to a number of indirect costs. These will include:

1. Their customers may become less ready to deal with them. This arises from the risk that the company's insolvency could result in a financial loss for a customer still awaiting the delivery of some service or product. For example, a number of airline passengers were left stranded when XL Airways collapsed in September 2008.

2. Their suppliers may also stop trading with a company in financial distress and at risk of insolvency. This is again because they will fear that they may not get paid for any goods or services supplied to an ailing business.

3. Their employees may start to leave. It is likely that the most marketable employees in a company facing financial difficulties will start to search for a safer career opportunity.

4. They may be forced to undertake speedy asset sales at a cut-down price. As the company is trying to raise funds, it might have to resort to selling its most liquid assets at a lower price.

It is clear that the direct and indirect costs of financial distress and insolvency are significant, with the result that companies may look to be far less reliant on debt capital than pure financial logic might dictate. The managers of a company might well end up with a less than optimal capital structure, but this must be balanced against the reduced risk of insolvency. There is a lot to be said for a good night's sleep! It is well worth the slightly higher costs of funding a business.

In the first article chosen for this section of the book we focus on how different types of capital are treated when a company gets into financial difficulties. In the second article we focus on the problems of business risk that face a particular UK retail company.

The following three articles are analysed in this section:

Article 16
MyTravel shareholders offered 4 per cent in £800 m debt-to-equity restructuring
Financial Times, 14 October 2004

Article 17
Blacks Leisure falls into the red
Financial Times, 4 May 2007

Article 18
UK investors dig in over pre-emption rights
Financial Times, 22 October 2007

These articles address the following issues:

- secured and unsecured bonds;
- convertible bonds;
- preference shares;
- business risk;
- gearing;
- rights issues;
- options for shareholders;
- calculating the ex-rights price;
- companies' cost of capital;
- role of the Monopolies and Mergers Commission.

MyTravel on the brink

In corporate finance it is essential to understand the important role that a company's capital structure plays in all its business activities. When a company looks to raise new finance, the choice is between the extremes of equity finance and debt finance. From the point of view of the company the issue of more share finance is much less risky as the company makes no financial commitments to the shareholders. In contrast, the issue of new bond finance means that the company is now obliged to pay interest each year and it also has to repay the loan at a fixed date in the future. Financial risk is the name given to the type of risk associated with this commitment to the debt holder.

In recent years we have seen the development of a number of new financing products which are debt–equity hybrids. This means that they are somewhere between the two extremes of equity and debt finance. This includes the use of convertible bonds. In this article we will see how the various providers of capital are treated very differently when a company faces the prospect of severe financial distress.

Article 16

Financial Times, 14 October 2004   **FT**

MyTravel shareholders offered 4 per cent in £800 m debt-to-equity restructuring

Matthew Garrahan

MyTravel shareholders have been offered just 4 per cent of the embattled travel group under an ambitious proposal that would see £800 m of the company's unsecured debt converted into equity.

Following sharp declines in MyTravel shares, the price of the stock had already factored in dilution so yesterday's announcement will not come as a great surprise to investors.

Under the board's proposal, creditors have been offered 88 per cent of the enlarged share capital, with convertible bondholders in line for 8 per cent should they wish to accept it.

The rest of the shares would be retained by existing equity investors.

James Ainley, leisure analyst with Dresdner Kleinwort Wasserstein, said the restructuring would imply the issue of about 13 bn new shares. 'At the current 5 p price, this equates to £650 m additional equity or about 80 per cent of the face value of the debt', he said.

However, the move could come unstuck if convertible bondholders object to the terms.

Bank creditors will, in effect, receive the face value of their loans in new MyTravel shares. But convertible bondholders will only receive shares equivalent to 30 p for every 100 p invested.

Analysts said it was unlikely the bondholders would not accept the proposal.

One said: 'If they say no, they could derail the deal and the business may go into liquidation'.

MyTravel has proposed a timetable for the restructuring that would see it completed by the end of 2004.

On completion, the company's debt will

be approximately £140 m of aircraft finance leases.

In order to satisfy European Union rules as to airline ownership, MyTravel has also proposed issuing ordinary shares to creditors and bondholders from countries in the EU and European economic area.

Non-voting preference shares will be awarded to creditors and bondholders from outside this area.

Provided the bondholders and creditors accept the proposal, the company will have a new, five-year overdraft facility worth £167 m.

■ The analysis

The company MyTravel plc has run into serious difficulties. As a result there is now a proposal for a major restructure of the financing of the business. So who are the winners and who are the losers in this situation?

The debt holders in any failing business are always in the strongest bargaining position. They are higher up the creditor hierarchy than the preference shareholders or the ordinary shareholders. As a result, the plans from the company's board of directors would offer 88 per cent of the new enlarged share capital to the various debt holders. In effect, they will see 100 per cent of the face value of their debt converted into shares in MyTravel plc. So, the monetary value of their investment has been protected, although they now have seen the money that they were owed by MyTravel converted into equity finance.

The middle of the creditor hierarchy is represented by the convertible bond holders who are being offered a further 8 per cent of the share capital. This means that they would get back 30 per cent of their existing investment in the form of shares.

At the bottom of the hierarchy are the ordinary shareholders who are being offered just 4 per cent of the expanded share capital. In order to go ahead with this course of action the company's board of directors will need a positive vote in favour from the various bondholders. One analyst quoted in the *Financial Times* article speculates that a rejection could derail the deal and the business may go into liquidation. This would leave the various parties fighting over any assets that the company still owns.

This article shows perfectly the risks that are faced by ordinary shareholders. If a company is doing well, they reap the rewards in terms of capital gains through a sharp rise in the share price plus higher income in the form of rising dividend payments. However, if the company hits problems, they act as the shock absorber for the other providers of capital. In other words, in times of trouble they will see a sharp fall in the capital value of their shares while the bond holders will normally be insulated against the most severe consequences of corporate failure. As a counter to this lower risk the bond holders accept much lower potential returns.

In summary, this article shows the stark choice that investors face. If they purchase good-quality corporate bonds, they are normally getting a low-risk but also a low-return investment. In contrast, if they buy shares from the same company, they are getting a high-risk asset which carries with it the potential for very substantial returns. This investment decision is often driven by the attitude of the individual investor to risk and return. The final choice is yours!

■ Key terms

Capital structure This refers to the long-term finance that a business needs in order to trade. This is made up of debt and equity finance. The debt finance will normally be in the form of a bond that carries fixed-interest payments and a set date when it will be redeemed. In contrast, there are no guarantees of any financial returns to the providers of equity (the shareholders). If a company does well and is highly profitable, it is likely that there will be significant dividends paid to the shareholders. However, if the company runs into financial difficulties, the dividends will be cut back and they might disappear altogether. It should be clear that in terms of capital structure the shareholders take a greater risk than the debt holders. As a result, it is reasonable for the shareholders to expect a higher level of financial returns to compensate for this higher risk.

See Articles 2 and 3 to find these issues discussed in more detail. It shows how activist shareholders are increasingly seeking management changes in companies that do not perform in line with their expectations.

Convertible bonds On the face of it, these are just like conventional bonds as they are interest bearing and have set redemption dates. However, they give the holder the right to convert their bonds into the shares of the issuing company.

Hint: For a more detailed discussion of convertible bonds you should look at Article 13 which examines the Japanese convertible bond market. There is a more detailed definition of convertible bonds in the 'Key terms' section.

Secured and unsecured debt Companies will normally have a range of different types of debt capital. The lowest-risk form of debt capital will be secured debt. This means that the debt is secured on various assets owned by the business including property or plant and machinery. If the business goes into liquidation, the secured bond holders will have a claim on these assets so that their investment will be protected. In contrast, the unsecured debt holders do not enjoy this form of protection. They accept a higher degree of risk which must be compensated for by a higher level of return.

Non-voting preference shares In many ways preference shares can be seen to be very similar to bond finance. They normally pay dividends at a set percentage very much like the coupon on a bond issue, and in addition they will normally have a set redemption date. However, unlike bonds, the dividends on a preference share are paid at the discretion of the board of directors of a company. Most preference shares are non-voting, which means that the holders will not have the right to vote on corporate policy at the annual general meeting.

■ What do you think?

1. With reference to this article comment on the relative risk and reward profile of ordinary shareholders, preference shareholders, convertible bond holders and secured bond holders.

2. Explain why the ordinary shareholders receive only 4 per cent of the new expanded share capital.

3. It is often said that shareholders act as 'shock absorbers' for the company. In the context of this article explain what this means.

4. What is meant by the term 'convertible bonds'? What are the advantages for investors who buy convertible bonds rather than ordinary bonds?

5. What is meant by the term non-voting 'preference shares'?

6. Why are preference shares referred to as hybrid securities?

7. What are the likely outcomes if the bondholders reject the restructuring proposal?

■ Investigate FT data

You will need the Companies and Markets section of the *Financial Times*. Go to the London Share Price Service. This is normally the two pages inside the back page of the Companies and Markets section.

In 2007 Thomas Cook merged with MyTravel plc.

Answer these questions:

1. What is the current share price for Thomas Cook plc?

2. What is the high and low for this share price in the last 12 months?

3. What is the current P/E ratio for Thomas Cook?

4. How does this P/E ratio compare to other transport companies?

■ Research

Arnold, G. (2007) *Essentials of Corporate Financial Management*, Harlow, UK: FT Prentice Hall. Look at pp. 252–7 for a very clear introduction to different types of bond issues.

Arnold, G. (2008) *Corporate Financial Management*, 4th edn, Harlow, UK: FT Prentice Hall. You should look especially at Chapter 11, pp. 441–3 to get more information about convertible bonds. It sets out very clearly the advantages of convertible to both the issuers (companies) and the investors.

Berk, J. and DeMarzo, P. (2009) *Corporate Finance*, Harlow,UK: FT Prentice Hall Financial Times. The topic of preferred stock is explained on p. 755.

Gitman, L. (2009) *Principles of Managerial Finance*, Harlow, UK: Pearson International Edition. There is a clear discussion of the differences between equity and debt capital starting on p. 330.

McLaney, E. (2009) *Business Finance Theory and Practice*, Harlow, UK: FT Prentice Hall Financial Times. There is a brief introduction to preference shares on pp. 13–14.

Pike, R. and Neale, B. (2006) *Corporate Finance and Investment*, 6th edn, Harlow, UK: FT Prentice Hall. You should look at Chapter 16.

Watson, D. and Head, A. (2007) *Corporate Finance Principles and Practice*, 4th edn, Harlow, UK: FT Prentice Hall. You should look at Chapters 4 and 5.

5

CAPITAL STRUCTURE

Blacks Leisure hit by global warming

Business risk is an important concept in corporate finance. This is the general risk that applies to all companies that operate in any business environment. For example, a company might see a sharp drop in sales because a rival business brings out a better product, or another company might be hit by a change in tax laws that has a negative impact on the profitability of a business. No matter what a company does, it is impossible to remove all business risk. It is a fact of life for companies. Instead, they must do their best to protect themselves against the most severe damage that might be caused to their businesses.

In this example we focus on Blacks Leisure, which has seen a sharp downturn in its financial performance as a result of a change in weather patterns. The company blames this business risk on the impact of global warming.

Article 17   *Financial Times*, 4 May 2007 **FT**

Blacks Leisure falls into the red

Tom Braithwaite and Maggie Urry

Background

Retailers are fond of blaming the weather when things go wrong. Blacks has gone a step further by blaming climate change.

'Blacks and Millets have historically benefited from the traditional British climate of somewhat wet summers and cold winters', it said yesterday as it reported a loss for the year that was 'the warmest and driest on record'.

Moreover, the new year had seen unseasonably warm spring weather'.

Blacks Leisure has slashed its dividend as it tries to stabilise the troubled business, heaping more misery on both its shareholders and those of Sports Direct.

Results for the year to March 3 showed the outdoor wear group just managed to break even, with underlying profit of £100 000 on sales little changed at £298 m, in line with expectations after its most recent profit warning.

However, Blacks went into the red following an exceptional charge of £13.9 m, the cost of closing about 45 loss-making stores, which mainly trade under its worst performing Millets fascia.

Investors in Sports Direct, the sportswear group that floated in February, are exposed to the fortunes of Blacks via a 29.4 per cent stake. Mike Ashley, the controversial founder and majority shareholder of Sports Direct, bought the stake in his own name last year but rolled it into the company upon flotation.

Both companies have suffered a significant sell off this year: shares in Blacks are down 37 per cent, while those in Sports Direct have fallen 25 per cent since it joined the market in February.

Shares in Blacks fell 2 p to 259 p yesterday, while those in Sports Direct closed down 3¼ p at 226 p.

Russell Hardy, chief executive of Blacks, said there had been 'some pleasing signs of good growth from the camping business' but that the company had endured a 'tough April'. In the first eight weeks of the new financial year, to April 28, sales were up 2.7 per cent and like-for-like sales had increased 0.8 per cent.

Blacks has traditionally performed well in wet summers and cold winters and claims that 'global warming' has brought about much of its weaker performance.

'In terms of weather proofing the business, we've done a lot of work for this season but my sense is it's going to take another couple of seasons to put the business in a position where it can cope with consistently drier weather', said Mr Hardy.

Blacks is cutting its final dividend by 6 p to 2 p, leaving the total for the year at 5.3 p, down from 11.3 p last time.

The board said it regarded 'the reduction in the final dividend as a proper measure reflective of the poor trading performance'.

During the year, like-for-like sales fell 2.7 per cent and high operational gearing meant margins fell sharply.

After taking the £13.9 m charge, Blacks reported a pre-tax loss of £13.8 m (£21.4 m profit). Losses per share were 29.7 p (earnings of 34.6 p).

■ The analysis

Anyone who has been on an outdoor activity holiday will know the name Blacks. For many it is the shop of choice for walking and climbing gear. The last time I was in a Blacks store getting some new trekking boots I remember being most impressed by its indoor walking ramp which is used to try them out. It is probably a slight simplification but, as a business, Blacks Leisure can be split into two main parts. The core activity is the outdoor leisure retail product market including clothing and boots. Perhaps less widely known, it also sells boardwear gear as it is the UK's distributor and retailer of O'Neill products.

This *Financial Times* article focuses on its latest very poor set of financial results which were for the year to 3 March 2007. In this period the company broke even on sales of £298 m. This was very much in line with the market's expectations following a very recent profit warning. However, an exceptional charge of some £13.9 m took the company into the red. This charge resulted from the closure of a significant number of loss-making Millets stores. Shareholders in the group have suffered a sharp fall of 37 per cent in the Blacks share price in the last year.

The chief executive, Russell Hardy, saw some encouraging signs despite these bad figures. He claimed that the company had suffered in the face of the impact of climate change. A company like Blacks performs best with wet summers and cold winters, so the onset of drier summers and milder winters hits sales badly. The company was attempting to insulate itself from the impact of global warming. This is most easily achieved through product diversification.

This is a classic example of a business risk damaging a company's performance. As usual, it is the shareholders who take the biggest hit. In this case they have seen the final dividend slashed by 6 p to 2 p. So, the total dividend for the year fell from 11.3 p to just 5.3 p. This dividend reduction combined with the sharp fall in the share price means that business risk has resulted in a disastrous year for Blacks' shareholders. As the advertisers of certain financial products are forced to say 'always remember the price of shares can go down as well as up'. What they do not say is that the cause is normally business risk.

■ Key terms

Business risk This refers to the general risk that can impact on a company's cash flow or profitability. It could be caused by general economic conditions (consumer spending, level of interest rates, etc.) as well as more specific company factors (changes in key staff, strike action by employees, etc.).

Hint: If you look at Topic 11 you will see more discussion of the risks facing companies. Article 31 shows how companies can manage some forms of currency risk.

Break-even A company achieves break-even when its sales revenue equals total costs. These costs will include some fixed costs as well as the variable costs that will be dependent on the level of sales.

Gearing This refers to the proportion of debt in the company's capital structure. A company is termed 'highly geared' if it has a large amount of debt finance compared to a small amount of equity finance. In contrast, a low-geared company will be largely financed by equity finance.

■ What do you think?

1. What is meant by the term 'business risk'? Select any five FTSE 100 companies and identify an example of business risk that might impact on them in the next year.
2. Explain what is causing the business risk associated with Blacks Leisure.
3. What steps could Blacks Leisure take to try to minimise this type of business risk?
4. Just about a year ago you advised a friend (perhaps, now a former friend!) to purchase 1000 shares in Blacks Leisure. Write a short report (300 words max) explaining the negative performance of these shares in the past year. Give a view on their likely performance in the year ahead.

Hint: Get hold of the company's latest report and accounts and visit its website.

■ Investigate FT Data

You will need the Companies and Markets section of the *Financial Times*. Read through the first few pages of this section in today's edition of the *Financial Times*.

Attempt this short activity:

1. Identify any two examples of a company's share price being impacted by a form of business risk.

Hint: If you cannot see an example in the various company reports look instead at the Markets Report at the back of the Companies and Markets section. This shows the main share prices movements in London and gives a reason for the change in most cases.

Research

Arnold, G. (2007) *Essentials of Corporate Financial Management*, Harlow, UK: FT Prentice Hall. Look at pp. 396–8 to see business risk defined.

Arnold, G. (2008) *Corporate Financial Management*, 4th edn, Harlow, UK: Prentice Hall Financial Times. You should especially look at Chapter 21, p. 803 to get more information about business risk.

Berk, J. and DeMarzo, P. (2009) *Corporate Finance*, Harlow, UK: FT Prentice Hall Financial Times. The link between leverage and risk is on p. 492.

Gitman, L. (2009) *Principles of Managerial Finance*, 12th edn, Harlow, UK: Pearson International Edition. There is a look at the popular sources of risk affecting financial managers on p. 229.

McLaney, E. (2009) *Business Finance Theory and Practice*, 8th edn, Harlow, UK: FT Prentice Hall Financial Times. You will find a section on risk and business finance on p. 5.

Pike, R. and Neale, B. (2006) *Corporate Finance and Investment*, 6th edn, Harlow, UK: FT Prentice Hall. You should look at Chapter 7, pp. 163–4 to see an explanation of the different types of risk.

Watson, D. and Head, A. (2007) *Corporate Finance Principles and Practice*, 4th edn, Harlow, UK: FT Prentice Hall. You should look at Chapter 8, p. 224 to see a section on business risk.

5

CAPITAL STRUCTURE

Looking for the 'right' way forward

When I am setting an exam question for my second year Finance students I always look for a real corporate finance activity that requires them to demonstrate a combination of good writing and quantitative skills. That is why I always tend to incorporate some aspect of a real rights issue into a question about capital structure.

People who buy shares in a company get few financial promises or guarantees. This is in sharp contrast to the bond holders who get a firm commitment from the company to pay them a certain amount of interest each year (the coupon) as well as the eventual repayment of the loan (the principal). The shareholders hope the company will perform well which will result in them receiving substantial dividend payments as well as a rise in the capital value of their shares. One of the few promises that a company does make to its shareholders is now coming under threat. This is where a company decides to raise additional finance through the issue of more share capital. The existing shareholders must be given the first opportunity to buy any new shares. This is important as it guarantees that they will be able to maintain their existing percentage of the company's share capital if they decide to exercise their right to purchase any extra shares that they are offered.

Article 18   *Financial Times*, 22 October 2007   **FT**

UK investors dig in over pre-emption rights

Kate Burgess

European Union authorities have infuriated UK investors by suggesting that pre-emption rights – the right of first refusal to new share issues that most investors regard as sacrosanct – could be removed.

'Investors jealously guard their pre-emption rights. If there is one way of infuriating the City, it is threatening to take them away', says a corporate broker at a US investment bank.

The latest assault on shareholders' sensibilities comes from the European Commission's review of European company law that enshrines the principle of pre-emption.

The review is nearing the end of its consultation stage, with responses due this month. The commission is working towards a deadline of next March for the first draft of new legislation.

It comes just three years after the UK government asked Paul Myners, former chairman of Marks and Spencer, to look at whether pre-emption rights hampered businesses from 'raising finance to innovate'.

Mr Myners concluded that the rights were a 'cornerstone of company law' that should not be removed. Pre-emption was an important safeguard for shareholders although they needed to be more flexible about waiving their rights on occasion, he said.

He argued that pre-emption instilled confidence among investors and therefore had a direct impact on lowering companies' cost of capital. In the US, for example, where these rights are less entrenched, the risks are higher and the costs of raising capital greater.

Mr Myners' findings echoed the conclusions of the Monopolies and Mergers Commission investigation, which five years earlier concluded that the rights were no more expensive than non-pre-emptive issues.

His conclusions allowed investors to breathe a sigh of relief. They could buy shares safe in the knowledge that their holdings would not be diluted without their agreement by companies selling equity at preferential prices to third parties. It meant investors could call a halt to profligate spending of shareholder funds. And when shareholders said no, companies could not gainsay them by issuing new shares to more management-friendly groups.

The present rules in the UK insist if companies wish to issue more than 5 per cent of their existing equity capital in a year, or 7.5 per cent over three years, they must get shareholders' approval.

But now, the European Commission has reopened the debate as part of a wider exercise to overhaul and simplify company laws that have been around for more than 20 years. Pre-emption rights, which were introduced in the UK in the 1980s, are part of the review. The commission has suggested that pre-emption rights could be modified or even repealed and the UK government has asked for responses.

The biotech industry has in the past argued that pre-emption rights were cumbersome, time-consuming and expensive, and companies needing regular cash injections quickly say that tapping the same investor base for the necessary funds can add to the costs of capital.

These companies have pushed hard for the same kind of freedom US rivals have to issue shares. But in the US fees on equity fund-raisings are usually substantially higher – as much as 6 per cent – and shares fall to discounts after a placing.

By comparison, rights issues in the UK attract fees of less than 3 per cent. So far, the voices of those in favour of pre-emption seem to be drowning out those against.

The CBI has written to the European Commission arguing that pre-emption needs to apply across the EU as part of a uniform set of core principles to develop a single market.

The CBI was minded to suggest modification at the wider EU level, because it could be retained in domestic regulation.

But, says Rod Armitage, head of company affairs: 'Pre-emption rights are a long-established feature of the investor-company landscape. None of our members lobbied for change and they were not in favour of them being done away with.'

The London Stock Exchange has also weighed in, pointing out that safeguards such as pre-emption rights play a significant part in London's competitiveness as a financial market.

'Pre-emption rights are an important and highly regarded aspect of investor protection', says Adam Kinsley, LSE director of regulation.

The most heated response has been from UK investors.

Karina Litvak, head of corporate governance at F&C Asset Management, says: 'This is a non-negotiable for most investors.'

The Association of British Insurers, backed by the UK's biggest shareholder groups, including Morley and Insight, has written to the government and the commission outlining investors' concerns.

It argues that pre-emption rights are 'vital in protecting investors' and have an EU-wide impact, affecting anyone investing across borders in EU companies.

However, the decisive factor will be the position the government takes. And,

$\rightarrow$

worryingly for many investors, they have detected a persistently lukewarm support from the government for pre-emption rights.

As Peter Montagnon, director of investment affairs at the ABI, says: 'We want to make clear to the government the strength of feeling on pre-emption rights so that it will have no doubt over what position to take in discussions with other member states.'

■ The analysis

Not for the first time the European Union authorities are proposing to take some action that will upset part of the UK population. Normally the targets are the fisherman facing yet more quotas and the market-stall holders still wanting to sell their fruit and vegetables in old-fashioned pounds and ounces. In this case the affronted group are the investors in companies who face the threat of losing their much coveted pre-emption rights. As the corporate broker is quoted as saying in the *FT* article:

> Investors jealously guard their pre-emption rights. If there is one way of infuriating the City, it is threatening to take them away.

The latest threat comes from a review of European company law that was getting close to the end of its consultation period.

This is not the first time that rights issues have been threatened in recent years. The *FT* article reports that just three years ago the ex-chairman of Marks and Spencer, Paul Myners, had been asked to look into the question of whether pre-emption rights had a detrimental effect on the UK companies' ability to fund new investments. He concluded that they were in fact a 'cornerstone' of UK company law, which should be safeguarded. In fact he went as far as to suggest that their existence re-enforced the confidence of shareholders and this actually reduced the cost of capital for UK companies. So, if you took rights issues away, the cost of company finance would actually rise. The result of this report combined with the outcome of a Monopolies and Mergers Commission Report was that UK investors were able to sleep easy in their beds safe in the knowledge that rights issues would remain. As a result, there was no danger that companies would be able to dilute the value of existing shareholdings by issuing additional share capital to new investors.

The article usefully includes the rule that UK companies must get shareholders to formally approve any share issues that involve more than 5 per cent of the existing share capital in any year, or 7.5 per cent over a three-year period. It also shows that this issue is still important for a number of bodies that look out for the interests of UK shareholders. The London Stock Exchange is quoted as saying:

> Pre-emption rights are an important and highly regarded aspect of investor protection.

Other support for the status quo comes from the Confederation of British Industry (CBI) and the Head of Corporate Governance at Foreign and Colonial Asset Management who says this is 'non-negotiable for most investors'. Against this background this looks like one battle the European Commission might not win. It looks like rights issues are here to stay which is good news for me as I start to plan my next exam paper!

■ Key terms

Pre-emption rights This refers to one of the very longstanding principles of corporate law. It gives all shareholders the first right to buy any additional shares being sold by companies. The new shares would be offered to existing holders in direct proportion to their existing holdings. So that if you owned 10 per cent of the existing shares in a company you would be given the right to buy 10 per cent of the new shares being sold via a rights issue. These additional shares are normally sold at a significant discount to the existing market share price to ensure a successful completion of the transaction.

The shareholders involved have three choices:

1. They can exercise their right, which means that they agree to buy the additional shares.

2. They can formally renounce the right, which will result in the company selling their rights on their behalf.

3. Finally, they can do nothing. In this case the company will still normally sell the rights on behalf of the shareholder anyway.

Corporate brokers These are important financial institutions that will make a market in a company's shares. This means that they must be willing to quote both buy and sell prices, enabling investors to deal in the shares. They could also act as an adviser to a company that was organising a new share issue.

Investment bank An investment bank acts as an intermediary between the issuers of capital (governments and companies) and the investors in capital (pension funds and insurance companies). The staff employed in an investment bank will work either in the investment bank division (IBD) which deals with the new issues of debt and equity capital or the markets division which deals with the investors in new bond and equity deals.

Shareholders In most companies the shareholders provide the bulk of the long-term finance. This makes them the key stakeholders in the business. They are the owners of the business and the managers must always remember that they are merely acting as agents working on behalf of the shareholder who are the principals. We normally assume that the primary objective of a company is to maximise the wealth of its shareholders. In practice, this is simplified to maximising the company's share price. The shareholders range from private investors with small stakes in the business right up to the large financial institutions that often own a significant percentage of the equity of a business.

Companies' cost of capital This refers to the financial return that is expected by an investor in a company's debt or equity issues. It is easy to understand if you think about it from the investor's point of view. The cost of capital is seen as the annual percentage return that an investor would expect if they were buying shares or bonds issued by a company. Let us look at an example:

Say we have a company called RBL plc.

They might have a 50/50 split between the amount of their equity and debt capital. We would expect the shareholders to demand a higher rate of return on the equity finance than the bondholders because it is much more risky.

RBL's cost of equity finance might be 10 per cent. This means that shareholders would only hold their shares if there was a reasonable expectation that the shares would give them an annual return of at least 10 per cent.

At the same time the cost of debt capital might be just 6 per cent reflecting the lower risk faced by the bondholders.

This means that the company's overall cost of capital is a simple average of the two which gives us a figure of 8 per cent.

Monopolies and Mergers Commission The Competition Commission actually took the place of the Monopolies and Mergers Commission in 1999. In simple terms, the MMC had the task of ensuring that the market in the provision of various goods and services remains competitive. They were required to undertake investigations and make recommendations in the case of takeovers to ensure that no single company had a dominant influence over a particular market.

Diluted (shareholdings) This arises when a company issues additional share capital. The result is that the existing shareholders see a diminished value in terms of their voting power and their value.

Shareholders' funds Put simply, this is a measure of the total value of the shareholders' stake in the company. It is made up of the total share capital plus any reserves.

Gainsay This means to deny or contradict something or somebody. In this context the *FT* article suggests that the need to get shareholder approval for a new share issue prevents companies from acting against the interests of their shareholders by going to 'more management-friendly' investors to fund a new share issue.

Equity fund-raising This simply refers to the company raising additional finance through the issue of extra share capital.

London Stock Exchange (LSE) This is the main stock exchange in the UK. It enables companies to raise new equity finance through their initial public offer (IPO) and subsequent share issues (rights issues). In recent years it has become increasingly international with companies from all over the world raising finance on the LSE.

Investor protection This refers to the defence of shareholders' rights including in this case the first opportunity to buy any new shares issued by the company.

■ What do you think?

1. What is meant by the term 'pre-emption rights'?

2. Why are rights issues usually made at a discount to the current market share price?

3. Explain the argument that the existence of pre-emption rights might result in a higher cost of capital for companies.

4. What is the normal level of fees that a company should expect to pay to an investment bank that organises and underwrites a new rights issue for them?

5. Why might the existence of rights issues actually reduce the cost of capital for UK companies?

6. The *FT* article suggests that the 'biotech industry has in the past argued that pre-emption rights were cumbersome, time-consuming and expensive, and companies needing regular cash injections quickly say that tapping the same investor base for necessary funds can add to the costs of capital'.

Discuss the arguments in favour of this viewpoint.

■ Investigate FT data

You will need the Companies and Markets section of the *Financial Times*. Go to the London Share Price Service. This is normally the two pages inside the back page of the Companies and Markets section.

Now go to the Telecommunications sector. Look at the current share price data for British Telecom.

Answer these questions:

1. If BT were to announce a 1 for 5 rights issue at 20 per cent below the current market share price, what would the price of each additional share be?

2. If a shareholder had 500 BT shares, how much would they have to pay in total to exercise their rights fully?

3. What would you predict would be the value of the BT shares after the rights issue process has been completed (ignore all other influences on the share price)?

Research

Arnold, G. (2007) *Essentials of Corporate Financial Management*, Harlow, UK: FT Prentice Hall. Look at pp. 212–15 for a very clear introduction to rights issues.

Arnold, G. (2008) *Corporate Financial Management*, 4th edn, Harlow, UK: Prentice Hall Financial Times. You should especially look at Chapter 10 to get more information about rights issues. pp. 383–6 are the most important.

Berk, J. and DeMarzo, P. (2009) *Corporate Finance*, Harlow, UK: FT Prentice Hall Financial Times. Rights issues are explained on pp. 770–1.

Gitman, L. (2009) *Principles of Managerial Finance*, 12th edn, Harlow, UK: Pearson International Edition. There is a discussion on the process of organising a rights issue on pp. 332–3.

McLaney, E. (2009) *Business Finance Theory and Practice*, 8th edn, Harlow, UK: FT Prentice Hall Financial Times. There is a section on rights issues on p. 229.

Pike, R. and Neale, B. (2006) *Corporate Finance and Investment*, 6th edn, Harlow, UK: FT Prentice Hall. You should look at Chapter 16, pp. 427–32.

Watson, D. and Head, A. (2007) *Corporate Finance Principles and Practice*, 4th edn, Harlow, UK: FT Prentice Hall. You should look at Chapter 4, pp. 1031–1110.

Equity finance

In corporate finance equity finance is represented by the ordinary shares that a company issues. These are generally the main providers of long-term finance with the holders receiving high returns in good times but suffering large losses when a company's prospects take a dive. The ordinary shareholders are the owners of the company and as such have a number of important rights.

1. **The rights of shareholders:**

   ■ They get to vote at a company's annual general meeting (AGM). This will include issues such as the make-up of the board of directors.

   ■ They will be asked to approve any strategic corporate moves being considered by the company. These will include proposals for mergers and takeovers.

   ■ They are entitled to receive their share of any dividends paid by the company. It should be noted, however, that no company is obliged to distribute any annual dividends. The level of these payments will reflect the trading performance of the company and the investment opportunities that are open to it.

   ■ They will get the first option to buy any new shares issued by the company.

   ■ Finally, they can expect to be kept informed of the performance of the company. At a minimum this will mean that the company sends them an annual report and set of accounts.

2. **Equities are risk capital.** When you read the Companies and Markets section of the *Financial Times* you will quickly understand that ordinary shares are a perfect example of what is meant by the term 'risk capital'. So that when the company is doing well the shareholders will see their wealth grow rapidly through dividend payouts and share price appreciation. However, the other side of the coin means that when a company starts to run into difficulties, it is the holders of equity finance who have most to fear. In the first instance, any dividend payments will be reduced or maybe cut out altogether. The ultimate risk is, if the company goes into liquidation, the shareholders are last in the queue to receive their money back. Indeed, in most cases they get nothing. The message is that, if the shareholder is wise or lucky, or both, then buying equity finance can open up the possibility of an individual becoming very rich as the company prospers. At the same time, if they buy into a business on the slide they can soon see their wealth go up in flames. Always remember that equity finance is high-risk and high-return finance. For investors the warning is clear. If they do not like risk they should invest their money elsewhere.

3. **Authorised shares**. When a company is first established, the total number of shares that it can issue will be set. This is known as the 'level of authorised shares'. In practice, they will not issue anything like this amount initially. The rest of the shares are known as the authorised shares that are as yet unissued. These shares can be issued by the company's board of directors at any stage in the future through what is known as a 'rights issue' or a 'placing'.

   At the outset new shares are assigned a par or nominal value; however, in contrast to bonds this is of little practical significance. In the case of bonds the par value is what is received by the holder on maturity. This is not the case for shares. The company's market share price is of far greater importance. So, if you look at a company's set of accounts it will show the issued share capital at this very low par value. To get an accurate gauge of the value of these shares you must add in the share premium account, which is a measure of the difference between the price the company sold its shares for and their much lower par value.

4. **Limited liability**. If the shareholders are the providers of risk capital, they do at least know that their maximum financial loss is represented by the amount that they invested in the shares. This is because they have what is known as 'limited liability'. As a result, anyone who is owed money by a company that goes into liquidation cannot turn to the ordinary shareholders for redress. If you invest £10 000 in the shares of a business that goes bankrupt, your maximum loss will be the amount that you invested in the shares. This may be of some comfort.

5. **Preference shares**. Before we start to analyse the articles in this section we should finally discuss preference shares. From their name you might think that they are just another form of equity capital, but this would be wrong. Although they are part of shareholders' funds, they should not be regarded as being equity finance. One important difference between preference shares and ordinary shares is that the former normally carry no voting rights.

Preference shares get their name from their two key characteristics:

1. They have their dividends paid before any payments to ordinary shareholders.
2. If the company is wound up, they will come before ordinary shareholders in terms of any capital repayment.

There are four main types of preference shares:

1. **Redeemable**. Most preference shares have a fixed date when the company will repay the initial capital invested in them.
2. **Cumulative**. This means that any preference share dividends not paid in one year will accumulate to be paid in the next year. So, if the normal 10p dividend was due in year 1 but could not be paid, this would result in 10p extra being paid in year 2. The company would not be allowed to pay any ordinary dividend until these arrears are paid in full.
3. **Participating**. Here the holder receives a preference dividend plus a percentage of

the ordinary dividend. This gives the holder of these preference shares a potential significant upside if the company prospers.

4. **Convertible**. The holder of a convertible preference share has the option to trade their preference share for an ordinary share on a specific date and for a fixed price. For example, they might be able to trade three preference shares for one ordinary share.

If you want to see what shares a company has issued in practice you should consult the London Share Service (this normally covers a couple of pages inside the back page of the Companies and Markets section of the *Financial Times*). A good sector to look at is the Banks.

For example, on the day I wrote this Lloyds Banking Group had the following:

Ordinary shares priced at 65 p.
8.0884% Preference shares priced at £545
6.475% Preference shares priced at 59
9 ¼% Preference shares priced at 78.50
9 ¾% Preference shares priced at 90

In our analysis of equities the following four articles are discussed in this section:

Article 19
IPO values Hargreaves at £750 m
Financial Times, 12 May 2007

Article 20
Hargreaves Lansdown soars on debut
Financial Times, 16 May 2007

Article 21
Valuing Sainsbury's
Financial Times, 17 May 2007

Article 22
Woolies investor opposes sale
Financial Times, 20 November 2008

These articles address the following issues:

- the definition of listing;
- initial public offer;
- the use of unit trusts;
- some key financial ratios;
- private equity bidders;
- share valuation techniques;
- property assets;

- sale and leaseback;
- emerging markets;
- impact of economic slowdown on retail sector;
- business and financial risk;
- leases.

Hargreaves' founders float all the way to the bank

These two articles show the rewards on offer to individuals who are willing to take the risks involved in creating a new business. Back in 1981 Peter Hargreaves and Stephen Lansdown combined to establish a company that sold financial investment products to private clients. Over the years they have built up a discounted broker business that has challenged the more established financial institutions and allowed their clients to buy investment products free from the normally exorbitant initial fees. This new share issue enables the founders to release part of their equity stake in the company, however, even now they remain significant shareholders as well as key executives.

Article 19

Financial Times, 12 May 2007 **FT**

IPO values Hargreaves at £750 m

Sarah Spikes and Lina Saigol

Hargreaves Lansdown, the Bristol-based private-client stockbroker and financial adviser, will list 25 per cent of its shares on Tuesday in an offering that will value the company at about £750 m, making it the biggest UK financial services initial public offering since Standard Life last year.

Peter Hargreaves, chief executive, said he expected the shares to be priced near the upper end of the 140 p to 160 p indicative range that the company gave earlier this month.

He said the offering was heavily subscribed. 'It was well received by most private and institutional investors on our roadshow.'

Private-client customers of Hargreaves Lansdown are taking a third of the offering while institutional investors are buying the other two-thirds. Nearly all of the institutional investors buying shares are UK-based, as the company marketed the offering almost exclusively in the UK. The group is raising no new money.

Mr Hargreaves founded Hargreaves Lansdown with Stephen Lansdown, the company chairman, in 1981. Both are chartered accountants.

Jonathan Bloomer, the former chief executive of insurer Prudential, is among the company's non-executive directors, along with Mike Evans, formerly chief operating officer for Skandia UK, a unit of the Swedish insurer taken over by Old Mutual last year.

If the shares list at the top of the range at 160 p a share, the market value would be £759 m, giving the group a price to earnings ratio of 15 times. This is above the level at which many UK-listed institutional stockbrokers trade but still below the ratings of some private-client stockbrokers.

Mr Hargreaves and Mr Lansdown together own about 80 per cent of the company and plan to remain significant shareholders.

Their holdings after the listing will be worth about £600 m.

In the six months ended December 31, revenue grew 35 per cent to £43.3 m. Since 1997, revenue has increased by at least a fifth each year.

| **Article 20** | *Financial Times*, 16 May 2007 | **FT** |

Hargreaves Lansdown soars on debut

Sarah Spikes

Shares in stockbroker Hargreaves Lansdown soared by more than 30 per cent on their London Stock Exchange debut, as investors piled in hoping to profit from increasing savings rates in the UK.

Shares opened at 160p and rose to close at 209½ p, adding £232.4 m in value to the 26-year-old Bristol-based financial adviser and stockbroker which finished the day with a market capitalisation of £991.4 m.

Founders Peter Hargreaves and Stephen Lansdown gained an extra £139 m more than anticipated, as the 60 per cent holding they retained increased in value from £455.4 m to £594.8 m.

The price–earnings ratio implied by 160 p was about 14 times 2009 earnings, roughly in the middle of the range between the highest and lowest rated UK stockbrokers and asset managers. But at the end of trading, the company was trading at more than 19 times estimated 2009 earnings.

Investors said that Hargreaves Lansdown merited a premium rating because it was serving a market that is not well targeted by other companies: investors with between £50 000 and £200 000 of assets to invest. Private client stockbrokers tend to target wealthier clients.

'There are 6.9 m mass-affluents (in the UK), many fed up with years of poor service from life (insurance) companies', analysts at company broker Citigroup said in a note.

They added that Hargreaves Lansdown has the only quoted platform in the UK that markets directly to investors. It has 350 000 clients. The main products that Hargreaves Lansdown sells to its clients are unit trusts.

Clients often pay 5 per cent of the investment upfront when they invest in unit trusts through brokers. But about ten years ago Hargreaves Lansdown innovated and started to offer unit trusts with large discounts to this 5 per cent rate and now charges no upfront fees on unit trusts.

■ The analysis

Peter Hargreaves and Stephen Lansdown founded their business 'Hargreaves Lansdown' in the early 1980s. They established a discount broker to serve private investors looking to invest their spare cash. Their unique selling point was that they did not target the super rich who were traditionally served by the private banks, but instead reached out to the growing middle classes who had an increasing amount of disposable income and a desire to invest in financial markets.

Unit trusts are one of the main financial products that they offer to their investors. The big attraction of using a broker to purchase these funds is that they offer significant discounts on the initial charges. If you go direct to a unit trust provider they will take an upfront charge which can often amount to 5 per cent of the total investment. This acts as a powerful disincentive to private investors. A few years back Hargreaves Lansdown opened up this market by initially offering big discounts on these charges and then virtually eliminating them altogether.

The first of the articles previews the initial public offer (IPO) for Hargreaves Lansdown. The shares were expected to be offered at a price somewhere in a range of 140–160 p. The final price would be determined by market conditions on the actual day of the sale. In advance the issue was being heavily marketed in the UK to both private and institutional investors. The Chief Executive, Peter Hargreaves, was reported as saying 'It was well received by most private and institutional investors on our roadshow'. The company had one massive advantage as it came with an already established list of potential investors from their existing clients who by definition were likely to be interested in a new share issue.

The second article reports on the outcome of the IPO with the shares selling at the top end of the range at 160 p. A positive trading environment saw them rise further to close at 209.5 p by the close of the day's activity. This gave the business a relatively high price earnings ratio of 19 times (based on its forecast 2009 earnings). This might be justified if the company was able to continue to grow the business by exploiting the type of newer investors that had been largely ignored by existing financial services companies.

Key terms

List This refers to the companies whose shares are quoted on the Main List of the UK Exchange. Companies who want to be listed must meet the very exacting criteria which are contained in the Stock Exchange's 'Yellow Book'. These criteria include the number of shares that have to be in the public's hands ahead of trading in the shares, the company's trading and financial history and the suitability of the board of directors. The Official List is intended for medium or large companies as there are high initial launch costs in addition to significant annual charges.

Initial public offer (IPO) When we examine any major stock market it is useful to split it into two aspects. The first is to see it as a primary capital market which enables companies to raise new share capital. In contrast a stock market must serve a vital function as a secondary market providing liquidity to the existing shares which can be traded. In this way existing shareholders can sell some or all of their holdings to new investors who want to buy a stake in the business.

An IPO refers to the situation where a company first sells its shares by listing on the stock exchange. This gives it a much wider access to increase its shareholder base. In addition, it provides much great liquidity in terms of the trading of the shares in the company. Companies considering a new IPO will appoint an investment bank to manage the process. They will meet the company and be heavily involved in valuing the shares, preparing a prospectus and getting investors interested in the new issue. The investment bank will be very well rewarded for this work with substantial fees often being paid to ensure a successful IPO.

Unit trusts If you pick up the Companies and Markets section of the *Financial Times* and go to the section called 'Managed Funds Service', you will see page after page of data relating to investments offered to private investors by professional fund managers. These will include a vast number of unit trusts which are a very important form of collective investment. They allow private investors to get exposure to a range of different sectors including the standard equity funds, bond funds, money market funds and various property funds. The attraction of unit trusts is that they allow fairly small investors to spread their risk across a more diversified portfolio.

All unit trusts are called 'open-ended', which means that the ultimate size of the fund is determined by the amount of cash that investors want to put in it. As more money flows in, the fund just keeps growing in size, which allows more money to be invested in the designated markets.

The basic principles can be easily explained with a simple example:

> A new unit trust 'KB special opportunities fund' is created. It has a clear investment strategy as it is looking to invest in the UK equity market with a strong bias towards smaller companies. Nearly all unit trusts actually have two prices – an offer price and a bid price, with a significant spread between them. The offer price is the price that a new investor must pay to buy a unit. The bid price is the price that an investor receives when selling a unit. As the spread between the buying price and the selling price of each unit might easily be as much as 5 per cent, you can see the need to view these investments as being relatively long term. If they are sold very soon after purchase, the investor stands to lose this initial spread even if the actual units are still at the same price.
>
> The ultimate price of the units will depend on the performance of the fund manager. If they are successful the value of the fund will grow and so each unit will appreciate in value.

Price–earnings ratio (PE ratio) The PE ratio is calculated by taking the market share price and dividing it by the company's earnings per share.

Institutional investors These are the large pension funds and insurance companies that are the key investors in financial markets. They look to invest in long-term assets to match their long-term liabilities (paying out pensions). These investors have flourished in recent years due to the greater wealth of the private sector. In contrast the private clients refer to the individuals who invest on their own behalf.

■ What do you think?

1. The *FT* article quotes a range of 140–160 p as an indicative range for the new IPO in Hargreaves Lansdown. What factors determined the final price for this new issue?

2. At the end of the first day's trading the PE ratio for this issue was around 19. How does this compare to other similar companies listed on the UK stock market?

3. What is the main advantage for investors in buying unit trusts through a firm like Hargreaves Lansdown rather than direct from the unit trust fund?

■ Investigate FT data

You will need the Companies and Markets section of the *Financial Times*. Go to the Managed Funds Service. This is normally about halfway through the Companies and Markets section.

Look at the section covering the fund manager Artemis:

Answer these questions:

1. What is the selling price of a unit in the Artemis Capital Fund?

2. What is the buying price of a unit in the same fund?

3. You are nervous about the outlook for the UK stock market, which Artemis unit trust funds might you look to invest in?

■ Go to the web

Go the official website of Artemis: www.artemisonline.co.uk.

Find the section called 'filmclub'.

What are the latest views of the main fund managers in relation to the investment outlook?

■ Research

Arnold, G. (2004) *The Financial Times Guide to Investing*, Harlow, UK: FT Prentice Hall. You should look especially at Chapter 5, pages 72–80 to get more information about unit trusts.

Arnold, G. (2007) *Essentials of Corporate Financial Management*, Harlow, UK: FT Prentice Hall. You should look at pp. 370–75 to find out more about price–earnings ratio.

Arnold, G. (2008) *Corporate Financial Management*, 4th edn, Harlow, UK: FT Prentice Hall. You should look at pp. 584–5 to find out more about price–earnings ratio.

Atrill, P. (2007) *Financial Management for Decision Makers*, 5th edn, Harlow, UK: FT Prentice Hall. You should look at Chapter 7. The offer for sale process is set out on pp. 283–5.

Berk, J. and DeMarzo, P. (2009) *Corporate Finance*, Harlow, UK: FT Prentice Hall Financial Times. The topic of new share issues is covered in Chapter 23.

Gitman, L. (2009) *Principles of Managerial Finance*, 12th edn, Harlow, UK: Pearson International Edition. There is a discussion of the process of 'going public' on p. 338.

McLaney, E. (2009) *Business Finance Theory and Practice*, 8th edn, Harlow, UK: FT Prentice Hall Financial Times. You should consult Chapter 8 for some coverage on new share issues.

Pike, R. and Neale, B. (2006) *Corporate Finance and Investment*, 6th edn, Harlow, UK: FT Prentice Hall. You should look at Chapter 2, pp. 30–31 to see a useful discussion of the role of the London Stock Exchange.

Watson, D. and Head, A. (2007) *Corporate Finance Principles and Practice*, 4th edn, Harlow, UK: FT Prentice Hall. You should look at Chapter 4, pp. 96–102 on the listing process.

Good value at Sainsbury's?

It is very common for the Lex column to consider the current stock market valuation of a company. Several of the valuation techniques commonly set out in corporate finance text-books will be applied. In this article the Sainsbury's market share price (560 p) is compared with a more realistic value of just 400 p/share based on a discounted cash flow approach. Lex argues that the higher price can only be justified by the assumption that there are bidders in the wings who will be prepared to offer significantly more than this funda-mental valuation. It concludes that the current business structure of Sainsbury's does not allow it to realise the full value of the company's extensive property assets.

Article 21   *Financial Times*, 17 May 2007   **FT**

Valuing Sainsbury's

Lex column

The numbers were almost beside the point. Even so, J Sainsbury's 2006 results, released on Wednesday, helped to clarify the market's position on the UK's third biggest food retailer. There was hope that the company's management might at least hint at property sales, especially having just let a potential 585 p per share private equity bid pass it by. But Sainsbury, quite rightly, reiterated the case for keeping control of its prop-erty assets and its shares closed unchanged on the day. At least this demonstrates an efficient market: whether or not a retailer owns its sites should not alter its value beyond some minor financial tweaking.

A share price of 560 p shows that investors are fully expecting another approach. Few analysts' discounted cash flow valuations are above 400 p. Mostly, this is owing to a low terminal growth rate as Sainsbury has no exposure to emerging markets and is underweight in faster-growing non-food retail. Applying an appropriate earnings multiple results in a yet lower price.

Although there will be upgrades fol-lowing Wednesday's encouraging results, operating margins are still well below Sainsbury's rivals. At best, margins are expected to improve from 2.5 per cent today to about 4 per cent by 2010. But Tesco's margin is already in excess of 6 per cent. This is the crux of Sainsbury's problem. It has to improve margins while also lowering prices and boosting top-line growth. But even assuming Sainsbury's upgraded sales targets can be met, Tesco is growing faster, further widening its scale advantage.

No wonder investors' hopes turn to Sainsbury's £8.6 bn property portfolio – equivalent, excluding debt, to about 470 p per share. Sure, it is possible for a third party to extract this value. But given the interdependence of property and retail operations, this cannot be achieved without damaging the operating company – perhaps irrevocably.

■ The analysis

In this article the Lex column reflects on the correct valuation of Sainsbury's shares. Earlier in the year there had been a sharp rise in their share price following a proposed move by a private equity bidder to buy the company. At this time David Sainsbury, the single largest shareholder, was thought to have ruled out such bids at least until they hit the 600 p level.

In order to understand these bids it is important to grasp the concept that private equity firms are actively looking for companies with strong cash flow and key assets which are not being fully exploited by the existing management team. Sainsbury's meets both these criteria with strong earnings from its stores and an impressive portfolio of property assets, which are a big attraction to private equity companies because they can see their potential. It is likely that any bidder would look to sell a large proportion of Sainsbury's stores, and then lease them back. Such a move would generate a massive amount of cash for a private equity firm. When the previous bid was made, the existing managers stated that these property assets would remain part of the current business. As Lex says 'At least this demonstrates an efficient market: whether or not a retailer owns its sites should not alter its value beyond some minor financial tweaking'.

The column goes on to argue that the fact the share price is still at 560 p firmly suggests that the market is still pricing in another bid approach. The normal discounted cash flow valuation would arrive at a share price nearer to 400 p. These techniques are based on the following key financial variables: the company's cash flows, the discount factor and, crucially, the growth rate. This latter factor is assumed to be much lower for Sainsbury's than its main rival Tesco which has far more exposure to both high-growth emerging markets (in Eastern European and South-East Asia) and also non-food retail products (clothes, electrical goods, etc.).

The article finally looks at 'Wednesday's encouraging results' which it expects to prompt some brokers to upgrade their share price valuations. However, it still compares unfavourably the margins achieved by Tesco (6 per cent) and the much more modest 4 per cent (at best) for Sainsbury's. In conclusion, Lex claims that Sainsbury's £8.6 billion property assets, excluding debt, might be worth some 470 p per share. While it is possible that an outside bidder could achieve this value from the property assets, it would be less straightforward for Sainsbury's with its current structure to exploit this possibility. As the article points out, if Sainsbury's was to sell all its retail outlets, this would change the whole nature of the business and perhaps cause irreversible damage.

■ Key terms

Private equity This term is used to describe the activities of a group of companies that invest in businesses that are already privately owned or ones that the buyers intend to remove from the stock market as soon as possible. See Article 24 for a full explanation.

Property assets Accountants like to distinguish between current assets (these are very short term and will last less than a year) and fixed assets (longer term and will last more than a year). The key fixed asset for Sainsbury's will be their vast property portfolio. This will include many high street stores as well as distribution warehouses.

Sale and lease back This is a very common transaction used by companies that want to extract the value of any significant assets. A company can sell its property (in this case the stores owned by Sainsbury's) and then lease them right back from the buyer (normally a financial institution) in the same transaction. This enables the owner to get the cash from the sale but at the same time still use the property to carry out their business. The financial institution that buys the property is guaranteed a long-term income from the leases on the property.

Efficient market This refers to the way that share prices react to new information. A stock market is efficient if it reacts quickly and accurately to a new market-sensitive announcement. So, if a company announces a surprise increase in dividends, its share price should rise immediately. If instead it reacts very slowly or indeed even falls in price, the share price will be highly inefficient. There are different levels of share price efficiency. You should read Arnold, *Corporate Financial Management*, FT Prentice Hall, p. 691 to learn more about this topic.

Discounted cash flow valuation Put very simply, this is where we take the future cash flows which will be earned by a company and multiply them by an appropriate discount factor to get their present value. This is a widely used technique to place a value on the share price of a particular company.

Emerging markets This refers to the financial markets of developing nations. In general, these markets have not been trading for long and as a result they are seen as being more risky than traditional financial markets.

Upgrades The investment banks employ analysts who research the prospects for a company and then place a target value for their share price. When the prospects for a company improve, these analysts will raise their forecasts. This is called a 'profit upgrade'. It might follow a new investment opportunity or a change in the company's business strategy.

Margins This is the difference between the company's average selling price for its goods or services and the costs that are required to produce them.

■ What do you think?

1. Why might a private equity bidder value Sainsbury's at 585 p compared to a value of just 400 p based on a discounted cash flow technique?

2. What is meant by the term 'sale and lease back' in the context of corporate finance deals?

3. What data would you need to calculate a valuation of Sainsbury plc using the discounted cash flow method?

4. Why is Tesco plc able to achieve a much higher margin and growth rate than Sainsbury plc?

■ Investigate FT data

You will need a copy of the Companies and Markets section of the *Financial Times*. Go to the London Share Price Service. Locate the Retailers section.

Answer the following questions.

1. What are the current share prices of Sainsbury plc and Tesco plc?

2. Compare the volatility of these two share prices in the last year.

   Hint: Look at the high/low data.

3. Compare the P/E ratios of these two companies. What do these figures say about the current stock market valuation of them both?

■ Research

Arnold, G. (2007) *Essentials of Corporate Financial Management*, Harlow, UK: FT Prentice Hall. You should look at Chapter 10. The dividend growth model starts on p. 372.

Arnold, G. (2008) *Corporate Financial Management*, 4th edn, Harlow, UK: FT Prentice Hall. You should especially look at Chapter 20. The dividend growth model starts on p. 756.

Atrill, P. (2007) *Financial Management for Decision Makers*, 5th edn, Harlow, UK: FT Prentice Hall. You should look at Chapter 12. You will see a very good introduction to the valuation of shares on pages 501–12. The dividend valuation method is explained on pp. 508–9.

Berk, J. and DeMarzo, P. (2009) *Corporate Finance*, Harlow, UK: FT Prentice Hall Financial Times. The dividend discount model is set out on pp. 249–56.

Gitman, L. (2009) *Principles of Managerial Finance*, 12th edn, Harlow, UK: Pearson International Edition. There is an introduction to the dividend valuation model starting on p. 512.

McLaney, E. (2009) *Business Finance Theory and Practice*, 8th edn, Harlow, UK: FT Prentice Hall Financial Times. There is a good guide to price earnings ratios on pp. 60–61.

Pike, R. and Neale, B. (2006) *Corporate Finance and Investment*, 6th edn, Harlow, UK: FT Prentice Hall. You should look at Chapter 12. The dividend growth model is on p. 297.

Watson, D. and Head, A. (2007) *Corporate Finance Principles and Practice*, 4th edn, Harlow, UK: FT Prentice Hall. You should look at pp. 326–7 to see the dividend growth model explained.

6

EQUITY FINANCE

As Woolworths died we try speed-dating for the last time!

On the day that Woolworths finally died I could not help but feel slightly nostalgic recalling my own childhood when a definite highlight would be the occasional visit to buy sweets from their garish 'pick and mix' counters. On the evening of their demise I was attending my youngest daughter's final parents' evening at the school that she had attended for the previous seven years. At one point in the evening as we were waiting to see her French teacher, I took the chance to stand back and look around the large hall for one last time. As I did so I could not help but wonder at what point the traditional parents' evening had given way to what now looked more like a speed-dating event. For those of you who have yet to endure such occasions these days the parents move from teacher to teacher, spending no more than two to three minutes with each one. This time allocation allows you to do little more than exchange a few pleasantries before the teacher anxiously looks to move you on so that they can meet the next in line.

If the school system was going through a period of change, the collapse of Woolworths was a clear sign that the credit crisis was also leading to major change in the look of the UK high street. Almost every new day bought fresh headlines of another store in severe financial difficulty. It became clear that after the boom years we were now heading for the inevitable bust. The shortage of available bank finance led to many casualties including chains like Whittards, Zavvi, the Pier and the furniture giant MFI. It became clear that the UK high street had grown too fat in the good years as consumers had gone on a debt-fuelled spending spree. In the more austere times caution had set in and high street sales were collapsing. The damage impacted on the whole range of goods from luxury items sold by chains like Mulberry and Chanel all the way to the more value-focused retailers. At this bottom end of the high street were Woolworths who had long been in difficulties but now had finally collapsed under a mountain of debt. The loss of one of the oldest UK store groups sent shock waves through the rest of the high street. For many the demise of Woolies removed one more pillar from their fading childhood memories.

Article 22

Financial Times, 20 November 2008 **FT**

Woolies investor opposes sale

Tom Braithwaite

Woolworths' biggest shareholder yesterday criticised talks between the retailer and Hilco UK, the retail restructuring company, arguing the group's stores were worth much more than the nominal price under discussion.

Shares in Woolworths fell to their lowest-ever level after the company acknowledged it was in talks to sell its 800-store retail division. Hilco UK, which invests in troubled companies, has indicated it would pay a £1 for the stores and assume part of the group's debt.

Ardeshir Naghshineh, the Iranian developer who owns 10.2 per cent of Woolworths, said the proposed deal was unacceptable.

'It's ridiculous to sell the whole retail division for £1', said Mr Naghshineh, whose Targetfollow company owns Centre Point tower in central London.

'We are obviously experienced in property', he said. 'We know that it's worth hundreds of millions of pounds. I know stores at the moment where landlords are prepared to give millions of pounds in premiums to get Woolworths out.'

Shares in Woolworths plunged 38.3 per cent, or 1.46 p, to 2.35 p after being suspended yesterday morning to give the company time to release a statement announcing the talks.

Some analysts have long believed the retail division is worth nothing, weighed down by onerous leases, heavy debt and increased competition from supermarkets and internet rivals.

Mr Naghshineh said Steve Johnson, the new chief executive, should be given time to turn the stores round and urged the board not to talk to Hilco.

'Obviously there's an alternative deal', said Mr Naghshineh, who declined to say whether he would be part of a rival bid.

As the exclusive talks continue, Hilco UK is offering to take on part of Woolworths' debt and all the leases, although some of the onerous leases could be shed if the potential bidder opts for a pre-pack administration.

The pension fund deficit and much of the debt would remain with the rump of the company, which includes a profitable wholesale distribution business and a DVD publishing joint venture with the BBC.

While Mr Naghshineh's objections will figure in the board's discussions, directors believe that the deal may be the best to protect dwindling shareholder value and prevent the whole business from falling into the hands of creditors.

The analysis

In the wake of the credit crunch a number of UK retailers came under severe pressure. In truth, one of the biggest casualties was Woolworths who had been one of the iconic names on the UK high street. Their troubles came to a head in late November 2008 when the company announced that trading in the retailer's shares had been suspended as they continued with talks in an attempt to save the business. In a statement the company said that it was having discussions with a view to sell some of its 840 stores. The article that I have included here is from the previous week when the *FT* ran a story indicating that Woolworths could be sold for just £1 to Hilco UK. This proposed sale was fiercely opposed by Woolworths' largest shareholder, Ardeshir Naghshineh, who owned 10.2 of the company's shares. He felt that the proposed deal was a massive undervaluation of the business.

The Woolworths business was dominated by its retail division with some 800 stores employing around 30 000 people in the UK. Despite its significant presence on the high street, many felt that this part of the company was worthless. This situation was due to a combination of severe business and financial risk.

- ■ **How did business risk impact on Woolies?**

  This refers to the general risk that can impact on a company's cash flow or profitability. It could be caused by general economic conditions (consumer spending, level of interest rates, etc.) as well as more specific company factors (such as changes in key staff or strike action by employees). In the case of Woolworths the company showed all the signs of being hit by severe business risk. Much has changed within the retail sector over the past few years and Woolworths ended up by losing out to the many Internet retailers which had taken over a substantial share of the market. This led many to wonder what exactly the purpose of Woolworths was.

- ■ **How did financial risk impact on Woolies?**

  This is the risk that applies to any company that has debt finance (see Topic 4) as a significant part of its capital structure. It refers to the possibility that a company will face financial distress due to the inability to pay either the annual interest or the principal on an outstanding debt issue. In the case of Woolworths the business had some £385 m of debt that had to be financed in very difficult market conditions.

  The only upside for Woolworths was that it did have two profitable parts of the business. These were a wholesale distribution business and a DVD publishing business which was a joint venture with the BBC. At the time of the article the sale of these businesses seemed to be the only way to save the company and to offer any financial value to the company's shareholders. In the end the company was formally taken into administration on the 6 December 2008 with debts of £385 m. Sadly a buyer could not be found and as a result its stores were shut and thousands of their employees joined the growing band of the unemployed.

■ Key terms

Nominal price This refers to the very low price that was being offered by Hilco UK who were looking to buy Woolworths.

Leases This is a very common transaction used by companies that want to extract the value of any significant assets. A company can sell its property (in this case the stores owned by Woolworths) and then lease them right back from the buyer (normally a financial institution) in the same transaction. This enables the owner to get the cash from the sale, but at the same time they can still use the property to carry out their business. The financial institution that buys the property is guaranteed a long-term income from the leases on the property.

Rival bid This is where there is a corporate takeover in progress and a new bidder emerges to challenge the current company that is looking to buy a business. In this case the bidder would be a rival to Hilco UK who hoped to buy Woolworths for just £1.

Pension fund deficit This refers to the crisis that affected companies in the wake of the financial market weakness of 2008. This led to many companies having inadequate financial provision in order to cover the liabilities to their employees in terms of future pension payments. As a result many companies were being forced to divert some of their profits in order to re-finance the pension funds.

■ What do you think?

1. In the context of this article explain what corporate financiers mean when they use the terms 'financial' and 'business' risk.

2. What is the dividend valuation model and how is it used to place a value on a company's shares? Would the use of this model help to explain why a major UK retailer with over 800 high street stores was being offered for sale to Hilco UK for just £1?

3. Why did Woolworths' largest shareholder believe that the proposed deal to sell the business for just £1 to Hilco UK was a bad deal?

4. What were the main factors that had led to the problems that Woolworths was experiencing at this time?

5. A week later shares in Woolworths were once again suspended on the London Stock Exchange. Explain what this means in practice and why it is important for companies to be allowed to do this.

6. Did the performance of Woolworths' share price suggest that they were behaving in a way that was compatible with at least the semi-strong level of stock market efficiency?

■ Investigate FT data

You will need a copy of the Companies and Markets section of the *Financial Times*.

Go to the London Share Price Service.

Find the latest price–earnings (P/E) ratios for the seven UK retailers listed below:

	P/E ratios (October 2008)	What are they now?
Clinton Cards	2.4	
Carphone Warehouse	10.2	
Debenhams	4.2	
Marks and Spencer	4.6	
Tesco	13.3	
J Sainsbury	14.2	
Woolworths	4.8	

You are required to explain what a P/E ratio is and show how it can be used to place a value on a company.

In addition you should try to explain the change in the levels of the P/E ratios from October 2008 to the present.

■ Research

Arnold, G. (2007) *Essentials of Corporate Financial Management*, Harlow, UK: FT Prentice Hall. You should look at Chapter 11. Business and financial risk are discussed on p. 396.

6

EQUITY FINANCE

Arnold, G. (2008) *Corporate Financial Management*, 4th edn, Harlow, UK: FT Prentice Hall. You should especially look at Chapter 13. Business risk is defined on p. 527.

Atrill, P. (2007) *Financial Management for Decision Makers*, 5th edn, Harlow, UK: FT Prentice Hall. You should look at Chapter 8. You will find a discussion of the impact of high gearing on company performance.

Berk, J. and DeMarzo, P. (2009) *Corporate Finance*, Harlow, UK: FT Prentice Hall Financial Times. The concept of risky debt is covered on p. 710.

Gitman, L. (2009) *Principles of Managerial Finance*, 12th edn, Harlow, UK: Pearson International Edition. There is a section on changes in risk on p. 358.

McLaney, E. (2009) *Business Finance Theory and Practice*, 8th edn, Harlow, UK: FT Prentice Hall Financial Times. There is a good guide to financial/business risk on p. 297.

Pike, R. and Neale, B. (2006) *Corporate Finance and Investment*, 6th edn, Harlow, UK: FT Prentice Hall. You should look at Chapter 7. The concepts of business and financial risk are explained on p. 163.

Watson, D. and Head, A. (2007) *Corporate Finance Principles and Practice*, 4th edn, Harlow, UK: FT Prentice Hall. You should look at p. 192 for a definition of financial risk.

Go to **www.pearsoned.co.uk/boakes** to access Kevin's blog for additional analysis of recent topical news articles and to post your comments. Download podcasts containing short audio summaries of the main issues relating to each article and check your understanding of in-text questions with the handy hints provided.

Stock market efficiency

Like most university lecturers I am increasingly being encouraged to make use of various web-based platforms to communicate with my ever-growing numbers of students. The main vehicle at Kingston is something called StudySpace which enables the students to access course documents as well as join in various activities like discussion boards and class tests. It also has a very useful facility which allows me to make announcements to all the students registered on the course. Recently I used this device to demonstrate a key theory of corporate finance in action.

This is how it worked:

- **Step 1**: I announced that the lecture in a week's time would be focusing on a key topic that they should expect to see heavily tested in their end of course exam. I stressed to them that this was an important session and that they should make every effort to attend.
- **Step 2**: I followed this up with a short individual e-mail to each student with a similar message.
- **Step 3**: A week later I walked into the lecture theatre for the year 2 Finance lecture and I could not help smiling as I looked around the room. After a quick headcount it was clear that the attendance was around 110 compared to the usual 70–80 students.

My pleasure came from the realisation that not only had my message convinced a significant number of students to get up early to come and attend this 9 a.m. lecture, but in addition I could now show them how their behaviour would be a perfect example of what today's topic was all about. That morning I was going to introduce them to stock market efficiency.

Every day at the back of the *Financial Times* you will see in the Markets section the daily changes in individual share prices. For example, Scottish and Newcastle dipped 1.7 per cent as takeover hopes faded or Unilever rose 1.6 per cent as traders took the view that it might be the next company to be targeted by an activist shareholder. Both of these show how company share prices react to relevant news stories or possibly just to rumours. This takes us into the area of share price efficiency as we see whether the share prices react quickly and correctly to these pieces of information.

In the context of stock markets the term 'efficiency' is used to define the situation where any new information about a company's prospects is quickly and accurately reflected in its share price. For example, if a company cancels an expected final dividend to shareholders, you would expect to see its share price fall immediately as it absorbs this piece of bad news. The share price change should be rapid and logical. If it takes some time for the share price to react to any published information, then the markets are deemed to be highly inefficient. The message of stock market efficiency is that it should not be possible for investors to make money by making their investment decisions on the basis of information that is already in the public domain.

The creation of the efficient markets theory (EMT) in the mid-1960s can be traced back to the work of Eugene Fama, the well-respected US economist, who was widely touted as a possible Nobel Prize winner in 2008. Indeed, but for the financial meltdown in existence at that time he would almost certainly have been the winner. The EMT actually defines three different levels of share price efficiency:

1. Weak-form efficiency where current share prices fully reflect all past share prices. This means that you should not be able to trade successfully on the basis of using a chart of previous share prices to try to predict the future price movements.

2. Semi-strong efficiency builds on the first level by adding the condition that share prices must now fully reflect all published information. This will include important news stories like profits figures, new investments and dividend decisions.

3. Finally we have strong efficiency, which now adds the condition that share prices also reflect all inside information. This covers any important information that is privately held by insiders like important staff within the company. Such a position would mean that even these people could not use their inside information to make abnormal profits by trading in their company's shares.

While few people would argue that most share prices are strongly efficient, it is widely accepted that they do meet the conditions necessary for semi-strong efficiency. This has important implications for investors. It is especially important that they should note that it is not normally possible to use publicly available information to make abnormal profits by trading the stock market. This means that they might do just as well by investing in a broad range of shares rather than by trying to select a portfolio of stocks that they believe will outperform the market. This has contributed to the growth in so-called 'indexed funds' where investment managers purchase a group of stocks that are designed to be a close match to a particular stock market index. These indexed funds have the major attraction of relatively low charges to the fund holders.

So, how did my example of encouraging wider attendance of students at my lecture demonstrate the EMT in action? It is simple, really. By announcing the special importance of this lecture to all students and strongly hinting that it would be examined in the summer, I was hoping to see the students reacting in a logical manner. They did this by turning up in large numbers eager to learn all about the EMT. As a result, in the summer exam no student should be able to achieve an abnormal mark simply by focusing on this topic, as the public announcement of the significance of the lecture meant that virtually all students will have the information needed to answer this question well. It is good to see that my students are logical and rational. In fact they are at the very least semi-strongly efficient students!

The following article is analysed in this section:

Article 23
Stock splits: time to query decades of dogma
Financial Times, 8 April 2007

This article addresses the following issues:

- nominal share price;
- stock dividends;
- stock spread;
- financial intermediaries.

Company shares split down the middle

In *Midsomer Murders*, the long-running ITV crime show, they seem to need at least five dead bodies per episode to satisfy their viewers. If the writers ever get tired with the usual poisonings, shootings or vicious knife attacks, I can suggest a rather more sophisticated way of bumping off the next victim. This is how it might work. The person involved is a retired colonel living in the country. He has a known heart condition and has just recently invested his entire fortune in the shares of Shadowlands plc. As students of corporate finance will know, it is never a good idea to put 'all your eggs in one basket'.

One morning as he reads the *Financial Times* over breakfast he suddenly sees that his shares have halved in price overnight. His face turns white and he collapses in agonised pain head first into his bowl of cornflakes. What starts out as a routine death soon becomes a murder enquiry as rumours surface of foul play? After weeks of unsuccessful investigations the police call in the Professor of Finance at Badgers Drift University. With surprising efficiency for an academic he solves the case and identifies the murderer.

It turns out that the colonel's nephew is in fact the Chief Finance Officer at Shadowlands plc and he had just organised a 2 for 1 stock split for the company's shares that had just hit £10 in the market. As a result the shares fell to £5 overnight. Since the colonel did not understand this transaction, he failed to realise that he in fact owned twice as many shares as he did previously. So what was the nephew's motive? Simple: he was the only surviving relative of the colonel and he stood to inherit his fortune including a country estate that he had always coveted.

Article 23   *Financial Times*, 8 April 2007 **FT**

Stock splits: time to query decades of dogma

John Authers*

This is a holy juncture. Christians are celebrating Easter while Jews are celebrating Passover. These festivals strengthen and reassert faith, but they do so in large part by questioning it.

At a less profound level, self-questioning and disciplined doubt can be good for an investment portfolio, not just for the soul. So let's take this opportunity to question one time-honoured ritual of equity investing: stock splits. What is the point of them?

Stock splits are meant to keep a share price at a manageable level. A two-for-one stock split involves replacing every outstanding share with two, and making no other changes. It is a complicated operation (although not wildly expensive: it generally costs up to $1 m for a large company), whose only effect is to halve the nominal price of the shares.

The habit is ingrained. General Electric's share price at the end of 1935 was $38.25. Exactly 70 years later, it was $35.05. According to research by a group of academics from the University of California at Los Angeles, Cornell

University and the University of Chicago,** GE would by this point have traded at $10 094.40, had it never paid stock dividends or split its stock.

I once interviewed a nonagenarian US investor, who had started his portfolio during the Depression. He tallied the success of his investments by the number of shares he had 60 years later, rather than by their value – so much was it taken for granted that companies would split their stock to keep the nominal price at about $40.

No constituent of the Dow Jones Industrial Average has a share price of less than $19, or more than $95.

In the UK, people like the nominal price of their shares to be even lower. Prices are quoted in pence, not pounds. No constituent of the FTSE-100 has a share price of more than 2680 p, or less than 310 p.

There are obvious disadvantages. Splits get in the way of comparisons of share price performance over time (although decent data providers can overcome this).

Sometimes they are self-defeating. Lucent Technologies probably wished it had not bothered to keep its share price at a 'manageable' level after it was caught up in the collapse of the internet bubble. For years, until its merger with Alcatel of France last year, its share price stood at about $2. It almost always had the highest volume of shares traded on the New York Stock Exchange.

This is important, because stock exchanges and other intermediaries charge fees based on the number of shares traded, rather than on the amount of money that changes hands. So splitting stock increases costs for investors. The researchers from Cornell and elsewhere found that GE investors would have saved 99 per cent in brokerage commissions if the company had not split its stock. About 5 bn GE shares traded in 2005, so this is equivalent, they say, to about $100 m – big money, even for big investors.

Are there good reasons for this? None stand up to examination. One is that there might be an 'optimal' trading range, at which individual investors can afford to buy a round number of shares. But this should logically at least have risen with inflation, so that average nominal prices now would be ten times their level of the 1930s. And in any case, individuals mostly now hold stocks through mutual funds, which don't find high share prices a deterrent.

Another possibility is that there is an effective minimum ratio between the 'tick' size, or spread between bid and offer prices, and the share price. Below a certain ratio, on this argument, nobody will be prepared to make a market in the stock. This will keep the share price down.

The problem here, the researchers point out, is that exchanges have introduced decimalisation in recent years, in place of fractions. This helped to reduce the average tick size from $0.125 per share to about $0.01 over the last decade. But instead of falling by more than 90 per cent, as this theory would predict, average share prices stayed the same.

A final argument is that a low share price, despite the attendant costs, signals to investors that a company is of high quality. But a low share price can be embarrassing. And the researchers found splits tend to come just as earnings have peaked – not a time when companies need to send out positive signals.

So has anybody had the nerve to go against the orthodoxy? They have, and their identity is revealing. Warren Buffett, the world's most successful investor, has never seen the point of stock splits. A share of Berkshire Hathaway, his main investment vehicle, will cost you $100 000. This has not harmed demand for the stock over the long term. Beyond the Buffett empire, the two highest share prices belong to the Chicago Mercantile Exchange (which has been as high as

→

$593) and Google (which has been as high as $513), the two most successful stock market debutants of this century. Neither has felt any need to bring its share price down to a lower level, and neither has been punished for this by investors.

So this is one case where questioning faith leads to a surprising result. Despite a century of dogma, companies should not split their stock, and investors should not reward them when they do.

Notes

*john.authers@ft.com

**Working paper: 'The Nominal Price Puzzle', by Shlomo Bernatzi, Roni Michaely, Richard H. Thaler and William C. Weld, University of California at Los Angeles.

■ The analysis

Liquidity is a very desirable characteristic for a financial market product. When it comes to company shares there is always a concern that once it hits a very high market share price this will impact negatively on its tradability. As the *Financial Times* article says 'Stock splits are meant to keep a share price at a manageable level'. So how does it work? It is easiest to understand with an example. Suppose a company's share price reaches £20. The finance team at the company might start to worry that this 'heavy' share price will inhibit trading the shares. So they opt for a 2 for 1 stock split. This means that every existing share will now be converted into two shares. However, as a result of the split each share is now worth half of its previous value, i.e. £10. Simply put, if I were to replace each £20 note in your wallet with two £10 notes, this would represent the outcome of a share split. You would have the same amount of money in your wallet, but in the form of more notes.

The *Financial Times* article uses the example of General Electric (GE) share price to illustrate stock splits in practice. So, their share price was $38.25 in 1935 and 70 years later it is almost exactly the same at $38.05. The article quotes some research from the University of California at Los Angeles to say that 'GE would by this point have traded at $10 094.40, had it never paid stock dividends or split its stock'. So how widespread is this practice? The *Financial Times* article states that 'No constituent of the Dow Jones Industrial Average has a share price of less than $19, or more than $95'. If you look at the London Share Price Service in the *Financial Times*, you will see very few FTSE 100 shares with a price of more than £20.

There are some clear disadvantages in share splits. First, they make price comparisons over time much more difficult. You must always first make the relevant adjustments to the share prices to take full account of any share splits. In addition, the share splits raise dealing costs because these fees are based on the number of shares traded rather than their value. So how can we explain the great enthusiasm for share splits? One possibility is that there is some ideal range for the level of market share prices, and if you were to go outside this it would discourage private investors buying a company's shares. The search for this enhanced liquidity must always be tempered by the concern about raising dealing costs.

Second, the *Financial Times* article argues that 'there is an effective 'tick' size, or spread between the bid and offer prices and the share price. Below a certain ratio, on this argument, nobody will be prepared to make a market in the stock. This will keep the share price down'. This is refuted by the claim that since decimalisation was introduced into share prices the average tick price has declined significantly. However, despite this average share prices have remained static and not fallen as this theory would have predicted.

Third, there is the argument that share splits are a clear signal from the company to investors that prospects are favourable and that a further sharp rise in the share price is expected. This article challenges the claim by stating that most share splits actually take place when compare profitability is at a peak rather than a low. This suggests that any positive signal suggested by a company's share split is often misleading.

The article ends by citing one share that has never been split. Warren Buffet, a well known international investor, does not support the advantages of stock splits. He just lets his share price rise so that one share in his investment company, Berkshire Hathaway, costs around about $100 000. I had better start saving to buy one of those, or perhaps it is time for me to pay a visit to my dear old Aunt Agatha who lives in the country!

■ Key terms

Nominal share price This is merely a value given to a company's share which is only used for accounting purposes. Unlike the par value of a bond it has no direct link to the market price.

Nonagenarian This refers to a person who is aged between 90 and 99 years old.

Stock dividends This is an alternative to an ordinary cash dividend. In this case the dividend is paid in the form of extra shares. For example, a 5 per cent stock dividend means that each shareholder gets an extra five shares for every 100 they own.

Intermediaries These are financial institutions that act as a middleman between those cash surplus units in the economy (the lenders) and the cash deficit units in the economy (the borrowers). Put simply, they enable people with money to meet people who need money.

Borrowers:	*Lenders*:
Govts	Pension Funds/Insurance Companies
Companies	Banks
Individuals	Individuals

Brokerage commissions If you wish to use the services of a stock broker in order to buy or sell shares you must pay them fees. This 'brokerage commission' is normally a set percentage of the total transaction or some kind of flat-rate charge.

Spread (tick size) In most financial markets if you ask a market maker for a price they will quote both an ask price (buying price) and a bid price (selling price). The market maker makes a profit by setting the ask price above the bid price. This means that they can sell the security for a higher price than they buy it for. We call the difference between the ask and bid price the 'spread'.

Suppose the ask price for a particular share is £14 and the bid price is £14.20 p, then the 'bid–ask spread' is 20 p.

This can also be called the 'tick' size.

■ What do you think?

1. Explain what is meant by a two for one stock split.

2. What are the advantages and disadvantages to the company and its shareholders of splitting the shares if the share price hits £20/share?

3. If a company decides to split their shares when they hit £10, what could this signal in terms of the future prospects for the company?

■ Investigate FT data

You will need a copy of the Companies and Markets section of the *Financial Times*.

Go to the London Share Price Service.

Now find the Travel and Leisure and the Real Estate sections.

1. Calculate the average share price in each section.

2. Identify any shares in these sections that might be likely to see a 'share split' in the near future.

■ Research

Arnold, G. (2007) *Essentials of Corporate Financial Management*, Harlow, UK: FT Prentice Hall. You should look at pp. 225–31 to see the efficient market hypothesis discussed.

Arnold, G. (2008) *Corporate Financial Management*, 4th edn, Harlow, UK: FT Prentice Hall. You should look at pp. 563–7 to see the efficient market hypothesis discussed.

Atrill, P. (2007) *Financial Management for Decision Makers*, 5th edn, Harlow, UK: FT Prentice Hall. You should look at Chapter 7. The efficient market hypothesis is discussed on pp. 269–75.

Berk, J. and DeMarzo, P. (2009) *Corporate Finance*, Harlow, UK: FT Prentice Hall Financial Times. The efficient markets theory is set out in Chapter 9. The key pages are 268–9.

Gitman, L. (2009) *Principles of Managerial Finance*, 12th edn, Harlow, UK: Pearson International Edition. The efficient market hypothesis is on p. 344.

McLaney, E. (2009) *Business Finance Theory and Practice*, 8th edn, Harlow, UK: FT Prentice Hall Financial Times. There is a section on the efficient markets theory in Chapter 9.

Pike, R. and Neale, B. (2006) *Corporate Finance and Investment*, 6th edn, Harlow, UK: FT Prentice Hall. You should look at Chapter 2 pp. 34–7.

Watson, D. and Head, A. (2007) *Corporate Finance Principles and Practice*, 4th edn, Harlow, UK: FT Prentice Hall. You should look at Chapter 2, especially pp. 34–41 to see the efficient markets hypothesis explained.

 Go to **www.pearsoned.co.uk/boakes** to access Kevin's blog for additional analysis of recent topical news articles and to post your comments. Download podcasts containing short audio summaries of the main issues relating to each article and check your understanding of in-text questions with the handy hints provided.

Private equity finance featuring management buyouts

Sadly these days, in the world of finance and financial markets mainstream TV programmes seldom provide a useful teaching resource. In the past I have used programmes such as the BBC's *Money Programme* and Channel 4's *Business Daily*. The nature of the former programme has significantly changed and the latter has disappeared off our screens altogether. However, I do have some ageing videos of a BBC series called *The Adventurers* which focused on the role of a venture capital company. It showed us the business from the inside. When I last showed the programme to my students, they thought that the dated clothes worn by the firms' executives were highly amusing. It was rather like watching the TV programme *Life on Mars* and seeing just how quickly fashions and peoples' attitudes change. In recent years I have used the *Dragon's Den* series. While it is far from perfect, it does give some insight into this topic. You do get to see what the Dragons look for before they are willing to put their own cash into a new business. If nothing else it gives the students a well-earned break from having to listen to me!

When I was working on the first edition of this book, private equity was a relatively new finance topic that was starting to dominate the business headlines. This was in sharp contrast to earlier years when this term had been used only occasionally in the context of a few specialised areas like management buyouts or venture capital. However, in the spring of 2007 the topic of private equity moved from the fringes of corporate finance right into the mainstream. Even back then the shadows of the credit crisis were starting to hover on the horizon, and all too soon they would fundamentally fracture the confidence of financial markets, pushing the private equity sector right back into the margins. The explanation for this change was quite simple. Whereas we had the perfect financial conditions for these deals from early 2005 to the spring of 2007, since then the picture has completely changed.

So what are the necessary conditions for these deals to prosper?

1. You need rising stock markets and immense confidence that this will continue. This is required to encourage the people who will come in and buy the businesses.

2. You need the availability of cheap debt finance.

Most of these deals are reliant on large amounts of borrowed money to fund the transactions. If this is too expensive or simply not available, they will not happen.

Before we move on to analyse the chosen articles in this section of the book, it might be helpful to explain a few key concepts that are used in private equity and venture capital deals. In terms of corporate finance these activities often stem from the desire for a company to divest itself of part of its business. This can be motivated by the need to raise cash or simply to allow the company to focus on what they perceive as their core operations.

We can identify four main forms of divestment activities:

1. **Spin-offs**. We use this term where a single part of a large company is being separated off. This might be where this part of the business is no longer considered as a 'core activity '. In most cases the host company will retain an equity stake in this new business. This process will often take the form of a demerger. At a later stage the demerged business that was subject to the 'spin-off ' might well be sold on to another company.

2. **Sell-offs**. In contrast, with a 'sell-off ' a non-core part of a company is identified and then sold for cash. This move can be justified when the price achieved results in a clear financial gain for the company's shareholders. For example, in February 2009 a struggling ITV company raised £1m by selling its stake in a spectrum management company. This deal was part of its programme of non-core assets disposal.

3. **Management buyouts (MBOs)**. Put simply, this is where the existing senior managers of a company offer to buy the whole company or a section of the business from the current owners. A strongly related corporate activity is known as a management buy-in (MBI). This is similar to a MBO but is used where the managers of the business being sold lack the necessary skills to be able to run the enterprise independently of the parent company. So, in this case there will be a new team of managers, from outside the company, who buy a controlling stake in the business. In the case of a MBI the managers must have no previous direct connection to the target company.

4. **Leveraged buy-out (LBO)**. In this case the use of the term LBO suggests that the MBO (MBI) is almost entirely financed by borrowed money. To be honest the vast majority of such deals will fall into this category as the managers will often find it very difficult to find sufficient equity finance.

■ **Why do these deals work in practice?**

Whatever the precise label attached to the deals, there is little doubt that many of these corporate activities have been highly successful in practice. It is generally recognised that this has sometimes been because part of the business was sold too cheaply by the parent company. However, in many cases the explanation might be a little more complex; it can be due to a massive increase in the managers' motivation when they become the owners. You should not find this too surprising. If you know anyone who runs their own business just think how much harder they work compared to those people are employed by a company.

■ **The financing of MBOs.**

A key issue with MBO-related transactions is the complex financing required to get these deals done. Generally speaking, the managers can only invest a small amount of the cash needed to buy the business. However, they are often able to gain a disproportionate share of the equity. This is through the existence of so called 'ratchet ' deals where they are given more equity in the business as a reward for meeting various financial targets. The rest of the equity comes from venture capital firms who are sometimes willing to take a significant stake in these companies. They can prefer MBO-type ventures rather than ordinary new start-up businesses as they tend to be less likely to fail. However, they will seek very high returns, often over 25 per cent pa. In addition, they will also be keen to arrange early exits, ensuring that they can make sufficient funds quickly and then move on to re-invest in other ventures.

The rest of the finance will be through various forms of debt capital. As we saw in the introduction to Topic 4, the highest-quality debt is termed 'senior debt' and this will be obtained from commercial banks and investment banks. There might also be some high-yield finance which ranks after senior debt in terms of any pay-outs in the case of the business failing. This is sometimes called 'mezzanine' finance as it refers to the layer of debt between the senior debt and the equity capital. The lenders will normally maintain close contact with the new venture and they can place restrictive covenants on future borrowings. These will prevent the company from issuing any additional capital that pushes the existing debt holders further down the debt hierarchy.

I have selected two articles to cover this topic. With the first, the aim is to provide a detailed overview of the private equity industry as we examine the deal for Boots the Chemist that hit the headlines in spring 2007. The second article takes a look at the state of 3i, Europe's biggest listed buy-out firm, as their share price tumbles and confidence in the group hits rock bottom.

The following two articles are analysed in this section:

Article 24
Boots provides takeover acid test
Financial Times, 21–22 April 2007

Article 25
3i chief Yea quits following steep fall in shares
Financial Times, 29 January 2009

The articles address the following issues:

- private equity finance;
- internal rate of return;
- how private equity is financed;
- leveraged buyouts;
- impact of credit crunch on private equity;
- buyout deals;
- growth capital deals;
- early-stage venture capital deals;
- infrastructure deals.

Private equity firm fills its Boots

If during early 2007 you were searching most leading corporate finance textbooks for a useful guide to private equity deals, you would have been very disappointed. At best you might have got a few pages on management buyouts and venture capital. This all changed with the corporate finance textbooks published from 2008 onwards, which started to reflect the increased focus on private equity deals in the real world. This was a part of finance that had moved from the fringes of corporate finance right into the mainstream and the academic writers had to reflect this development.

Despite this increased prominence, it is clear that private equity remains one of the most misunderstood concepts in corporate finance. The first article here examines the case of the first ever UK FTSE 100 company to fall into the hands of a private equity financier. It will explain the motivation behind the deal.

Article 24   *Financial Times, 21/22 April 2007*   **FT**

Boots provides takeover acid test

Chris Hughes, Tom Braithwaite and Andrew Taylor

Whether Alliance Boots falls to KKR or Terra Firma, any potential deal would become the acid test for private equity ownership of Britain's largest and most iconic companies.

The challenges are already apparent in the heady price of about £11 a share that the bidders are willing to pay for the pharmacist and retailer. And the more the winner pays, the harder it will have to drive the company to make acceptable returns.

That would not be a problem in a smaller deal. An advantage of private equity is the ability to take tough action

Revenue by segment*

£m	2005	2006
Retail	2,956	3,125
Wholesale	4,343	4,388
Other commercial activities	44	47
Total revenue	7,343	7,560
Retail outlets UK		2,586
Retail outlets international		372

* Note: Pro forma six months to September, inclusive of intra-group revenue

Sources: Company; *Thomson Datastream*

that would be off limits for a public company, such as extensive lay-offs that can plunge it temporarily into the red.

The snag for the would-be owners of Alliance Boots is the sheer size of this deal. It would be Europe's biggest ever leveraged buy-out at close to £11bn.

Private equity executives admit that in transactions this big, they cannot behave as though they are answerable only to themselves. In November, Charles Sherwood, a partner at Permira, the UK's largest buy-out firm, said: 'The argument that private equity is private may hold for smaller businesses. But when you own the UK's ... largest private company ... people have different expectations on disclosure and that is understandable'.

Since then, a public furore has broken out about private equity's management methods following February's private equity approach for J Sainsbury, the supermarket chain. The takeover failed amid resistance from members of the Sainsbury family, some of whom had deep

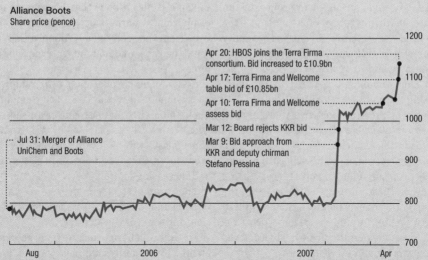

Alliance Boots
Share price (pence)

Apr 20: HBOS joins the Terra Firma consortium. Bid increased to £10.9bn

Apr 17: Terra Firma and Wellcome table bid of £10.85bn

Apr 10: Terra Firma and Wellcome assess bid

Mar 12: Board rejects KKR bid

Mar 9: Bid approach from KKR and deputy chirman Stefano Pessina

Jul 31: Merger of Alliance UniChem and Boots

Source: FT Graphic: Mario Lendvai

8

PRIVATE EQUITY FINANCE FEATURING MANAGEMENT BUYOUTS

suspicions about private equity owner-ship.

For its part, KKR is going into this situation with its eyes open. People familiar with the firm say it insisted on putting the name of Dominic Murphy, the partner leading the deal, on yesterday's statement. Others saw that as a risky disclosure. After all, Damon Buffini, the managing partner of Permira, has had to endure unions dragging a camel to his church in protest at his wealth.

There are already fears that while Sir Nigel Rudd, the chairman, has teased out a great price for Alliance Boots' shareholders, he has created a bigger problem for the current and retired work force. The worry is the new private equity owners will need to cut costs and use excessive debt funding to make the deal's maths add up.

Both KKR and Terra Firma are prepared to go on the front foot on this occasion, angry at what they see as unfair criticism. Their rationale for paying a huge premium to the share price is that Alliance Boots is a growth opportunity: pharmacies would be opened not closed; staff would be hired not fired.

But trade unions have already waded in. Brendan Barber, TUC general sec-retary, has told Sir Nigel, KKR and Stefano Pessina, the executive deputy chairman backing its bid, that the prospect of the deal would alarm staff and customers.

'Many such takeovers have hit staff and customers hard as the new owners seek to make the biggest and quickest possible buck at the expense of the long term', he said.

Paul Kenny, general secretary of the GMB, which has been at the forefront of the campaign against private equity, asked the government to ensure that pharmacies in outlying areas would not be closed to meet the cost of a highly leveraged buy-out.

He also attacked the existence of tax relief on interest payments, which will assist in the funding of any highly leveraged transaction. Taxpayers would be subsidising any deal by £144 m, he said. 'The union considers [the tax break] is the motor that is driving this takeover of Boots and other household names.'

It certainly does no harm to the economics of a bid but even with the tax break, City analysts are sceptical that private equity can make the numbers add up.

Nick Bubb, analyst at Pali International, said in a note to clients that

KKR would struggle to generate an internal rate of return of 20 per cent – the typical expectation of private equity investors – if it paid its proposed £10.90 a share for the company.

This would require KKR to lift operating margins from 4.5 per cent to 7.25 per cent over the next five years, judged 'very implausible given the pricing pressures in the business'.

People familiar with each bid proposal say neither plan involves cost-cutting beyond that already envisaged by the current management. The required margin uplift would come from a dramatic increase in revenues achieved by renewed investment and service levels.

Adopting such a strategy would not be possible if Alliance Boots stayed as a public company because its investors would baulk at increases in capital expenditure that could come at the expense of dividend growth.

There is also a hope that liberalisation of pharmacy markets across Europe will transform the sector – and Alliance Boots could become a dominant international force.

Restrictions on pharmacy ownership – long abandoned in the UK – are thought likely to be lifted in most European countries. And there is the hope that pharmacists will be given more power to prescribe medicines, drawing in patients and increasing footfall.

The grand strategic dreams of Mr Pessina and fellow travellers are not sufficient for some of the sceptics.

Mr Bubb believes that anyone paying about £11 a share would have to take 'an axe to Boots' HQ in Nottingham and the bigger stores'. Such a move would be likely to provoke a huge trade union backlash.

On the other hand, if Terra Firma or KKR do expand the company, they could kill off the political storm forever.

■ The analysis

At the outset we need to clearly identify the key players in this transaction. This record-breaking private equity deal was spearheaded by Stefano Pessina, an Italian billionaire with backing from the leading US private equity firm Kohlberg Kravis Roberts (better known as just KKR). Mr Pessina had built up from scratch his European drug wholesaling business called Alliance Unichem. This company merged with Boots in 2006 in a move that saw Mr Pessina becoming the deputy chairman of Alliance Boots and its largest shareholder. The additional financial muscle needed to win over the Boots' shareholders came from KKR, a leading player in US private equity funds.

The target for Mr Pessina and KKR was 'Boots the Chemists' which has been synonymous with the UK high street for as long as anyone can remember. No British high street is complete without a Boots store. The history of Boots began in Nottingham where the business was founded some 150 years ago by Jesse Boot. A committed Methodist, Jesse Boot believed in making medicinal products easily available to the working classes through the simple device of lowering prices. This philanthropic approach to business also saw substantial charitable donations and a paternalistic approach to his workforce. After the 2006 merger with Alliance Unichem, the newly named Alliance Boots plc employed some 100 000 people with around 3000 retail stores.

At the time of this article two potential players were competing to take Alliance Boots back into private ownership. KKR were up against a rival firm called Terra Firma headed up by Guy Hands, the former head of Principal Finance at Nomura International in London. Eventually KKR offered over £11 bn for the company which secured the deal as Terra Firma withdrew from the battle. However, the result of the bidding war was that the chairman of Boots, Sir Nigel Rudd, was able to obtain a truly astonishing price for the shares in Alliance Boots with the final offer for each share hitting over £11. This represented a premium of 60 per cent compared to the share price of 690 p just a year before. So, in the short-term the existing shareholders were the clear winners. They would be compensated very substantially in financial terms for losing their shareholding in the company.

This *Financial Times* article looks at this private equity deal by analysing four key issues:

Question 1: What is meant by the term private equity?

At the time of this rush of private equity deals it was common in the newspapers to see the leaders of private equity being presented as crazed barbarians going on a ruthless debt-fuelled acquisition spree and looking to earn millions on the back of the workforce who would face mass sackings. So is this a fair description of private equity?

Most corporate finance books begin by comparing companies that are private businesses with those that are public limited companies. The main difference is that in a public limited company there is a clear separation between the managers of the business and the wide range of shareholders who actually own the business. This means that the senior executives of a public company must ensure at all times that they are acting in the interests of their shareholders. After all, the shareholders are the owners of the business. In contrast, a private company is normally owned and run by the same person or small group of people. As a result we do not see the same conflicts of interest between the owners and managers of a private company.

Most of the time we read about private companies wanting to become public limited companies. The resulting stock market floatation sees the owners of the business turn some or all of their paper wealth into real money that they can spend. In contrast, in this article the reverse process is taking place. KKR is looking to return Alliance Boots to being a private company.

Question 2: How are such private equity deals financed?

The short answer to this is through a combination of a small amount of equity finance and a much larger amount of new debt finance. Make no mistake, these deals are highly leveraged. The equity finance came partly from Mr Pessina himself. The rest of the equity finance is in the form of 'bridge equity' with seven of the eight banks that are funding the deal each buying a stake in the equity themselves. At a later stage they will then look to sell these equity states onto a third party. This carries some degree of risk for the banks involved as their equity stakes could fall in value and they might also prove difficult to sell.

However, in the Lex column of the *Financial Times* on the 25 April it was argued that the banks' involvement in this equity part of the deal is the price they pay to be part of the syndicate of banks providing the debt capital for the new business.

The Lex article suggests that 'the equity to be underwritten in this transaction – estimated at about £1.5 bn – represents about £200 m for each of the participating banks . . . But the banks must regard it as a necessary evil rather than their preferred way to make money out of a deal'.

Question 3: What is the motivation for this deal?
Question 4: How can the deal makers justify paying over £11 a share for Alliance Boots plc?

The *FT* article hints at the justification when it says (paragraph 3) 'An advantage of private equity is the ability to take tough action that would be off limits for a public company, such as extensive lay-offs that can plunge it temporarily into the red'. This tells us much about the reasons for private equity deals. The aim of deal makers is to identify what they see as 'an undervalued company'. They then obtain the finance to mount a bid to buy the business outright from the existing shareholders. When the business is back in private hands, the new managers will set about raising the profitability of the company. This will normally involve substantial rationalisations with big cuts in costs (especially staff numbers) and some major re-focusing of the business. Then when the time is right, they will look to return the business as a public company, hopefully at a much higher market value. They can then repay their debt and make a substantial amount of profit in the process.

However, this article highlights some of the dangers in this particular deal. First, KKR have paid dearly for the Alliance Boots business. Most independent observers find it hard to believe that this price they have obtained is a bargain. As a result of paying such a high price it will be much harder to make the expected return on this particular investment.

Second, the *FT* article argues that it will be harder for the new owners of the business 'to take tough action that would be off limits for a public company'. So, as we have seen, a private company would normally be sharpening its knife ready to reduce its cost base. However, in this case it is argued that in the case of such a well-established and iconic business it is not realistic for the new owners to be able to take such actions without prompting a strong backlash from trade unions, loyal customers and even the government. As the TUC General Secretary, Brendan Barber, is quoted as saying: 'Many such takeovers have hit staff and customers hard as the new owners seek to make the biggest and quickest possible buck at the expense of the long-term.'

So what are the prospects for this deal? An analyst at Pali International is quoted as saying that KKR would struggle to generate an internal rate of return of 20 per cent if it paid £10.90 a share for the company. The final situation looks even less attractive as KKR ended up paying over £11 per share to secure the deal.

The current business plan of KKR was said not to involve cost-cutting plans any more than those currently planned by the existing management of Alliance Boots. In contrast, it is claimed that the long-term financial returns will result from a massive capital investment plan that would try to make Alliance Boots a dominant force on a global scale. We could see a major expansion in Europe, Latin America and Asia. The advantage of these plans being undertaken by a private company is that it can finance the substantial capital investment needed even at the expense of the dividend growth. If it was still a public company, many shareholders would be reluctant to give up their dividends now in return for the much riskier prospect of a higher share value at some time in the future. At this stage it is hard to be clear about the long-term prospects for the business. In reality, once it is out of the public glare it is hard to imagine that we will not see some major rationalisations of the business to generate the cost savings necessary to justify the large price paid for the shares.

■ Key terms

Private equity This term is used to describe the activities of a group of companies that invest in businesses that are already privately owned or ones that the buyers intend to remove from the stock market as soon as possible. Once they are removed from a quoted stock market, the private equity firms can then set about making a series of significant changes designed to increase their ultimate market value.

The term 'private equity' is also used to cover other areas such as venture capital where new start-up businesses receive finance in their early stages of development. Strictly speaking, private equity is different from venture capital as the deal size tends to be much larger and the investment is in more established companies.

We can trace the origins of private equity to the United States in the early 1980s. Many investment banks set up private equity divisions in the hope that they could acquire companies cheaply and later sell them on for huge profits. The biggest names in private equity have been spun off from these banks (for example, Permira was once part of Schroder's) or some private equity firms were set up by individuals from within the investment banks (for example, Kohlberg Kravis Roberts and Terra Firma).

Leveraged buyout The term 'leverage' refers to the capital structure of the new company being formed. A leveraged buyout suggests that the company will be financed largely with debt capital. This means that it will generally have a high degree of financial risk.

Tax relief on interest The tax treatment of long-term debt finance is very different to that of equity finance. The interest on long-term debt finance can be charged against pre-tax profits which effectively means that the taxpayer subsidises the cost of debt finance. In contrast, dividends are merely an appropriation of after-tax profits. As a result, any interest paid is an allowable deduction from profits chargeable to tax. The existence of this tax relief on interest payments has the effect of subsidising any highly leveraged deal.

Internal rate of return The internal rate of return (IRR) is a widely used method for companies to decide if a new business investment is worthwhile in financial terms. The IRR of a project is the discount rate that equates the present value of the expected future cash outlays with the present value of the expected cash inflows. As a result the project's net present value is zero.

■ What do you think?

1. Why might Alliance Boots be worth much more in financial terms to a private equity buyer than its previous stock market value?

2. What are the attractions to an investor who decides to invest part of their portfolio in a private equity fund?

3. What are the key financial conditions that are necessary to create a buoyant market in private equity deals?

4. What are the financial risks that face the banks that provided a significant share of the equity finance needed to fund this private equity deal?

5. It is clear that the existing Alliance Boots shareholders are big winners in this transaction. In addition, in the longer term Mr Pessina and KKR hope to make a significant

(margin, right side) **8**

PRIVATE EQUITY FINANCE FEATURING MANAGEMENT BUYOUTS

financial return on their investment. What stakeholders might be the biggest losers in this private equity deal?

■ Go to the web

Go to the official website of leading US buy-out fund Kohlberg Kravis Roberts. You will find this at: www.kkr.com.

Go to the KKR investments section.

a. Take a look at a range of new investments made by KKR.

b. Produce a quick overview of the type of companies that they like to get involved with.

c. What are the key characteristics of these companies?

■ Research

Arnold, G. (2008) *Corporate Financial Management*, 4th edn, Harlow, UK: Prentice Hall Financial Times. You should especially look at Chapter 11, pp. 435–8 to get more information about private equity.

Gitman, L. (2009) *Principles of Managerial Finance*, 12th edn, Harlow, UK: Pearson International Edition. The 'buyout binge ' is explained on p. 560.

Pike, R. and Neale, B. (2006) *Corporate Finance and Investment*, 6th edn, Harlow, UK: FT Prentice Hall. You should look at Chapter 20, pp. 597–603. This includes a nice section called 'criticisms of private equity'.

Watson, D. and Head, A. (2007) *Corporate Finance Principles and Practice*, 4th edn, Harlow, UK: FT Prentice Hall. You should look at Chapter 11 especially pp. 343–5 for a brief introduction to management buyouts.

Economic slowdown provokes unease at private equity firm

The first article in this section focused on the private equity business nearly at its peak with a rush of new deals coming almost on a daily basis and senior employees becoming millionaires in the process. Sadly for them, all good things must come to an end and this time the crash arrived in the wake of the credit crisis. In the second article we see the adverse impact that the declining liquidity in the credit markets was having on 3i, the biggest European private equity firm. With its share price going into freefall, their chief executive was edged out and a new boss faced the challenge of restoring the faith of 3i's anxious shareholders.

Article 25

Financial Times, 29 January 2009   **FT**

3i chief Yea quits following steep fall in shares

Martin Arnold

Philip Yea, chief executive of 3i, parted ways with Europe's biggest listed private equity group yesterday after its shares fell by almost three-quarters in a year.

The surprise move came as the only private equity group in the UK's FTSE 100 said it had written down the value of its 50 biggest investments by 21 per cent, or £864 m ($1.2 bn), as a result of the financial and economic downturn.

The group said the departure of Mr Yea, who will be replaced by 3i veteran Michael Queen, had been a 'mutually agreed decision taken after proper discussion'. Mr Yea is expected to receive a severance package worth about £1 m, in line with his salary.

Investors and analysts told the *Financial Times* that Mr Yea had come under pressure over worries about 3i's debt levels, which have driven the share price to record lows.

Mr Yea, a former finance director at Diageo, the drinks group, joined 3i in 2004 after a spell at Investcorp, the Bahrain-based private equity company.

The 54-year-old overhauled 3i's strategy, focusing on bigger mid-market buy-outs and growth capital deals, closing its early-stage venture capital activity, launching infrastructure and listed private equity arms and expanding in Asia and the US.

However, 3i shares have fallen sharply, along with most listed private equity groups, and are now worth less than half what they were when he took over. The shares fell 3½ p to 251¼ p yesterday, below the 272 p at which 3i listed in 1994.

Mr Queen is a 20-year veteran of the group and most recently set up and ran its infrastructure activity. He will face serious challenges to turn round 3i's share price.

The 47-year-old, who has also been finance director and head of growth capital for 3i, told the *Financial Times*: 'I have worked very closely with Phil and am absolutely aligned with him on the long-term strategic direction of the business'.

→

'Clearly, it is a tough economic climate out there but we've been through that before and we have a strong business.'

Analysts worry about 3i's £500 m of debt and £1 bn of capital calls that could fall due in the next three years, against £620 m of cash on its balance sheet in September.

Even though 3i's mid-market buy-out and growth capital focus means it typically uses less debt than its 'mega buy-out' rivals, investors also worry that it could be hurt by 'leverage on leverage'.

The group said yesterday that it had £2.1 bn of net debt and £839 m of cash deposits and undrawn banking facilities.

■ The analysis

In the analysis of the previous article we gained a clear insight into the workings of a private equity firm in the good times when profits are high and the rewards to the executives involved considerable. The second article is designed to provide some balance by looking at what happens when economic conditions deteriorate. The focus is on 3i, the only FTSE 100-listed private equity group based in the UK. The hard facts are that the value of its investment portfolio had fallen dramatically, resulting in a sharp decline in share price. As a result, the chief executive, Philip Yea, was leaving to be replaced by another '3i veteran Michael Queen'. The personal blow to Mr Yea would be offset by an exit financial package worth some £1 m, made up of salary and additional pension contributions. This was somewhat controversial as he had been in charge of 3i during the last year when 70 per cent had been wiped off its share price, thus seriously eroding the company's shareholder value.

1. **What was the history of 3i?** 3i had been formed back in 1945, as the Industrial and Commercial Finance Corporation, by the Bank of England and all the leading UK banks. It was designed to provide long-term investment cash aimed at smaller and medium-sized enterprises. The business was floated on the London Stock Market in 1994 at an initial share price of 272 p valuing the whole business at £1.5 bn.

2. **What were the main problems facing 3i in early 2009?**

   a. *Financial risk*: the article points to the severe worries about 3i's rising debt levels with the company reported to have a net debt of £2.1 bn. This gave rise to the possibility that 3i, like any other highly geared company, could even go bust if the current adverse market conditions persisted for several years and future refinancing was not forthcoming.

   b. *Business risk*: in the prevailing economic climate of that time private equity firms would always be likely to face a severe drop in returns with the credit crisis causing large write-downs in the value of their portfolio of investments. They might have had a share in a business valued at some £100 m a year or so ago. That same business could now be worth much less, resulting in a severe loss to the private equity firm. In addition the lack of available bank finance was making it much harder for private equity firms to borrow the money they needed to fund future deals. These were hardly the ideal conditions for a private equity firm to prosper.

c. *Regulatory risk*: as if the economic background was not bad enough, these firms also faced a future where they were becoming much more heavily regulated by governments around the world. The heady days of self-regulation were fading fast.

3. **How was 3i positioned against this background?** The short answer was while 3i was struggling, it was nevertheless in a somewhat better state than certain of its rivals who had much higher levels of debt to service. In addition, in recent years the strategy of the business had been refocused towards the sorts of deals that might be viewed as being more defensive:

    a. *Mid-market buyouts*: it is generally thought that it is safer to back new businesses where the existing managers are buying the business from its current owners. This is because they should have much better knowledge of the business looking from the perspective of an insider.

    b. *Growth capital deals*: by focusing on these sorts of companies, 3i was clearly looking for business opportunities that offered the prospect of above average growth in future years.

    c. *Early-stage venture capital deals*: these would be the more risky types of propositions as a significant number of these types of businesses would, sadly, fail to survive. In the market conditions prevailing in early 2009 these would be very hard to finance.

    d. *Infrastructure deals*: in these deals 3i would be taking a stake in new projects that were focusing on investments in schemes ranging from transport systems to new sports stadiums. In reaction to the economic downturn governments across the globe were keen to initiate such projects in order to provide vital new employment opportunities.

4. **What was the future like for 3i and other private equity firms?** In the immediate future all private equity firms had to face up to the fact that debt, the lifeblood of the industry, was virtually unobtainable. As a result, private equity firms that make use of a mix of investor funds and bank finance to buy companies had to alter their business plans. This was mainly by changing to deals that were much less reliant on debt finance or where no borrowing was required. Indeed there had even been some private equity deals done on an 'all-equity' basis. For example, in November 2008 the *Financial Times* reported one such deal with BC Partners €500 m+ buy-out of SGB Starkstrom Gerätebau, the German transformers maker which was done with debt. The attraction of such deals was that they were considered to be far less risky than traditional deals.

■ Key terms

Private equity groups Put simply this is a group of companies that raise finance from investors and then use this cash to buy a company which they will then remove from the stock market. This means they are holding unlisted, privately owned shares. A more complete definition is given in the 'key terms' section for the previous article.

FTSE 100 We start with the FTSE 100 which is the most widely quoted UK stock market index. It is based on the value of the 100 largest UK companies in terms of their market capitalisation. It started with a base level of 1000 in January 1984. This index is now quoted in real time on the various news information systems that serve the City traders.

Severance package This refers to the pay and benefits that an employee receives when their employment contract is terminated. It will normally be partly additional salary as well as some contribution to their pension fund.

Market buyouts This term is normally associated with the provision of finance to help the existing managers of a business take control of their company. The private equity firm will help them fund the buyout in the hope of generating a significant return for their shareholders.

Growth capital deals This refers to the provision of finance to those companies that seem to offer the prospect of particularly high rates of growth. This might be because of the type of service or goods that they provide. For example, a high-technology company might be viewed as being higher growth than a utility like an electricity supplier.

Venture capital activity This is the form of finance that is normally provided to young start-up companies. The idea is to help them survive and then expand in their early years of trading. In return, the hope will be that they might provide an exceptionally high rate of return for the venture capital company. This is a classic form of high-risk but high-return investment.

Infrastructure This is defined as investment projects that will focus on a nation's basic network of assets such as roads, railways, communications systems, etc.

Capital calls This can be defined as any additional money that equity holders will be required to provide to meet a financial deficit. In this case the worry is that 3i has £0.5 bn of debt plus an additional £1 bn of additional capital required in the next three years.

■ What do you think?

1. Why are the fortunes of private equity companies so sensitive to the general economic outlook?

2. What actions does a private equity firm take once it gains the ownership of a business?

3. Explain how a combination of financial and business risk has impacted adversely on the performance of 3i.

4. At this time 3i was generally regarded as representing the cautious face of private equity compared to the even more aggressive end of the private equity spectrum. What evidence can you find to support this view?

5. The article points out that 3i's share price has fallen sharply to hit a low of just over 251 p, which was below their initial price when they listed in 1994. Which factors might explain this sharp fall in their share price?

■ Go to the web

Go to the official website of 3i, Europe's biggest listed private equity group at: www.3i.com.

Go to the section marked Investment Approach. Take a look at each section:

a. buyouts

b. growth capital

c. infrastructure

d. quoted private equity

e. smaller minority investments

f. venture capital.

Now prepare one PowerPoint slide on each of the above private equity investment strategies being used by 3i. You should explain clearly how 3i uses this form of investment to generate value for their shareholders.

■ Research

Arnold, G. (2008) *Corporate Financial Management*, 4th edn, Harlow, UK: Prentice Hall Financial Times. You should especially look at Chapter 11, pp. 435–8 to get more information about private equity.

Fraser-Sampson, G. (2007) *Private Equity as an Asset Class*, Chichester, UK: Wiley Finance Series.

Pike, R. and Neale, B. (2006) *Corporate Finance and Investment*, 6th edn, Harlow, UK: FT Prentice Hall. You should look at Chapter 20, pp. 597–603.

Watson, D. and Head, A. (2007) *Corporate Finance Principles and Practice*, 4th edn, Harlow, UK: Prentice Hall Financial Times. You should look at Chapter 11. See the section on divestments on p. 341.

Wright, M. and Brining, H. (eds) (2008) *Private Equity and Management Buy-outs*, Cheltenham, UK: Edward Elgar Publishing Ltd.

Go to **www.pearsoned.co.uk/boakes** to access Kevin's blog for additional analysis of recent topical news articles and to post your comments. Download podcasts containing short audio summaries of the main issues relating to each article and check your understanding of in-text questions with the handy hints provided.

Dividend policy

There is always a great deal of pressure on companies to provide adequate rewards to their shareholders. This topic can be seen as part of the increased emphasis on 'value-based management'. This is essentially a managerial approach to corporate strategy that puts the primary focus on maximising shareholder wealth. In response to this trend, you will increasingly see a company's annual report and accounts making some explicit reference to the goal of maximising shareholder wealth.

A key aspect of most companies' attempts to maximise the wealth of their shareholders is the regular payment of income to them in the form of dividends. This subject plays a vital role in nearly all aspects of corporate finance. To illustrate, here are just three examples:

1. When we look to place a value on a particular company's share, the level of dividends it pays will lie at the heart of most of the financial models that are used. Indeed the most important of these is actually called the **dividend valuation model**.

2. In a similar way, whenever the topic of share price efficiency is discussed, the company's dividend policy has a significant impact on its share price. So, if a company is able to announce a sustainable increase in its annual dividends you can expect a sharp rise in its share price wherever an efficient market exists.

3. Finally, in the area of mergers and acquisitions it is common for companies that are being targeted by an aggressive corporate raider to seek to secure the loyalty of their existing shareholders by promising higher dividends either now or in the future.

It is clear from the above discussion that, if we want to learn about corporate finance, we need to understand the dividend policy of companies. We should start with the basics. The amount of annual dividends to be paid to shareholders is set by the company's board of directors and is subject to the approval of the shareholders. Most UK companies will split the annual dividend into an interim and a final payment paid six months apart. It is important to understand that not all companies will pay dividends. Any loss-making businesses will be unable to pay them and other fast-growing ones will choose to re-invest all available profits rather than make cash payments to their shareholders. This is quite sensible as long as the company senior managers are convinced that they can secure a better financial return on these investments than the shareholders could obtain if they were investing the cash themselves.

Sometimes instead of paying a cash dividend a company can opt to reward shareholders with additional shares. This is called a 'stock' or 'scrip dividend'. For example, a company might announce a 5 per cent stock dividend, which means that each shareholder gets an extra five shares for every 100 they own.

If a company want to return a particularly large amount of cash to its shareholders it can announce a special dividend payment. The intention is that, in labelling it 'special dividend', the shareholders will not expect it to be maintained in the future. For example, in March 2007 the Drax Group, the UK's largest coal-fired electricity generator, paid a special dividend after pre-tax profit more than doubled due to high power prices. The company announced that it would give 32.9 p a share, or £121 m, to shareholders as a special dividend as well as a final of 9.1 p a share.

Before we get into the particular articles chosen for this section of the book there are two further aspects of the company's dividend policy that can be important in practice. They are:

1. **The clientele effect**. If you ask someone why they own shares in a particular company, their answer can sometimes be highly revealing. Sometimes they will say that they like these shares because they pay a good level of dividends on a regular basis; while others might say they like certain shares because they have delivered a strong growth in the capital value over many years. This is the clientele effect in practice.

    Put simply, it says that there is a natural clientele for those shares that pay out a high proportion of earnings and another quite different one for those shares that have a low pay-out rate. This puts pressure on the management of all companies to produce a stable and consistent dividend policy that is in line with their shareholders' expectations. If they move away from this usual flow of dividends, this inconsistency will result in a fall in popularity with their normal client group.

    A classic example of a clientele shareholders group that is often highly reliant on dividend incomes is older retired people who use their shareholdings to bolster their pensions. As an example, when the UK government planned to purchase preference shares in a number of UK banks in the autumn of 2008, they ruled that the banks would be prevented from paying any ordinary dividends out until the government had their money repaid in full. This resulted in a number of complaints from pensioners, who stated that the loss of this income would have a very negative impact on their standard of living at a time of rising prices.

    It is sometimes argued that with an efficient capital market companies should not worry too much about maintaining a consistent dividend policy at all times. The claim is that shareholders can do just as well with holdings in companies where the focus is on share price growth rather than funding dividends. Shareholders in these companies can sell some shares each year, effectively making their own 'home-made dividends'. In reality, this process might be rather costly and inconvenient as many people will not want to be forced to sell small parcels of shares each year. They prefer their dividends which are more predictable.

2. **The information contained in dividend decisions**. Now we should move on to consider the kind of message that a company's dividend policy can signal to investors. There is little doubt that the annual dividend announcement is normally seen as an important signal of the future performance of the company. The senior managers who set the level of dividends are operating from inside the business,

which gives them greater information about the company's current trading. This means that the decision to increase dividends can be taken as a good signal as the senior managers perceive future earnings to be strong enough to sustain this trend.

If you read the Companies and Markets section of the *Financial Times* on a regular basis, you will certainly see that the announcement of dividends is seen as a vital process. A cut or missed dividend is viewed as a big event which results in a sharp fall in the company's share price.

I have selected two articles to highlight the key issues in the area of dividend policy. In the first we see what happens when companies actually have more cash than they need. In these cases they seek to return surplus funds to their shareholders. The article looks at the relative attraction of using share buybacks compared to the more common method of simply paying out cash dividends to shareholders. In the second article we look at a company, De La Rue, which is in an enviable position of having spare cash that it decides to distribute to its shareholders in the form of a special dividend.

The following two articles are analysed in this section:

Article 26
Shareholders taking a stand on handouts
Financial Times, 19–20 May 2007

Article 27
De La Rue pays special dividend
Financial Times, 23 May 2007

These articles address the following issues:

- dividends;
- special dividends;
- market capitalisation;
- capital expenditure;
- redeemable 'B' shares.

Have share buybacks gone too far?

Many corporate finance activities involve companies raising additional finance to enable them to invest in new capital projects. However, sometimes we see the reverse when companies actually have more cash than they need. In these cases they look to return surplus funds to their shareholders. The first article looks at the relative attraction of using share buybacks compared to the more common method of simply paying out cash dividends to shareholders. It suggests there is some evidence that companies which offer share buybacks might actually see their share prices underperform compared to those companies which instead used surplus cash to support the steady growth of dividends.

Article 26   *Financial Times*, 19–20 May 2007   **FT**

Shareholders taking a stand on handouts

Chris Hughes

Investors used to be grateful when companies promised to return buckets full of cash. These days they seem to shrug their shoulders at corporate handouts. Many are even rebelling against the most common method of cash-return – the share buy-back.

Last year was a record year for cash returns to investors, with UK companies funnelling £108 bn their way, according to Morgan Stanley. That includes £46 bn of share buy-backs, up from about £28 bn in 2005.

But fashions are changing and share buy-backs by UK companies are expected to be only £23 bn this year, although BT this week said it planned to spend £2.5 bn repurchasing its own stock.

Buy-backs took off because they were a simple and flexible means of distributing cash generated by rising corporate profitability.

They work like this. A company instructs its broker to purchase its shares in the stock market. These shares are then cancelled, which means the company's future profits are spread among fewer shares, so each remaining share becomes more valuable.

Background

Companies have enjoyed a strong recovery in profitability in recent years, creating surplus capital that they have distributed to shareholders. Many companies have chosen to do this via share buy-backs – repurchasing their shares in the stock market and cancelling them, thereby increasing earnings per share for remaining investors. Last year was a record for cash distributions by UK companies. However, companies are coming under increasing pressure to spend cash in other ways, such as by raising dividends or through capital expenditure.

Research from Morgan Stanley this month found that companies that pursued share buy-backs saw their shares underperform those that consistently raised dividends.

But buy-backs are not necessarily a good thing. They absorb cash that could be spent on higher annual dividend payments or capital expenditure.

If a company's stock is overvalued, the company wastes money buying it – just

Top 20 companies by buy-back yield

	Buy-backs (£m)	Buy-back yield*
Psion	84	83.0
First choice	200	26.1
Computacenter	75	15.5
Wetherspoon (JD)	79	13.9
Evolution	50	13.2
Biocompatibles	12	12.6
Enterprise Inns	388	12.6
Pennon	138	12.0
SurfControl	15	11.1
Rank	201	10.5
Hays	209	10.2
Burberry	192	9.8
Capita	245	9.0
Spirent Comms	42	8.6
Reuters	527	8.5
InterCont Hotels	307	8.4
Next	341	8.2
Vodafone	6457	7.2
Anglo American	2111	7.1
BP	8155	6.7

* Buyback to average market cap 2005 and 2006 results

Source: Morgan Stanley

like any other investor. And to the extent that stock repurchases are good for the company's continuing investors, they are correspondingly bad for those who sell out during the buy-back.

Shares in companies that have been growing dividends have performed better over the past decade than those pursuing buy-backs, according to Morgan Stanley.

Private shareholders have long opposed buy-backs because they think they cannot participate in them. This is a fallacy given that anyone can sell shares in the market during a buy-back and the price at which buy-backs are conducted is regulated.

At Royal Dutch Shell's annual meeting this week, a disgruntled shareholder drew applause when he thanked the oil company for stopping its share buy-back, citing Morgan Stanley's research.

'You've returned £16.3 bn in dividends and buy-backs. Thank you for my dividends, I have banked them', he said. 'Tell me, how do I bank my buy-backs? . . . Where is [the money] exactly?'

There was a similar incident at the Unilever annual meeting the following day.

Institutional investors are also taking a stand. Stuart Fowler, fund manager at Axa Investment Managers, says: 'We prefer dividends to buy-backs and we state that very plainly to companies that ask. You would have thought that by now more companies would have spotted what Morgan Stanley has found'.

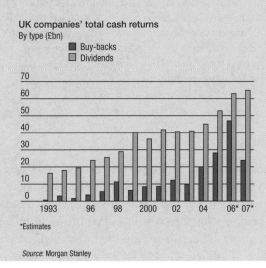

UK companies' total cash returns
By type (£bn)
■ Buy-backs
□ Dividends

*Estimates

Source: Morgan Stanley

He says that companies such as BPB, BAA, BOC might still be independent if they had paid higher dividends and therefore commanded higher share prices – a lesson for Rio Tinto, which is currently the subject of takeover speculation.

'Rio is the sort of company where putting the dividend up would help defend its borders', he says.

Euan Stirling, investment director, UK equities at Standard Life, says: 'There can be value creation from buying back cheap shares. But if companies have a permanent increase in their cashflows, dividends are the best way to distribute this to shareholders. There is plenty of scope for UK companies to grow dividends from here'.

Other investors want cash to be spent on capital expenditure instead. Robert Waugh, head of UK equities at Scottish Widows Investment Partnership, says: 'Buy-backs can make sense at the right price, but we prefer good management to invest more in the business. At the moment most investment is going on expensive acquisitions'.

Neil Darke, analyst at Collins Stewart, has campaigned against ill-judged share buy-backs, arguing that investment banks advise companies to do buy-backs because their equity desks make easy commission from them. He says other means of capital return – such as special dividends or redeemable 'B' shares – are preferable, since they do not differentiate between selling and buying shareholders.

But management at companies that have been buying back shares are quick to dismiss criticism.

Ted Tuppen, chief executive of Enterprise Inns, says investors seem to prefer buy-backs because they do not trigger a taxable event like a dividend.

'When we asked our shareholders, the overwhelming response was that they preferred share buy-backs. But fashions change, and you get to a point when it's not earnings enhancing.'

Mr Tuppen says companies are not being cajoled into buy-backs by bankers, since it is possible to negotiate very low commission rates with brokers.

Jim Clarke, finance director of JD Wetherspoon, says: 'Most of our long-term large shareholders have said they see buy-backs creating more value than putting up dividends'.

He says the company buys its shares when their free cash-flow yield exceeds its cost of borrowing.

Ian Burke, chief executive of Rank, says: 'There are a lot of factors that influence the decision about how you return capital. We have used both buy-backs and a special dividend'.

So should companies continue buy-backs? It depends. Collins Stewart research has found that buy-backs trigger share price outperformance when the company also has a low valuation, a reputation for disciplined capital investment and a strong balance sheet. 'A buy-back is only a catalyst for correcting undervaluation – it is not a value creator in itself', says Mr Darke.

■ The analysis

According to the US investment bank Morgan Stanley, 2006 was a record year for companies returning surplus cash to shareholders. The total figure of some £108 bn included share buybacks of £46 bn. This method is often favoured because it is cheap and easy to organise. A company just needs to instruct a broker to go into the market and start buying its own shares. These shares are then cancelled, which means that each remaining share is now worth more in line with the higher level of earnings per share.

This process benefits all shareholders through the rise in the capital value of their share holdings.

However, there are some problems with this method of returning value to shareholders. First, when a company decides to use spare cash to purchase its own shares, it is inevitably at the expense of paying higher dividends which is a more visible form of monetary return to shareholders. It is possible that some private shareholders do not fully understand the share buyback process. This might be the reason that some shareholders at recent company annual general meetings have been questioning the value of share buybacks. They argue that while they could bank their dividends they could not bank their share buy-backs. Even some leading institutional investors express a preference for dividends. Stuart Fowler at Axa Investment Management says 'we prefer dividends to buybacks and we state that very plainly to companies that ask'.

A second argument against share buybacks comes from the research at Morgan Stanley which suggests that companies that have been concentrating on growing their dividends have seen a better performance compared to companies that made share re-purchases. The argument seems to be that if a company has been able to produce a permanent increase in its cash flow, the correct response is to signal this greater confidence in their future prospects by raising dividends.

Finally, there is the argument made by Robert Waugh, head of equities at Scottish Widows Investment Partnership, who would like to see companies spend any spare cash on additional investment projects. In some ways a share buyback programme is a nega-tive outcome. The company is saying that it cannot identify any suitable investment projects so it is handing the cash back to shareholders to make their own investments.

If companies cannot readily identify any suitable investment projects, Neil Darke an investment analyst at Collins Stewart would like to see them make special dividends or to issue class B redeemable shares. The attraction is that these are highly visible and they are paid to all shareholders. The same firm identifies the perfect candidate for a successful share buyback, they must have 'a low valuation, a reputation for disciplined capital invest-ment and a strong balance sheet'. In this situation the share buyback can be seen as the starting point for a revaluation of the company.

■ Key terms

Share buybacks This is an increasingly common method for companies to return cash to their shareholders. The process is relatively simple. The normal technique is for companies to make a 'tender offer' to all shareholders inviting them to sell their shares back to the company at a set price. Second, a company might offer to buy from a particular group of shareholders. Finally, the company could make a stock market purchase of its shares. In this last case there will not be one set price, as this will vary depending on the exact timing of the share re-purchase. In all cases the company will cancel the re-purchased shares so that the earnings per share will increase, assuming that earnings remain the same and that there are now a reduced number of shares in existence. It should be noted that a share buyback is a voluntary arrange-ment for the shareholders. They can always decline the offer from the company and keep their shares.

Capital expenditure This is where a company spends money on various types of fixed assets such as property and plant and equipment. These assets cannot easily be turned into cash and are generally viewed as long-term investments.

Redeemable 'B' shares This refers to a type of share capital which has reduced or zero voting rights. These shares are generally redeemable which means that they have a fixed life unlike most ordinary shares which have an infinite life. In recent years a number of companies have given their shareholders redeemable 'B' shares instead of cash dividends.

■ What do you think?

1. From the point of view of shareholders what are the main differences between a company returning any surplus cash to them in the form of:

    a. Redeemable 'B' shares?

    b. A special dividend?

    c. A share buyback?

2. What are the main reasons that private shareholders and institutional shareholders might have different attitudes to the possibility of a company making a share repurchase instead of simply raising normal dividends?

3. Why is it argued in this article that paying higher dividends might protect a company from a possible takeover bid?

■ Research

Arnold G. (2007) *Essentials of Corporate Financial Management*, Harlow, UK: FT Prentice Hall. You should look at pp. 433–5 to see more information about share buybacks.

Arnold, G. (2008) *Corporate Financial Management*, 4th edn, Harlow, UK: FT Prentice Hall. You should especially look at Chapter 22, p. 853 to get more information about share buybacks.

Atrill, P. (2007) *Financial Management for Decision Makers*, 5th edn, Harlow, UK: FT Prentice Hall. You should look at Chapter 9, especially pp. 386–7.

Berk, J. and DeMarzo, P. (2009) *Corporate Finance*, Harlow, UK: FT Prentice Hall Financial Times. The payout policy for companies is set out in Chapter 17.

Gitman, L. (2009) *Principles of Managerial Finance*, 12th edn, Harlow, UK: Pearson International Edition. The dividend policy of companies is covered in Chapter 13.

McLaney, E. (2009) *Business Finance Theory and Practice*, 8th edn, Harlow, UK: FT Prentice Hall Financial Times. The dividend decision is covered in Chapter 12.

Pike, R. and Neale, B. (2006) *Corporate Finance and Investment*, 6th edn, Harlow, UK: FT Prentice Hall. You should look at Chapter 17, pp. 474–7 to see a very clear discussion of share buybacks.

Watson, D. and Head, A. (2007) *Corporate Finance Principles and Practice*, 4th edn, Harlow, UK: FT Prentice Hall. You should look at Chapter 10.

Printing money pays big dividends for De La Rue

This article looks at De La Rue plc, the company that makes its money by printing bank-notes all around the world. This company went through some tough times back in early 2003. The company issued three profit warnings in just over seven months. As a result the share price fell sharply to just over 190 p. However, times have changed and this company is now viewed as a very successful business. The company is at the forefront of new tech-nology and as a result earnings are very strong and the company is cash rich. It is therefore looking to return some of this money to shareholders through a special one-off dividend. Against this background the share price hit nearly 750 p.

| Article 27 | Financial Times, 23 May 2007 **FT** |

De La Rue pays special dividend

Tom Griggs

De La Rue, the banknote printer, is to pay a special dividend to shareholders as it pointed to a strong backlog of orders at both its currency and cash systems businesses.

Leo Quinn, chief executive, said new security features and innovative cash-counting machines had driven a 12.6 per cent rise in revenues to £687.5 m and a 34 per cent rise in pre-tax profits to £102.4 m.

He added that the group had generated cash flow of £144 m in the year to March 31, representing 140 per cent of operating cash flow.

De La Rue raised its dividend 12.4 per cent to 19.1 p with a 13.27 p final and announced plans for a special distribution of 46.5 p, worth about £75 m.

Mr Quinn said the group will have returned £283 m to shareholders over the past three years, representing 50 per cent of its market capitalisation from three years ago and double free cash flow over the period.

Stephen King, finance director, added that De La Rue had completed its pension review. The normal retirement age has been increased from 62 to 65, member's contributions will increase by 1 per cent by June 2008 and future increases in life expectancy will be borne by members by an adjustment to the pension accrual rate.

De La Rue has also agreed to pay off the current £57 m deficit over the next six years.

Two years ago it shifted two factories to China to cut costs. Mr Quinn said there was 'still a significant way to go' with cost savings.

Earnings per share rose to 43.9 p (31.4 p).

The shares added 1 p to close at 726 p.

FT comment: After a positive trading update, investors had expected Mr Quinn to announce the cash return. But the prospect of another good year will add a further support to the shares. De La Rue trades on a price/earnings multiple of about 16.8 times 2008 estimated earnings – which seems about right for the time being. The company is operating near to full capacity and future cost savings will be harder to find. After such a strong year, these results are going to be difficult to live up to next time around.

■ The analysis

The announcement of a special dividend can hardly have come as a big surprise to investors as it came just after a recent very positive trading update. De La Rue, the company that prints banknotes, has become a very successful business. It is a company with a licence to print money that has been able to translate this into real cash for its shareholders. The latest set of figures were very strong, with revenues up by nearly 13 per cent to £687.5 m. There was a sharp rise in earnings per share to 43.9 p. Even more significantly the company was full of spare cash with a positive cash flow of some £144 m in the year to 31 March 2007.

This very positive cash position has enabled the company to raise the normal dividend by 12.4 per cent to 19.1 p. In addition, it announced a special one-off dividend of some 46.5 p per share. The chief executive is reported as saying that the company has now returned £283 m to shareholders in the three years. This means that if you bought some shares in the company just three years ago, you would have now received 50 per cent of the purchase price back in the form of cash dividends.

The *Financial Times* comment piece gives a favourable outlook for the company. It suggests that it is trading at a price–earnings (PE) ratio of around 17 times estimated future earnings 'which seems right for the time being'. However, it suggests some caution ahead as in the longer term it might prove difficult to maintain this strong performance. As usual, the future is always more uncertain than the past.

■ Key terms

Dividends A normal dividend is simply the payment made each year to all shareholders in the company. The exact level is set by the company's board of directors. This payment will be made to all shareholders who are registered on a particular date. In most cases these dividends are paid in cash.

Stock dividend A stock dividend is where the company rewards its equity investors with additional shares rather than a cash payment.

Share buyback A share buyback is where the company uses spare cash to buy their own shares in the stock market with the explicit aim of increasing the share price.

Special dividend Finally, a special dividend refers to the situation where a company decides to return any surplus cash to shareholders through a one-off payment. This should be seen as an additional payment on top of any expected normal dividend. The significance of labelling this dividend as 'special' is that it is a signal from the company that it will not be able to maintain annual dividends at this higher level. It is a one-off benefit that shareholders should not see as becoming the norm.

Market capitalisation This gives the current overall stock market value of the company. It can be easily calculated by multiplying the numbers of shares in issue by their current market share price. In some cases companies will have more than one class of shares. In this case it is necessary to add together the different classes of shares to get the total value of the company.

Price–earnings ratio The PE ratio is calculated by taking the market share price and dividing it by company's earnings per share. This ratio is often used to compare the current stock market value of a company.

> So in this case what is the company's price–earnings (PE) ratio?
>
> This can be calculated by taking the share price (726 p) and dividing it by the company's earnings per a share (43.9 p). This gives us an answer of 16.5 to be precise.

■ What do you think?

1. It is often said that the dividend announcement made by a company is an important source of information about the future prospects for the business. In this case what signal is being given by De La Rue plc in the decision to raise the annual dividend by 12.4 per cent and in addition to announce a special one-off dividend of 46.5 p?

2. How else could the company have used this spare cash?

■ Investigate FT data

You will need the Companies and Markets section of the *Financial Times* for any Monday edition. Go to the London Share Price Service. This is normally the two pages inside the back page of the Companies and Markets section.

Take a look at the Bank's Sector.

Look only at the Banks in the FTSE 100. They are all shown in bold.

Answer these questions:

1. Which bank pays the highest dividend in pence?

2. Calculate the dividend yield for this bank based on its current market share price.

3. Which bank has the highest market capitalisation? Do not forget that you need to add all classes of shares. For example, HBOS has three different preference shares.

4. Which bank has the highest dividend cover?

5. Which bank has the lowest dividend cover?

■ Research

Arnold G. (2007) *Essentials of Corporate Financial Management*, Harlow, UK: FT Prentice Hall. You should look at Chapter 12.

Arnold, G. (2008) *Corporate Financial Management*, 4th edn, Harlow, UK: FT Prentice Hall. You should especially look at Chapter 22.

Atrill, P. (2007) *Financial Management for Decision Makers*, 5th edn, Harlow, UK: FT Prentice Hall. You should look at Chapter 9.

Berk, J. and DeMarzo, P. (2009) *Corporate Finance*, Harlow, UK: FT Prentice Hall Financial Times. The payout policy for companies is set out in Chapter 17.

Gitman, L. (2009) *Principles of Managerial Finance*, 12th edn, Harlow, UK: Pearson International Edition. The dividend policy of companies is covered in Chapter 13.

McLaney, E. (2009) *Business Finance Theory and Practice*, 8th edn, Harlow, UK: FT Prentice Hall Financial Times. The dividend decision is covered in Chapter 12.

Pike, R. and Neale, B. (2006) *Corporate Finance and Investment*, 6th edn, Harlow, UK: FT Prentice Hall. You should look at Chapter 17.

Vaitilingam R. (2006) *The Financial Times Guide to Using the Financial Pages*, 5th edn, Harlow, UK: FT Prentice Hall. You should look at Chapter 5. This has an excellent explanation of the London Share Price Service including market capitalisation, dividend cover etc.

Watson, D. and Head, A. (2007) *Corporate Finance Principles and Practice*, 4th edn, Harlow, UK: FT Prentice Hall. You should look at Chapter 10.

Go to **www.pearsoned.co.uk/boakes** to access Kevin's blog for additional analysis of recent topical news articles and to post your comments. Download podcasts containing short audio summaries of the main issues relating to each article and check your understanding of in-text questions with the handy hints provided.

Mergers and acquisitions

Mergers and acquisitions (M&A) play a very important role in corporate finance. For example, they help to ensure that the managers of a business act in the best financial interest of their shareholders by maximising the company's share price. If the share price starts to slide, they know that they risk another company coming in and making a takeover bid for the business which will almost certainly see the managers lose their well-paid jobs. M&A activity also enables companies to grow their business by being able to exploit opportunities for external growth. This is particularly important where the scope for internal growth is limited. For example, a particular company may be highly successful in growing their business, but in the end it reaches a point where the size of the total market for their product or services rules out any further expansion. In these situations there is little choice for the company but to seek out opportunities to expand their horizon by corporate mergers or takeovers.

At the outset it is important to set out clearly the terminology that is applied to this area of corporate finance. In practice, the terms 'merger' and 'acquisition' or 'takeover' are often used quite interchangeably. However, strictly speaking, 'merger' should imply a more friendly deal with both companies fully consenting to the combining of their assets. In contrast, when we refer to an acquisition or takeover there is a clear suggestion that one company is chasing the other in a more aggressive manner. The predator sees a clear financial gain to be made by securing the assets of the target business and using them to its advantage. This distinction is clear from the following well-used descriptions in this area:

- **A friendly merger**. The companies are normally of equal size and they see a mutual interest in the deal being made.
- **A hostile takeover**. Normally a larger company is attempting to take over a smaller business rival.

Having established the distinction between mergers and acquisitions or takeovers we can now define three categories within this type of corporate activity:

1. **Horizontal M&A activity**. In this case we have two companies from the same industrial sector both of which are involved at the identical stage of production. For example, when easyJet took over Go in 2002, it was a case of one budget airline taking over another.
2. **Vertical M&A activity**. Here we have two companies operating at quite different stages of production that merge their activities. For example, a new TV company might acquire a business that makes new programmes in order to ensure a run of high-quality content in the future.

3. **Conglomerate M&A activity**. In this last case we see two companies from unrelated business sectors coming together. This results in the creation of large industrial conglomerates like ArcelorMittal which employs over 320 000 people in over 60 countries. It has interests in steel, cars, construction, packaging and household goods.

Before we start to examine the articles included in this section we should briefly examine the economic reasons often used to justify M&A activity. We can list the main arguments as follows:

1. **Synergy**. Perhaps, the most powerful argument in favour of M&A is that it can lead to significant gains through the exploitation of the synergies that exist between the two companies involved. In this view the value of the combined business is going to be significantly higher than the simple sum of the values of the two companies. This can be because the new business will be able to make significant cost savings or enhanced revenue opportunities thanks to its more powerful position in the market. It is certainly the case that following virtually all M&A deals, there will soon be announcements of rationalisations as duplicated operations are shut down. If there are many winners from M&A deals, the losers are often the lowliest employees who find their services quickly becoming surplus to requirements.

    A great example of synergy in practice was provided by the Lloyds TSB bid for HBOS in the autumn of 2008. When they unveiled the updated terms of their bid on the 3 November 2008, they suggested that the combined new group would make cost savings of some £1.5 bn per year. Inevitably these would come largely in the form of significant job losses.

2. **Immediate access to new markets**. I can remember that, when the eurozone was about to be created with the introduction of the new single currency, an economist in an investment bank published a new research note titled 'the urge to merge'. His argument was that ahead of this development the easiest way into this new market was through the acquisition of a leading European company that already had a significant presence within this market. This shows how M&A activity can be viewed as one way to gain access to new market opportunities.

3. **The motives of ambitious managers**. It is often argued that much of M&A activity can be traced back to purely managerial motives. The directors of a business see it as being in their best interests to search for the opportunity to grow their business fast by the acquisition route. As a result they will find their status and remuneration on a fast upward curve.

4. **Spreading risk through diversification**. A better reason for M&A activity is that a company might be able to reduce its exposure to business risk through the expansion into a wider range of corporate activities. For example, if there is downturn in demand for gym memberships, this will have less impact on a range of sports clubs that also offer tennis courts, physiotherapy, health and beauty and hotel accommodation.

5. **The opportunity to buy an undervalued company**. It is often the case that the drive to launch a takeover bid might come from the perception that the target company has been significantly undervalued by the stock market. The aim will be to

buy up the business and re-focus it in some way so this hidden value can be better exploited. This is often the case when there is a general fall in share prices, which can result in an unjustifiably steep fall in a particular company's market value.

Whatever the reasons for M&A activity, there is something about it as a subject which always seem to intrigue students of corporate finance. It is most likely to be the fierce battle that often takes place as two or more rival bidders fight for the ownership of a company. The embattled company usually has to fight hard to maintain its independence, and in these articles we compare two different forms of tactics used to defend companies in the face of a hostile bid.

The following three articles are analysed in this section:

Articles 28
Discussions unlikely to yield white knight
Financial Times, 2 February 2006

Articles 29
Mittal goes on Arcelor charm offensive
Financial Times, 31 January 2006

Article 30
Poison pill's strength under analysis
Financial Times, 15 June 2007

These articles address the following issues:

- mergers, takeovers and acquisitions (MTA);
- financing of MTA;
- defence mechanisms;
- white knights;
- poison pills;
- warrants;
- greenmailer.

> **Sophisticated European company** into hot metal seeks more sympathetic partner to rescue them from a very unhappy prospective partner. No time wasters please. Call 0905 560 4000

In this first case we look at the charismatic figure Lakshmi Mittal, the owner of Mittal Steel, who launched a takeover bid for Luxembourg-based Arcelor in 2006. This was a strongly contested bid with Arcelor, proud of its position as Europe's leading steel producer, determined to maintain its independence. Indeed at this stage there was the possibility of the involvement of a so called 'white knight' in the shape of Nippon Steel. They might have formed an alliance with Arcelor in an effort to fend off the advances from Mittal steel.

Article 28   *Financial Times*, 2 February 2006 **FT**

Discussions unlikely to yield white knight

Mariko Sanchanta

When Akio Mimura, president of Nippon Steel, sits down in Paris today to speak with Guy Dollé, head of Arcelor, they will have more to talk about than just the state of their five-year-old technical alliance.

The long-set meeting comes less than a week after Mittal Steel launched its hostile bid for Arcelor.

The meeting has fuelled speculation that Nippon Steel might act as 'white knight' to help fend off Mittal's advances. Mr Dollé has said he is open to discussions with other companies about uniting and making things more difficult for Mittal.

But such an agreement might not make sense for Nippon Steel, Asia's leading steelmaker and the world's third largest. Analysts say a stronger union with Arcelor is likely to yield little for Nippon Steel, which has refused to join the wave of industry mergers.

Russ McCulloch of Steel Business Briefing, a trade publication, says the aim of the original arrangement with Usinor – later subsumed into Arcelor – was to provide Japanese car companies in Europe with similar grades of steel to Japan. 'In the late 1990s Nippon Steel had no alternative but to tie up with Arcelor, as they couldn't export their steel to Europe', says Mr McCulloch. 'Now, from Nippon Steel's point of view, what could Arcelor provide them with?'

Nippon Steel has emerged from Japan's recession of the 1990s and is on track to report a record profit for the second year, which reflects strong pricing power for its high-grade steel products despite a steep increase in raw material costs.

Nippon Steel's determination to remain independent has put it at odds with JFE, a Japanese rival, created in 2002 via a merger between NKK and Kawasaki Steel.

'Merging with a foreign steelmaker wouldn't make much sense for Nippon

Steel or JFE, because it wouldn't give them more clout over their biggest customer – the Japanese carmakers', says one Japanese steel analyst. 'It would make more sense to consolidate domestically. The only merit a merger with a foreign company would bring the Japanese makers is more sway over raw materials suppliers.'

Analysts added that it would be even less likely that JFE would align itself with Arcelor, since it already had a tie-up with Thyssen-Krupp.

Moreover, in 2001 Kawasaki Steel and Usinor negotiated for seven months over the supply of automotive steel sheet in Europe. The talks fell through and Usinor aligned itself with Nippon Steel.

According to Mr McCulloch: 'Japanese steel companies usually don't have short memories'.

Other large Asian steel companies seem unlikely to take a hand in the battle.

South Korea's Posco said it was not concerned about becoming a target, and had no plan to make a play for the European steelmaker. 'We do not have any plans or any intentions over Arcelor', Han Dong-hee, a spokesman, says.

Tata Steel, India's largest private-sector steel producer, has close relations with Arcelor and Nippon Steel. The Japanese company constructed a cold rolling mill in India for Tata Steel, which also has a technology-sharing arrangement with Arcelor.

However, Tata Steel is probably too small to make much difference in a potential alliance of steelmakers positioned against Mittal. The company's output is about 7 m tonnes a year, although it has plans to raise production.

Note: additional reporting by Khozem Merchant and Anna Fifield.

Article 29

Financial Times, 31 January 2006 **FT**

Mittal goes on Arcelor charm offensive

Peggy Hollinger

Lakshmi Mittal, the Indian billionaire, yesterday launched a charm offensive in France in an attempt to avert growing political opposition to his €18.6 bn (£12.7 bn) bid for Arcelor, Europe's largest steel producer.

Insisting there would be no job cuts or factory closures should his Mittal Steel group succeed in its hostile offer, Mr Mittal said he was determined to avoid conflict with the government.

He said: 'I have never confronted a government in my life. We believe there is strong industrial logic to putting these two companies together for the benefit of all stakeholders, including governments. I am sure we will convince them'.

Mr Mittal's comments followed a tense meeting with Thierry Breton, France's finance minister, who is openly hostile to the unsolicited nature of the bid for Arcelor, which employs about 23 000 people in France.

Mr Mittal said there had been a 'free exchange of views' at the meeting where he had explained his reasons for going hostile.

Mr Breton reiterated his 'profound concerns', saying the lack of discussion with

→

Arcelor had increased the risks that any merger would fail.

He said: 'In the 21st century, if you want such a transaction to be successful, you need to start with preliminary discussions between the companies involved, on a friendly basis'.

Dominique de Villepin, French prime minister, is understood to have banned members of his government apart from Mr Breton from speaking out, but wider political opposition appeared to be gathering steam yesterday.

The Socialist Party, with perhaps one eye on the presidential election in 2007, attacked the government for a 'truly weak response'.

Bernard Carayon, from the ruling UMP party, said the bid marked the 'hour of truth for Europe'.

Arcelor, formed from Franco-Spanish and Belgo-Luxembourg interests, had to be protected from predators 'even if it couldn't be protected legally'.

Yesterday, Pedro Solbes, Spain's economy minister, said he wanted more information on what the bid meant for Spanish workers. Mr Mittal is expected to meet Jean-Claude Juncker, the Luxembourg premier, today.

Meanwhile, Guy Dollé, Arcelor chief executive, insisted there was no industrial logic in putting the two businesses together and railed against Mittal Steel's unwelcome approach.

Referring to a private dinner at Mr Mittal's home on January 13, he said: 'It was made in four minutes just after the aperitifs. I think a deal of this size merits more than four minutes after the aperitif'.

■ The analysis

The first article sets out the strategy of the Mittal Steel group, headed by the Indian billionaire Lakshmi Mittal, who launched a bid of €18.6 bn for the Luxembourg-based steel maker Arcelor on the 26 January 2006. He argued that the deal made sound commercial sense and it would benefit all the stakeholders of Arcelor including various European governments. This approach was designed to reassure the French government, which was particularly hostile to the proposed bid. One serious concern was that any takeover would result in severe plant closures and job cuts in a country where about 25 per cent of Arcelor's employees were located. As the *Financial Times* says, there was a particularly hostile reaction from France's Finance Minister, Thierry Breton. With an election coming up in the spring of 2007 perhaps this was not that surprising.

The chief executive of Arcelor, Guy Dollé, is quoted as saying that he saw no industrial logic in putting the two businesses together. Indeed, he commented on the tactic employed by Mr Mittal in trying to explain the logic behind the deal over aperitifs at a private dinner at the latter's house. One potential escape route for Arcelor was the possibility of persuading a friendly company to combine with them in an effort to fend off the bid from Mittal Steel. The first article identifies Nippon Steel as a possible 'white knight'. However, industrial analysts are quoted as saying that such a merger would make little commercial sense for Nippon Steel. They saw far more merit in the Japanese-based company forming an alliance at home.

In early April 2006 Arcelor used more common tactics to fight off the takeover bid. They announced that they would increase the 2005 dividend and distribute a further £3.4 bn to shareholders. In addition they announced that they would transfer the shares that they owned in a Canadian firm (Dofasco) to a foundation which would make it much harder for Mittal Steel to sell this business if it succeeded in buying Arcelor.

In the end the European regulators which had investigated the proposed takeover gave the go-ahead in June 2006. As a result Mittal Steel was able to take over Arcelor although they ended up paying a significantly higher price. This created the world's largest steel-maker. The process of integrating the companies proved to be fairly trouble free. A new board of directors was created with three executives from each company. The vice-president of Arcelor, Roland Junck, became the head of the new firm. Aditya Mittal, son of the Mittal Steel chairman, became the firm's chief financial officer. It was perhaps signifi-cant that the chief executive of Arcelor, Guy Dollé, had no executive role in the new business.

The combined company's share price performed very strongly. A *Financial Times* article in spring of 2007 reported that it had outperformed the global index of all share prices by nearly 28 per cent. The article concludes with a cautious statement from a banker close to the business. He says that the takeover was still in the honeymoon period and considers that '. . . the real tests will come later in the year when quite possibly the steel market will start to soften and conditions for the company begin to look rather tougher'.

■ Key terms

Mergers This is where two companies decide that it would be to their joint benefit to come together to form a new business entity. With a merger the process is normally friendly with the full consent of both sets of shareholders.

Takeover This is the purchase of one company's ordinary shares by another company. In this process one company is seen to dominate the other.

Stakeholders This refers to the various parties who have a share or an interest in a company. This will include the shareholders, managers, employees, suppliers, government and the members of the local community.

White knight This is where the company being chased will seek out an alternative friendlier suitor that will form an alliance to act as a defence against the first bidder.

■ What do you think?

1. In early 2006 Mittal Steel launched a hostile bid for Arcelor, Europe's largest steel pro-ducer. Following the bid there was speculation that Nippon Steel might act as a 'white knight' to help fend off Mittal's advances. Explain what the function of a white knight is in mergers and acquisitions.

2. Why might a bidding company be prepared to pay a premium above the market value for the shares of a business?

3. In mergers and acquisitions what is meant by the term a 'winner's curse'?

■ Go to the web

Go to the European Union's website. You will find this at http://europa.eu/index_en.htm. Now go to the section on Competition.

Hint: You will find this in the section: 'What the European Union does by subject?'

Now go to the section on Mergers.

Hint: You will find this at the top of this page.

Now go to the overview section. Read this section and answer the following questions which are set out here. Make sure you use your own words.

a. Why do mergers need to be investigated at a European Union level?

b. Which mergers are examined by the European Commission?

c. When are mergers approved or prevented?

■ Research

Arnold, G. (2008) *Corporate Financial Management*, 4th edn, Harlow, UK: FT Prentice Hall. You should especially look at Chapter 23.

Atrill, P. (2007) *Financial Management for Decision Makers*, 5th edn, Harlow, UK: FT Prentice Hall. You should look at Chapter 12. You will see a very good definition of a 'white knight' on p. 497.

Berk, J. and DeMarzo, P. (2009) *Corporate Finance*, Harlow, UK: FT Prentice Hall Financial Times. You will find mergers and acquisitions explained in Chapter 28. You will see a definition of a 'white knight' on p. 890.

Gitman, L. (2009) *Principles of Managerial Finance*, 12th edn, Harlow, UK: Pearson International Edition. Mergers, LBOs, etc. are covered in Chapter 17.

McLaney, E. (2009) *Business Finance Theory and Practice*, 8th edn, Harlow, UK: FT Prentice Hall Financial Times. The topic of corporate restructuring is covered in Chapter 14.

Pike, R. and Neale, B. (2006) *Corporate Finance and Investment*, 6th edn, Harlow, UK: FT Prentice Hall. You should look at Chapter 20.

Watson, D. and Head, A. (2007) *Corporate Finance Principles and Practice*, 4th edn, Harlow, UK: FT Prentice Hall. You should look at Chapter 11.

Can Japanese sauce spice up US hedge fund?

Mergers and takeovers often involve fierce battles between the predator company and the target company. These stories tend to stay in the news for weeks as rival companies get involved in the bidding process and the company under attack mounts a strong campaign to defend its independence. In this case we have a clash of cultures on several levels. First, we have an aggressive hedge fund chasing a corporate prey. Second, we have the clash of continents with the hedge fund based in the US and the target company being Japanese.

In addition, this *Financial Times* article provides an insight into the use of complex financial market products in the area of mergers and takeovers. More specifically, it shows us how a poison pill can be used as a defence mechanism by a company in the face of a hostile takeover bid.

| Article 30 | Financial Times 15 June 2007 **FT** |

Poison pill's strength under analysis

Michiyo Nakamoto

Corporate litigation in Japan generally lacks high drama and is not something that arouses public excitement.

But the decision by Steel Partners to file an injunction against Bull-Dog Sauce's poison pill has thrown the spotlight on the judiciary.

Major Japanese companies that have adopted poison pills

Sector	Company
Electric	Matsushita, Sharp, Hosiden, Yokogawa Electric
Chemical	Shinetsu Chemical, Mitsui Chemical, Fuji Photo Film, Kaneka
Food	Nippon Meat Packers, Meiji Dairies, Yukijirushi, Snow Brand Milk Products, Kagome
Steel	JFE, Kobe Steel, Nisshin Steel, Maruichi Steel Tube
Pharmaceutical	Rohoto, Santen Pharmaceutical, Mochida Pharmaceutical
Non-ferrous metal	Mitsubishi Material, Sumitomo Metal Mining, Dowa
Paper	Nippon Paper, Oji Paper, Mitsubishi Paper
Other	Dai Nippon Printing, Kokuyo, Mitsubishi Estate, Keio, Nippon TV

Source: FT research

The move puts the burden on the judiciary to set a precedent that some say will test the integrity of Japanese capitalism and have far-reaching consequences for capital markets in Japan.

'This is a very important case', says Nobu Yamanouchi, partner at the Day Jones law firm in Tokyo. The way the poison pill was implemented gives Steel a strong hand, he thinks.

'But if poison pills are not going to be effective against someone like Steel Partners, then there won't be any hostile bidder that companies will be able to use them against', Mr Yamanouchi says.

'The judge is being put in a very difficult position.'

Steel Partners is seeking an injunction against a particular type of poison pill that Bull-Dog has adopted, known commonly as a rights issue but in Japan ominously dubbed SARS, for special acquisition rights.

The maker of Worcester sauce and other condiments is the target of an

→

unsolicited tender offer by Steel Partners, which has a 10 per cent stake and wants to acquire all the shares it does not own.

Bull-Dog, which reacted to the advances with outright hostility, unveiled its SARS plan, which it will put to the annual shareholders' meeting this month.

The Bull-Dog rights issue is unprecedented in Japan in several respects. Pending approval by shareholders, it intends to issue warrants that can be converted into shares at 1 per warrant. Shareholders, including Steel Partners, will receive three warrants per share.

For Steel Partners, it is bad enough that the rights issue will dilute its shareholding from 10 per cent to less than 3 per cent. But the scheme also singles out Steel Partners, which alone will not have the right to convert its warrants into shares but instead will receive ¥396 per warrant.

To make matters more galling, Bull-Dog reserves the option of converting Steel Partners' warrants into cash but has no obligation to do so. If Bull-Dog decides not to exchange Steel Partners' warrants for cash, the fund could be left with useless paper.

Steel Partners charges that the scheme represents 'a discriminatory act against [it] in violation of Japanese law', which it says states that 'a company should treat shareholders equally according to the contents and amounts of shares they have'.

It says the plan is 'only seeking ... to dilute [Steel Partner's] shareholdings and stop its tender offer'.

Many believe that if Bull-Dog's plan were approved it would send a strongly negative message to the investment community that the board, which in Japan is usually controlled by management, can choose the company's shareholders.

'Japan [would be] going back to the dark ages. It will really depress the stock market because what it effectively says is that a board can kick out a shareholder', one lawyer says.

The head of Japan mergers and acquisitions at a leading western investment bank says that, if the court approves Bull-Dog's measure, 'it's the end of the Japanese capital market'.

Japan allows poison pills under certain conditions but Bull-Dog announced the measure only after Steel Partners made its bid. 'That makes it look like the management is trying to protect their job', says Scott Jones, partner at Jones, Day.

In general, poison pills are allowed only in times of peace, when a company is not facing a hostile bid, Mr Yamanouchi says.

Bull-Dog was not available for comment yesterday. It has said it believes its defence measure was 'lawful and appropriate'.

The courts have ruled against warrants that companies have planned to issue to third parties in two cases out of three – a poison pill by Nireco in 2005 and plans by Nippon Broadcasting Systems to issue warrants to TBS.

But there is a possibility that Bull-Dog's poison pill will be allowed if Steel Partners is deemed to be a greenmailer. When the court struck down Nireco's poison pill, it also noted that poison pills could be allowed if they were targeted against greenmailers.

Steel Partners has had the blessing of Institutional Shareholder Services, which says: 'We do not believe that Steel Partners' offer is so clearly inadequate or otherwise abusive as to justify denying shareholders the option to tender their shares if they so choose'.

The question is whether the courts will look objectively at Steel Partners' record or pander to the public, which is against the US group.

Note: additional reporting by David Turner.

■ The analysis

In this case the Japanese company Bull-Dog Sauce was the subject of a hostile takeover bid by the US hedge fund Steel Partners. Steel Partners had already built a 10.5 per cent stake in the target company. It then offered ¥1584 for each remaining share which amounted to a 20 per cent premium on the company's stock market price at the time of the bid. This was the latest bid by increasingly activist shareholders who were forcing some Japanese companies to make moves which were designed to win favour with their shareholders. This included increases in share dividends and some modernisation of their corporate structure.

Following the move from the US hedge fund, Bull-Dog Sauce inserted a so-called 'poison pill' which would act as a strong disincentive to any bidder. The particular type of poison pill being used here is a complex form of rights issue which was rather worryingly termed a 'SARS' in Japan. In fact 'SARS' just stands for a special acquisition rights. So how does this product work in practice?

The Bull-Dog Sauce rights issue is very different from a normal corporate rights issue. True, it will allow shareholders to purchase additional shares in the company. However, this will be achieved via an issue of warrants. This is a financial instrument that gives the holder the right to purchase financial market securities from the issuer at a set price. In this case they will allow all Bull-Dog Sauce's shareholders, except Steel Partners, to buy new shares in the company at just ¥1 per warrant. Every shareholder, including Steel Partners, will receive three warrants per share. However, Steel Partners alone among the shareholders will not be able to trade their warrants in for shares. Instead they will receive ¥396 per warrant. This is a best-case scenario because, while Bull-Dog Sauce 'reserves the option of converting Steel Partners' warrants into cash ... [it] has no obligation to do so'. So it is possible that their warrants will turn out to be valueless instruments and, more importantly, due to the extra shares that have been issued, if this poison pill is allowed to take effect Steel Partner's equity stake will fall from 10 to 3 per cent.

This raises the big question of whether this process is legal in Japan. It would seem to violate the principle that companies should treat all shareholders the same. Within Japan, the *Financial Times* quotes Steel Partners as suggesting that the scheme represents "a discriminatory act ... in violation of Japanese law", which it says states that '"a company should treat shareholders equally according to the contents and amounts of shares that they have"'.

The *Financial Times* article expresses the fear that if this poison pill is allowed to stand it will seriously damage the Japanese Financial Services Industry. It might well undermine confidence both among domestic and international investors. Indeed the head of Japanese mergers and acquisitions at a leading western bank is quoted as saying if the court approves Bull-Dog's measure, 'it's the end of the Japanese capital market'.

Finally, the article seems to suggest that Bull-Dog Sauce's poison pill will only be allowed by the Japanese courts if they regard Steel Partners to be acting as a Greenmailer. This is where a company deliberately sets out to mount an unwanted takeover bid in order to force the target company to buy their equity stake at a significant premium. Foreign companies rarely bid for Japanese companies and therefore this move from a US hedge fund might well be seen as coming from just such an unwanted 'corporate raider'.

10

MERGERS AND ACQUISITIONS

■ Key terms

Poison pill When a company is subjected to an unwanted takeover bid, there are a number of measures that they can take to try to defend themselves. One such technique is called a 'poison pill'. This is where a company introduces some measure that will seriously damage the interests of the company making the takeover bid. This might, for example, be an issue of a new bond which following a takeover bid would give the bond holders the option to redeem their bond immediately at a significant premium to its par value. This will act to deter any bidder.

Tender offer This is simply where the takeover bid is made through a public offer which is open to all shareholders allowing them to sell their shares at a price that is usually well above the current market price.

Annual general meeting (AGM) All public companies must invite their shareholders to an AGM to vote on a number of important issues. This will include the approval of the annual report and accounts, the re-election of the directors and the dividend level.

This is the key forum allowing the shareholders to express their views to the managers of the company. For example, in recent years it has allowed some pressure groups to exert pressure on companies involved in the arms industry or other so-called 'unethical' sectors.

Rights issues This is where a company issues some additional shares on a pro rata basis to existing shareholders. The new shares are normally sold at a discount to the current market price. These issues provide no access to new shareholders.

Normal rights issues are popular because they can be made at the discretion of the board of directors. The shareholders like the discounts available and they leave the balance of voting rights unchanged.

Warrant This is a derivative instrument that gives the holder the right to purchase financial market securities from the issuer at a set price within a certain time period. They are commonly attached to certain new bond issues giving the holder the right to buy some shares in the issuing company. They were used a great deal in the 1980s when international investors were very keen to buy Japanese shares.

Greenmailer This refers to a very unusual situation in corporate takeover bids. It is where one company (the takeover company) deliberately builds up a large stake in another business (the target company) and then appears to launch an unfriendly takeover. This whole process is designed to force the target company to repurchase the stock at a substantial premium to prevent a takeover bid.

■ What do you think?

1. Briefly describe the main defences that can be used by a company after its board has received an unwanted take-over bid.

2. In the context of mergers and takeovers explain what is meant by a 'poison pill'. Give some examples of three poison pills that have been used in practice.

3. What is meant by the financial term 'warrant'?

■ Research

Arnold, G. (2008) *Corporate Financial Management*, 4th edn, Harlow, UK: FT Prentice Hall. You should especially look at Chapter 23.

Atrill, P. (2007) *Financial Management for Decision Makers*, 5th edn, Harlow, UK: FT Prentice Hall. You should look at Chapter 12.

Berk, J. and DeMarzo, P. (2009) *Corporate Finance*, Harlow, UK: FT Prentice Hall Financial Times. You will find mergers and acquisitions explained in Chapter 28.

Gitman, L. (2009) *Principles of Managerial Finance*, 12th edn, Harlow, UK: Pearson International Edition. Mergers, LBOs, etc. are covered in Chapter 17.

McLaney, E. (2009) *Business Finance Theory and Practice*, 8th edn, Harlow, UK: FT Prentice Hall Financial Times. The topic of corporate restructuring is covered in Chapter 14.

Pike, R. and Neale, B. (2006) *Corporate Finance and Investment*, 6th edn, Harlow, UK: FT Prentice Hall. You should look at Chapter 20 with p. 575 having a discussion of 'poison pills' as one of many potential takeover defence tactics.

Watson, D. and Head, A. (2007) *Corporate Finance Principles and Practice*, 4th edn, Harlow, UK: FT Prentice Hall. You should look at Chapter 11. Poison pills are explained on pp. 337–8.

Go to **www.pearsoned.co.uk/boakes** to access Kevin's blog for additional analysis of recent topical news articles and to post your comments. Download podcasts containing short audio summaries of the main issues relating to each article and check your understanding of in-text questions with the handy hints provided.

10

MERGERS AND ACQUISITIONS

Risk management and hedge funds

The last few years have seen a huge increase in interest in the concept of the many types of financial risk and in particular how they can be managed. This is hardly surprising in the light of the credit crisis and the resulting long list of bank failures across the world. Before we look at the risks that banks face we should pause briefly to define what is meant by the term 'risk' in the context of finance. Put simply, we define risk in terms of the possibility of incurring some kind of financial loss. This is the natural flip-side to the financial gains that are available in financial market investments. As we have seen, earlier investors in shares must be willing to tolerate the much higher degree of risk in order to give themselves a chance to make much higher gains than are available on safer investments like bonds or cash deposits.

For risk-averse individuals the advice is to stick with low-risk and low-return investments like government bonds or cash deposits in banks. In contrast, those investors who are more tolerant of risk should go for more equity-related investments which have historically offered the prospect of higher returns to compensate for their greater risk.

In this section of the book, in addition to the topic of risk, I have decided to include an extra section on the role of hedge funds. There are two reasons for this. First, they are a perfect example of a financial institution that is strongly associated with the concept of risk. Second, during my teaching I have found that this is one of the areas which elicit most questions from students. They seem to be intrigued by the activities of hedge funds.

The credit crunch showed us that the risks that banks face can have a very significant impact on the wider economy. This is largely due to the perceived threat that, if one bank goes under, it will almost inevitably result in other banks failing. This so-called 'domino effect' was the great fear that forced governments across the globe to spend billions in support of their domestic banking systems during 2008. These fears explain the heightened public concern that centres on bank failures and the resulting trend towards even tighter regulation of the activities of banks.

So what are the major types of risk facing banks?

1. **Credit risk**. This is the risk that a party to a financial contract fails in some way to fully discharge the terms of the contract. In the case of banks this form of risk is most strongly linked to their lending activities. The credit risk refers to the possibility that the bank will not see these loans repaid in full. In addition to this form of credit risk there is also a strong link to the banks' tendency to hold a wide range of financial assets. A perfect example would be where a bank owns a bond market instrument and the issuer of that financial market security fails to make timely payments of

interest or the principal on the maturity date. We can also call this 'default' risk. In the *Financial Times* 'High-Yield & Emerging Market Bonds' table you will see the use of the symbol 'DEF' next to a bond issuer to signify that they are in default. This was sadly the case for Argentina's emerging euro-denominated issue in October 2008.

In order to counter this form of risk, the banks will use the services of the various credit-rating agencies (including Moody's and Standard and Poor's). Their function is to assign credit ratings to various bond issuers. This acts as a measure of the risk that they will default on the terms applying to the issue. The highest credit rating allocated by Moody's is triple A (AAA) which indicates the issuer's 'capacity to pay interest and principal is extremely strong'. The banks will typically also employ their own in-house credit rating teams to provide another view on this form of risk.

2. **Market risk**. This occurs where there is the possibility that the prices of a financial market security may decline over a period of time due to any general economic factors or some other change in market conditions. As an example, a bank might be the holder of a significant number of shares in a particular airline. They are likely to see a sharp decline in the financial value of these holdings if an economic downturn results in the need for the airline to lower profit margins in order to prevent a large loss in passenger numbers.

3. **Interest rate risk**. As we have seen earlier, banks hold a wide variety of financial assets. The value of these securities is likely to change following any movement in interest rates. For example, the price of government bonds would be expected to fall in reaction to any increase in interest rates. This price fall will maintain the competiveness of their yields compared to the higher level of interest rates.

4. **Liquidity risk**. In financial markets this term refers to how easily an asset can be turned into cash. Notes and coins are the most liquid financial assets. Liquidity risk occurs when the holder of an asset is prevented from being able to realise the full value of it when they need to sell. For example, a bank might be forced to offer a significant discount when they become forced sellers of a large number of financial market securities in order to raise additional finance. This is a very important form of risk for banks as they will be required to keep a large amount of liquid assets to cover their day-to-day needs. In practice, the demand from their customers for cash will be fairly predictable as they tend to only look to access a small percentage of their total deposits held with the bank. If a particular bank experiences a higher than normal demand for money, it can normally access extra liquidity by borrowing in the inter-bank markets. It was only when this market effectively stopped functioning during the credit crunch that a number of banks got into severe financial difficulties.

5. **Operational risk**. The efficient operation of the banking system is increasingly dependent on complex computer systems. This form of risk comes into play when a failure in a bank's systems results in some kind of financial difficulty. In the US the Federal Reserve Bank makes emergency loans available to any qualifying banks that are facing these sorts of technical difficulties.

6. **Fraudulent risk**. Sadly, all banks face the risk that one person or a group of their employees will engage in some activity that causes them a significant financial loss. For example, in early 2008 the news broke that a single rogue trader had lost Société Générale €4.9 bn (£3.7 bn) in fraudulent futures trades.

7. **Exchange rate risk**. This is the risk that a bank might incur as a result of adverse movements in foreign exchange rates. This is a major issue for many banks, because they tend to hold large amounts of foreign currency assets and liabilities in their balance sheets.

8. **Legal risk**. This is the risk that arises from any contracts that a bank finds impossible to legally enforce. As a result the business of the bank could be significantly interrupted.

9. **Systemic risk**. This is the risk that the entire financial system might face the possibility of contagious failure following the collapse of one particular bank. The worry is that the collapse of this bank starts to have a domino effect which impacts on other banks in the system.

Banks are associated with many different types of risk. In the above discussion these rights have been identified as separate and independent, but in practice they will be far more interrelated. For example, if there is a sharp increase in interest rates (interest rate risk) this is likely to lead to many more loan defaults (credit risk). In the light of the recent credit crisis it is not surprising that banks are now putting huge resources into attempts to manage the many risks that they face.

Another financial institution that involves large amounts of risk are **hedge funds**. One key characteristic of many of them is their innate secrecy. You will have a long search if you are hoping to see adverts for their services on TV or radio or in the popular press unless you are reading *Millionaires Weekly*. The reason for this is that they focus on high net-worth individuals to provide their client base. The hedge funds have been around for a surprisingly long time with their origins going back to the early 1940s primarily in the USA. The first time I came across them was when one of their star names, George Soros, made a financial killing at the expense of the UK government when sterling exited the exchange rate mechanism in September 1992.

So what do they do? In essence their business model is quite simple. They look to raise sizeable amounts of cash from wealthy individuals and then invest this money in almost anything that they believe will make them profitable. So, in many ways they are rather like any normal fund manager who looks to invest cash for the financial benefit of their unit holders. However, there are two important differences. I will set these out briefly here and develop these themes in the analysis of the related article later.

1. They tend to take far more risk with their investments, often employing some unusual investment strategies. For example, they are heavily associated with the practice of short selling. This is where a hedge fund would sell shares that they do not yet own. In other words they have not yet made an offsetting purchase. This is a very risky activity because, if the price of the financial market security rises, the

hedge fund will have to pay an ever higher price to secure the stock. In this case the traders are betting on the shares falling in price. For example, they might sell 1 million shares at £5. If the share price now falls to £4 the fund makes £1 m. However, if instead the share price rises their risk is infinite.

2. They charge very high fees for their services. This is normally taken as a percentage of the profits made by the fund. So, if a particular hedge fund makes a profit of £300 m for their clients, do not be surprised to see the owners of the fund take 20–30 per cent of this cash to share between themselves. In good times hedge fund managers can get seriously wealthy very quickly.

In this section of the book I have included two articles. The first focuses on the well-established topic of the impact of foreign exchange rates on companies. In contrast, the second article looks at the relatively new area of hedge funds. In this article you will clearly see that hedge funds attempt to maximise their returns but often at the cost of much greater financial risks for their fund holders. I have also tried to give a clear guide to the main activities and investment strategies of hedge funds.

The following two articles are analysed in this section:

Article 31
Exporters curse dollar's drag on profits
Financial Times, 14 May 2007

Article 32
Facing down the threat of tighter rules
Financial Times, 20 June, 2007

These articles address the following issues:

- types of currency risk;
- economic risk;
- translation risk;
- impact of currency movements on dividends;
- role of hedge funds;
- investment strategies of hedge funds;
- long-short equity;
- activist hedge funds;
- macro-trading strategy;
- regulation of hedge funds.

The $2 pound puts pressure on UK companies

The *Financial Times* has over the years traced the rise and fall of the pound on the foreign exchange rate markets. As a survivor of numerous sterling crises in the 1980s and early 1990s it has always seemed to me that it has done far more falling than rising. Indeed the article makes reference to the famous day on Wednesday 16 September 1992 when the UK government gave up trying to defend the pound's value in the old exchange rate mechanism. The Chancellor allowed interest rates to go back to a more reasonable level and the pound fell sharply. It was the day when the media claimed that the international financier George Soros called the Bank of England's bluff and the Bank blinked first.

Almost 15 years later (can it really be that long ago?) this article looks at the subject of corporate foreign exchange rate risk. It examines how the UK economy is being affected by the advent of the $2 pound. Even more telling is the perspective of the individual companies who are dealing with the daily problems of living with a pound that has appreciated so strongly against the backdrop of a very weak dollar.

Article 31

Financial Times, 14 May 2007 **FT**

Exporters curse dollar's drag on profits

Chris Hughes

The pound's strength against the dollar is a boon for British consumers planning luxury mini-breaks to New York. But some UK companies are cursing the toll the exchange rate is taking on their profits and competitiveness.

The issue came to prominence last month when the pound breached $2 for the first time since the UK withdrew from the exchange rate mechanism in 1992. In fact, the currency has been strengthening steadily over the past five years, and especially the past nine months.

About 22 per cent of the sales of the FTSE-350 are directly exposed to the US, while a further 11 per cent come from regions closely tied to the dollar, according to Citigroup.

So how is UK plc holding up? The victims will fall into one or more of three categories. First, exporters serving dollar markets are at a competitive disadvantage if their cost base is located in the UK and denominated in sterling. The weak dollar crimps their revenues, but wages still have to be paid in pounds. That creates a painful squeeze

Second, companies that serve US markets through local operations will see dollar costs and dollar revenues move in tandem, but their dollar profits still take a hit when converted into sterling.

Finally, the exchange rate reduces the sterling dividends of companies that report their financial results in dollars. That applies to many large UK companies, such as GlaxoSmithKline, BP and HSBC.

It is companies in the first camp that are being hit the hardest. The strong pound is not just reducing the profits and dividends paid to investors. It is affecting

→

177

their long-term competitiveness and may even lead to loss of market share to US or Asian rivals.

One such victim is Arm Holdings, the Cambridge-based designer of semiconductors, an industry whose global currency is dollars. Warren East, chief executive, estimates that the dollar has wiped £1 bn from the company's stock market value. 'We are at the acute end of the scale. The last three years have been pretty horrid', he says. 'The only way you can respond is by matching your cost base [to the dollar]. That means jobs going outside the UK. We have gone as far as we can and about 50 per cent of our costs are now overseas.'

Arm has also taken advantage of relatively low-cost skilled labour in India. Headcount there has risen from two to 230 since 2004.

'There is a lot of intellectual capital in the business that's in Cambridge and will never leave. This is still very much a UK company at heart', Mr East says.

Meanwhile, other companies in a similar position have responded by hedging – buying derivatives off banks that offset the impact. CSR, the Bluetooth technology group, hedges about 40 per cent of its cost base, fixing it on a rolling 12-month basis.

Economists have nevertheless been surprised by the resilience of UK plc as a whole. The latest quarterly survey of industrial trends by the CBI, the employers' organisation, found that export orders were holding up well and company optimism about exports was at its highest in two years.

Ian McCafferty, chief economist at the CBI, says companies have learnt lessons from previous jumps in the pound, and most UK companies remain more reliant on Europe than the US or Asia.

'Anecdotally, the strong pound is putting pressure on profit margins but it is not affecting volumes. UK companies lived with a strong exchange rate after 1998 across the board. That led to a great deal of efficiency improvements', he says. 'British industry is a little bit more competitive even at these exchange rates than we feared.'

As for the wider stock market impact, it depends where you look. Citigroup research has found that over the past six months, shares of companies with more sales in the US have underperformed. Meanwhile, looking at the market as a whole, Morgan Stanley estimates that for every 10 per cent rise in sterling against the US dollar, stock market dividend growth is reduced by 2.5 percentage points. That means dividend growth this year could be zero.

And are there any winners from the weak dollar? Clothing retailers such as Next benefit from cheaper textiles costs in Asia, while much of the manufacturing industry enjoys lower raw material costs, such as steel and chemicals.

The snag is that companies benefiting from the weak dollar may also come under pressure to pass savings on to customers. Bauer Millett, a Manchester-based car importer, looks as though it is a sweet spot. Not so, says Chris Harris, one of its directors. 'Yes, we have been able to buy US cars for less. But customers expect to buy them at half price because that's what they see in the headlines.'

■ The analysis

With the often wild movements in foreign exchange rates there are always some winners and some losers. In the case of the pound rising in value against a weak dollar, UK consumers delightedly head west in their masses to buy up all the goods that retailers such as

Bloomingdales and Macys can offer them. The losers are the many UK-based companies which export to the US or to other parts of the world that have their exchange rates linked to the dollar.

The reasons for the weakness of the dollar are not made clear in the article. There are a number of theoretical models that are used to explain currency movements. In the research section I have provided a reference to a very clear explanation of these theories (see Pilbeam book). At this particular time there is no doubt that a major factor behind the weakness of the dollar was the concern about problems in the US mortgage market which it was feared would cause a slowdown in the world's largest economy. Against this background the Fed was expected to keep its key short-term interest rates unchanged, while in contrast we were seeing increased interest rates in both the eurozone and the UK. The foreign exchange markets were focusing on the resulting change in the interest rate differential between the US and these European markets. Investors were being attracted by the higher interest rates available in both the euro and sterling money markets and were selling dollars fast as they liquidated their US money market investments. The expectation that other key central banks would increase interest rates while the Fed held US rates steady was expected to result in a continued period of dollar weakness.

The core of the article identifies three main types of currency risk that face corporate treasurers. The first is economic risk, which is caused by the rising value of the pound making all UK goods and services more expensive when they are being sold into the dollar-based markets. In effect it is the reverse impact of UK consumers flocking to buy cheaper goods in US stores. Now at $2 to the pound US customers will look elsewhere for much cheaper merchandise, which results in the UK companies losing market share to companies based in other countries which have not seen their exchange rates appreciate against the dollar.

This article relates this economic risk to the UK-based company Arm Holdings plc. The Cambridge-based company designs semiconductors; this is an industry that almost more than any other is dollar-based. Their chief executive is quoted as saying that 'the dollar has wiped £1 bn from the company's stock market value'. Companies respond to economic 'exchange rate risk' by keeping their prices as competitive as possible, which means keeping a firm hold on their cost base. Labour costs are pivotal, so Arm Holdings have sought to relocate some jobs to India with the company's labour force there rising from just two in 2004 to currently 230.

The *Financial Times* article reports that other companies in a similar position to Arm Holdings have attempted to offset the impact of sterling's rise against the dollar. They have looked to employ the various sophisticated hedging techniques which are on offer from the banks. These can be used to minimise some of the economic risk. The downside is that they are very expensive and they do not always suit this type of risk that is by its nature very uncertain.

The second type of currency risk is translation risk. This occurs where companies that supply the US markets through local operations will see their dollar revenues and costs move together. So far so good; however, the companies will take a financial hit when their dollar profits are finally converted back into sterling.

As an example, if we have a UK-based company that has a US-based subsidiary to deal with the United States market. It is successful and generates profits of some $200 m per year.

Where the exchange rate is £1 = $1:
These $200 m profits will translate into £200 m for the UK accounts.

However, where the exchange rate is £1 = $2:
The same $200 m translates into just £100 m for the UK accounts.

The final type of currency risk discussed here applies to those companies that report their financial accounts in dollars. There is a direct impact on the sterling value of dividends announced in dollar terms. The rise in the value of the pound against the dollar reduces the value of the dividends received in terms of the local currency. This applies to a number of the biggest UK companies including GlaxoSmithKline, BP and HSBC.

The article moves on to express surprise that, despite these examples, the UK economy as a whole has been remarkably resilient in the face of the appreciation in the pound. The most recent CBI industrial trends survey shows that export orders are holding up well and optimism about future exports remains strong. Its chief economist thinks that 'companies have learnt lessons' from the past and that they have protected themselves by strong efficiency gains. The resulting reduction in UK costs has countered some of the negative impact of an appreciating pound.

In addition, the article points out that UK companies have reacted to sterling's appreciation against the dollar by looking to sell more to other markets such as the rest of Europe and Asia. This is a perfectly viable strategy in this case as the dollar was generally weak against these other currencies as well. This means that all other exporters to the US were facing the same problem of their currencies appreciating against a weak dollar. Therefore, they were all losing competitive advantage, which means that UK exporters were not losing out compared to other international exporters selling to the US. They were all losing competitiveness against US producers.

The article ends with a useful attempt to quantify the impact of currency movements on dividends. They cite Morgan Stanley estimates that for every 10 per cent rise in sterling against the US dollar, stock market dividend growth is reduced by 2.5 percentage points. Despite this gloomy assessment there are some more winners. These are the UK companies that see a sharp fall in the costs of their raw materials which are priced in dollars. Companies like Next, for example, will be paying much less for textiles coming in from South-East Asia. However, their customers will be demanding ever lower clothes prices, otherwise they will be heading back across the Atlantic again with their empty suitcases!

■ Key terms

Exchange Rate Mechanism (ERM) In the days before the existence of a single European currency there was a very complex system set up to control exchange rate fluctuations between participating currencies. For a very brief time the UK became part of this system and this caused severe problems for the UK economy which was then in recession. The government had to keep interest rates very high in the middle of this downturn in a vain attempt to defend the pound's value. This policy came to a dramatic end on Black Wednesday in September 1992. The pound crashed out of the ERM and interest rates fell sharply.

Currency risk This comes in three main types: transaction, translation and economic (see below).

Transaction risk This is the risk associated with a particular financial commitment entered into by a company that will involve a currency transfer. For example, if a UK company borrows money in the US dollar and it is committed to make interest payments in dollars they are exposed to transaction risk. So that each $1000 interest payment will cost £500 at an exchange rate of £1 = $2. However, if the pound falls sharply in value so that £1 = $1, the $1000 interest payment will now cost £1000.

Translation risk This applies to multinational companies which see their consolidated financial accounts being affected by exchange rate movements. This might occur when a company has various overseas subsidiaries and exchange rate volatility impacts on its consolidated accounts when the subsidiaries' figures are combined into the group's overall financial results.

Economic risk This is caused by exchange rate movements impacting on the competitiveness of a company. Put simply, if a company's home currency appreciates, this will make it less competitive as its goods and services become more expensive in overseas markets. It is normal to see economic risk described as being a much more general risk than either transaction or translation risk.

Hedging This term is widely used in financial markets to indicate that an investment in a financial market product is being made to minimise the risk of any unfavourable movement in the price of a particular financial asset. In the context of the foreign exchange market hedging refers to the process of a company attempting to protect itself against an adverse movement in the foreign exchange market. The most commonly used hedging technique in this context is the forward foreign exchange market. When a company is concerned about foreign currency risk, it can use the forward market to sell or buy in advance a specific amount of currency at a fixed rate on a specific date in the future. This is suitable if a company knows with 100 per cent certainty the amount of foreign currency they will need to buy or sell on that particular date.

FTSE indices First we have the FTSE 100 index. This is the most widely quoted UK stock market index. It is based on the value of the 100 largest UK companies in terms of their market capitalisation. It started with a base of 1000 in January 1984.

Second we have the FTSE 250 index. This is simply an index of the next 250 companies in terms of their market capitalisation.

And then we get to the FTSE 350 index. Put simply, it combines the FTSE 100 and the FTSE-250 indices.

CBI surveys The Confederation of British Industry (CBI) is widely described as the employers' organisation. It is a voluntary group made up of around 1500 UK-based manufacturing companies. It carries out a wide range of surveys to gauge their members' views on the current state of economy activity. It provides a useful overview of the state of manufacturing industry.

11

RISK MANAGEMENT AND HEDGE FUNDS

The surveys are sent out at the end of each quarter and the results are published about three weeks later.

■ What do you think?

1. Define the main types of risks faced by banks.

2. What is the difference between liquidity risk and a liquidity trap?

3. Explain what is meant by the term foreign exchange rate risk.

4. Describe the three main types of currency risk that impact on companies in the UK. Give real examples in each case.

5. Companies have learnt lessons from the previous jumps in the pound and most UK companies remain more reliant on Europe than the US or Asia.

> 'Anecdotally, the strong pound is putting pressure on profit margins but it is not affecting volumes. UK companies lived with a strong exchange rate after 1998 across the board. That led to a great deal of efficiency improvements.'

This paragraph is from the article with the quote from Ian McCafferty, chief economist at the CBI.

You are required to explain what types of measures have been taken by UK companies in recent years to protect themselves from these adverse exchange rate movements.

■ Investigate FT data

You will need the Companies and Markets section of the *Financial Times*. Go to the back page.

Take a look at the Daily Markets Report. Find an example of a company's share price that moves as a result of a movement in the foreign exchange markets.

■ Go to the web

Go the official website of GlaxoSmithKline: www.gsk.com.

Find the latest annual report. Look at the section titled 'Financial position and resources'.

Scroll down to the section on foreign exchange risk management.

a. Write a short note on the types of currency risk faced by GlaxoSmithKline.

b. How does the company manage these risks?

■ Research

Arnold, G. (2008) *Corporate Financial Management*, 4th edn, Harlow, UK: FT Prentice Hall. You should especially look at Chapter 25, pp. 969–91 to see more on the main types of currency risk and how they can be managed.

Berk, J. and DeMarzo, P. (2009) *Corporate Finance*, Harlow, UK: FT Prentice Hall Financial Times. You will find exchange rate risk covered on pp. 939–43.

Gitman, L. (2009) *Principles of Managerial Finance*, 12th edn, Harlow, UK: Pearson International Edition. There is a superb section on exchange rate risk on pp. 817–25.

McLaney, E. (2009) *Business Finance Theory and Practice*, 8th edn, Harlow, UK: FT Prentice Hall Financial Times. The topic of foreign exchange is in Chapter 15. The various types of FX risk start on p. 418.

Pike, R. and Neale, B. (2006) *Corporate Finance and Investment*, 6th edn, Harlow, UK: FT Prentice Hall. You should look at Chapter 21, pp. 620–30 for a superb explanation of 'transaction exposure, translation exposure and economic exposure'.

Pilbeam, K. (2006) *International Finance*, 3rd edn, Basingstoke: Palgrave Macmillan. This has a very clear introduction to the theories of foreign exchange rate determination. You should look in particular at Parts 1 and 2 which cover the balance of payments theory and practice and exchange rate determination: theory, evidence and policy.

Van Horne, J. and Wachowicz, J. R. (2008) *Fundamentals of Financial Management*, 13th edn, Harlow, UK: FT Prentice Hall. You should focus on Chapter 24, pp. 641–55 for a comprehensive coverage of exchange-rate risks.

Watson, D. and Head, A. (2007) *Corporate Finance Principles and Practice*, 4th edn, Harlow, UK: FT Prentice Hall. You should look at Chapter 12. The key section is on pp. 365–6.

11

RISK MANAGEMENT AND HEDGE FUNDS

So tell me, what do these hedge funds actually do?

It used to be the case that ambitious parents would dream of their kids becoming international sports stars scoring the winning goal at the San Siro or sinking the winning put at Augusta to claim their third 'green jacket'. This was their path to glory and financial security. Sadly, these parents might soon start to dream of their offspring setting up a new hedge fund because this seems to be the quickest route to joining the super-rich. We might even see the '101 things you need to know about hedge funds' replace Harry Potter as the bedtime reading of choice.

But what is a hedge fund? In simple terms it is an extreme form of fund management. Hedge funds raise a small amount of initial capital from investors and then borrow money from financial institutions and take much greater financial market risks in the search for spectacular returns both for their clients and also themselves. These funds are often on the front pages of newspapers when they buy a stake in an underperforming company and then demand major changes in their corporate strategy. The company's senior managers are axed and this is then followed by significant rationalisations of the business much to the anger of the employees and the trade unions.

The hedge funds appear to be quite secretive. Certainly their websites contain very little information about their activities. However, the one thing we know for sure is that the amount of money managed by these funds is growing rapidly. It has been estimated that there has been a growth of 25 per cent pa in the cash in these funds since the early 1990s. Their attraction is obvious. In a rising market they can secure vastly superior returns by using complex financial products to maximise their gains and they can even turn falling markets to their financial advantage. Some governments have become concerned about their increasing power and the potential risk that they pose to the world economic order. The worry is that confidence in the financial system could be undermined if one of the larger hedge funds went bankrupt. This article shows the response of the hedge fund industry which is looking for voluntary controls rather than a system of strict official regulation.

Article 32

Financial Times, 20 June, 2007 FT

Facing down the threat of tighter rules

James Mackintosh

When the biggest hedge funds in the world team up, the target is usually quaking in fear at the power wielded by the shadowy asset managers.

But when 13 of the biggest European funds got together yesterday – supported by a score or more of smaller participants – the move was defensive, intended to

Working group members

Brevan Howard, London. Nagi Kawkabani, CEO

Brummer & Partners, Stockholm. Klaus Jäntti, CEO

Centaurus Capital, London. Bernard Oppetit, CEO

Cheyne Capital, London. Stuart Fiertz, president

CQS, London. Michael Hintze, CEO

Gartmore, London. Jeffrey Meyer, CEO

GLG Partners, London. Manny Roman, co-CEO

Lansdowne Partners, London. Paul Ruddock, CEO

London Diversified, London. Rob Standing, founding partner

Man Group, London. Stanley Fink, deputy chairman

Marshall Wace, London. Paul Marshall, chairman

Och-Ziff Capital, New York. Michael Cohen, Europe, CIO

RAB Capital, London. Michael Alen-Buckely, chairman

head off an assault on the industry by regulators.

Hedge fund managers have been watching with increasing horror as political pressure on the private equity industry has ratcheted up, particularly as many critics lump hedge funds in with the buy-out groups they accuse of pillaging companies and endangering jobs.

When Germany unsuccessfully tried to push the Group of Eight to tighten oversight of the industry – already regulated in Europe, but only lightly regulated in the US – that prompted Marshall Wace, one of London's biggest funds, to start calling rivals.

Sir Andrew Large, the former deputy governor of the Bank of England who is heading the working group, said: 'The G8 may have helped to crystallise the process but the recognition that something along these lines was desirable had been developing for some time.

'The idea is really designed to enhance confidence in the sector in the eyes of investors, in the eyes of supervisors, and more generally.'

The funds will look at the various guidelines issued by different groups, such as trade bodies and regulators, and either endorse them or come up with their own voluntary standards, using the 'comply or explain' model from Britain's Combined Code on corporate governance.

The focus of the group is on valuation, disclosure and risk management, all areas of concern to regulators.

It got off to a good start. Before it has even had its first formal meeting Germany, which has been pushing for greater transparency in the industry, and the European Central Bank, welcomed the move.

Peer Steinbrück, German finance minister, said: 'Naturally, I welcome the plan by the hedge funds on self-regulation. I see it as a confirmation of our G8 transparency initiative'.

Germany's G8 move was shot down by other countries, particularly the UK and US, which argued against more government interference in the booming sector.

But it is far from clear that trenchant critics of hedge funds – including left-wing politicians and trade unionists – will be satisfied by the group's review.

Activist hedge fund attacks on underperforming companies, which have led to union protests and criticism of hedge funds as 'locusts' in Germany and Holland, is unlikely to feature in recommendations due next year, said Sir Andrew, who chairs MW Tops, the listed hedge fund.

The group is not likely to become a voluntary regulator, or a self-regulatory body along the lines of the Securities and Investment Board, the Financial Services Authority's predecessor, run by Sir Andrew for five years.

Hedge funds involved in the group have dismissed the idea, raised by Germany last year, of a global database of hedge fund holdings.

'You have to ask the question of disclosure to whom, and about what', Sir Andrew said.

For now, the detailed results of the review remain no more than speculation.

→

But Sir Andrew is hopeful they could form the basis of standards not just for the UK – where 80 per cent of European hedge funds are based – but elsewhere, even though the review is focused on the UK regulatory environment.

'If London hedge funds take the view that this is a good way to go then I hope that others might feel that it could be a sensible way to go as well', he said.

■ The analysis

Many people reading this will be surprised to know that they are already hedge fund investors. If you are working and you have a pension fund the chances are that some of it will be invested in one of the big hedge funds. The best way to analyse this article about the role of hedge funds is to answer five important questions:

1. **What are hedge funds?** Hedge funds have been around for some time but they first came to prominence in the late 1990s when one particular fund got into financial trouble. This was Long-Term Capital Management (LTCM) which had been set up by the former head of bond trading at Salomon Brothers. LTCM borrowed huge amounts from the banks to finance some complex trades in the government bond market. In the wake of the Asian financial crisis they ran up huge losses of some $4.5 bn in 1998. The New York Reserve Bank organised a rescue package involving many major financial institutions which enabled the fund to close without too much of an adverse impact on the world's markets.

    Although hedge funds are engaged in managing funds, they are very different from a traditional pension fund. For example, they are judged in absolute terms, which is in sharp contrast to normal investment funds which see their performance compared to a standard benchmark like a stock market index (for example, the FTSE 100). It could be argued that this makes more sense because a conventional UK equity fund manager is seen to have done well if his fund falls by 20 per cent when the index he is tracking has fallen by much more. This is precious comfort to a fund holder who reads his annual report and sees a sharp fall in the value of his pension fund.

2. **What investment strategies do hedge funds use?**

    (a) *Long-short equity*. How does this work? Let us take the example of the UK stock market. Our hedge fund manager believes that the retail sector is overvalued and it will correct itself shortly. He is especially sure that the share price of Tesco will fall sharply. So he borrows some Tesco shares from a broker and then sells them to a third party. If he is right the shares will soon fall in value. He waits for this to happen and then buys them back at a much lower price. He can then return the stock to the broker that he borrowed them from. The trick is that he buys back the shares at a lower price compared to the price at which he sold the shares when he borrowed them. The message is that the hedge fund can make money if Tesco's share price falls. With this strategy, if Tesco's share price rises, he will lose money.

In reality, this is even simpler than it sounds as the financial engineers who work in the City have designed special products that enable them to 'take this bet' in a much easier way.

So hedge funds can make money from a falling market. In contrast, traditional fund managers tend to either hold shares (if they think they will rise) or at best do nothing, i.e. keeps their money in cash until they think the time is right. So the hedge fund manager has a more flexible investment strategy and can do just as well in a falling as a rising stock market.

(b) *Activist hedge funds.* Some hedge funds will take a large stake in a company and become heavily involved in the day-to-day running of the business. They might believe that the existing senior management team is making poor decisions and so the hedge fund will seek changes. In short, they aim to ensure that the managers of a public company are working every second of every day to maximise the wealth of their shareholders. If you picked up the *Financial Times* almost any day in the spring and early summer of 2007, you would find examples of activist hedge funds in action somewhere in the world. No wonder the managers of businesses are afraid of hedge funds building up a stake in their companies. They know that they will be under pressure to deliver superior returns to the shareholders or face the sack.

(c) *Global macro strategies.* This investment strategy covers a wide range of high-profile areas. The hedge fund manager might use various financial products to take a bet on the next move in interest rates, exchange rates or oil prices. A good example would be the Quantum Fund under the management of George Soros, who made around $1 bn by betting that the UK government could not defend the pound's value against the Deutsche Mark in September 1992.

3. **How do the hedge managers make their money?** They charge substantial fees. This includes a normal annual charge of 2 per cent per annum (management fee). However, what is distinctive about hedge funds is that they also take a percentage of any profits that they make from their investments (typically 20 per cent). This explains the incredible level of returns for the partners in these funds. It is not unusual to see them share annual bonus pools of some £400–500 million split between 30–40 partners. This is not bad work if you can get it.

4. **Why do the regulators want to control them?** Much of the pressure for greater regulation has come from the Group of Eight countries led especially by Germany, which is looking to see far greater control imposed on the hedge funds. However, as the *Financial Times* article says, 'Germany's G8 move was shot down by other countries, particularly the UK and the US, which argued against more government interference in the booming sector'. The concern from Germany is that hedge funds might pose a threat to the global economy. One fear might be that, if they were to make substantial losses and even fold like LTCM, this could have a domino effect on the whole of the banking industry. It should be remembered that many banks have made substantial loans to the hedge funds.

5. **What controls are proposed?** So far the leading hedge funds have tried to propose a system of self-regulation in an attempt to fight off moves for more serious official regulation. Under the chairmanship of Sir Andrew Large, former deputy governor of the Bank of England, the hedge fund's working group is to look into a system of voluntary standards for the UK where the bulk of hedge funds are based.

■ Key terms

Hedge funds This refers to a particular type of investment management where the fund manager will employ a range of different investment tools in an attempt to maximise the returns or try to make gains even in a falling market. The fund will rely on large amounts of borrowing and will use derivative markets and short selling to achieve these aims.

Fund managers The fund manager's main role is to build a successful investment strategy enabling them to optimise the value of the investment portfolio. They will have to monitor financial markets and constantly assess market risks. In addition, they will have to communicate their objectives with their clients.

Activist hedge funds This is very similar to an activist shareholder. An activist hedge fund manager will target companies that are seen to be underperforming compared to their rivals. They will then build up a stake in the business and use their power to demand significant changes in the way the business is being run. This might include an attempt to oust the existing managers or close down loss-making activities.

■ What do you think?

1. What are hedge funds?

2. What are the main differences between a hedge fund and a traditional pension fund?

3. Outline three of the most popular investment strategies used by hedge funds.

4. Why is there growing pressure to see the hedge fund industry much more regulated and controlled?

5. What impact would there be on the UK banking system if a number of large hedge funds were to fail at the same time?

6. In March 2009 a number of hedge funds started to invest in gold. Many people saw this as a way of betting against the policies being adopted by the central banks in response to the economic downturn. The *FT* said at the time that 'a bet on gold is a bet against paper currencies'. Explain why gold might prove to be a good investment if there was a serious risk that there would soon be a significant rise in worldwide inflation due to the actions of the central banks.

■ Research

This is a relatively new type of investment management, so there is only limited coverage so far in the main corporate finance textbooks. The best place to learn more about hedge funds is through reading the *Financial Times* regularly. There are articles most weeks on their performance and regulation.

Coggan, P. (2008) *Guide to Hedge Funds: What they are, what they do, their risks, their advantages*, London: Economist Books.

Peston, R. (2008) *Who Runs Britain and Who's to Blame for the Economic Mess We're /In*, London: Hodder Paperbacks.

Stefanini, F. (2006) *Investment Strategies of Hedge Funds*, Chichester: The Wiley Finance Series.

Go to **www.pearsoned.co.uk/boakes** to access Kevin's blog for additional analysis of recent topical news articles and to post your comments. Download podcasts containing short audio summaries of the main issues relating to each article and check your understanding of in-text questions with the handy hints provided.

Bank failures featuring Northern Rock and Citigroup

The first edition of this book was written largely against the backdrop of the economic boom of 2006 and early 2007. This accounted for the optimistic articles on investment banking, private equity and hedge funds. It was a time of ever-rising City bonuses when the Labour government embraced the importance of the City to the UK economy. The one exception was the topic based on the demise of Northern Rock, which was a late addition in the last few months before publication. In many ways that topic is the bridge that takes us into this new updated edition which inevitably reflects the economic recession. One strange anomaly of this period is that, though there were some corporate bankruptcies (such as Woolworths covered in Topic 6), given the severity of the downturn relatively few companies went bust. Indeed, if you examined the constituents of a major stock market index from mid-2007 and compared it to the same one in mid-2009, you would find the names looked very similar.

The one exception to this would be in the banking sector, which went through a period of unrivalled consolidation and change. The banks that led the rush into reckless mortgage lending either went bust or had to be saved by another financial institution or the government. There was an almost total collapse of confidence in the banking system internationally which resulted in the rush of bank failures. A number of iconic banking names disappeared forever, and it became clear that the general public would never fully trust their banks and the promises they made ever again.

Some of the bank failures
Lehman Brothers fails.
Northern Rock nationalised.
Bradford and Bingley nationalised.
Alliance and Leicester taken over.
AIG bailed out.
Royal Bank of Scotland (record losses of £24 bn in 2008) bailed out.
Bank of America bailed out.
Citigroup bailed out (partial nationalisation: the US government becomes largest shareholder with a 36 per cent stake).
Merrill Lynch taken over.
HBOS taken over.
Freddie Mac and Fannie Mae both bailed out.
Lloyds TSB bailed out.

In discussing this topic, I have chosen to focus on just two examples of bank failure in order to highlight the reasons behind these catastrophic events and to analyse the role of governments in trying to prevent the banks' demise since it would have led to financial and economic meltdown. We start by updating the story of Northern Rock, which still provides important lessons about the problems caused when uncontrolled greed meets an almost total absence of risk management. You can read more on risk in Topic 11.

In the first article we see the origins of the crisis in the sub-prime market in the United States which led to the deepening credit crisis and its consequences for financial markets across the world. In the second and third articles we focus on the repo and interbank markets at a time when banks were no longer willing to lend to each other. In the fourth article we see how the UK authorities were finally forced to act to save Northern Rock. They realised that they could not allow a major bank to go bust. Such an event would have had far-reaching consequences for the reputation of the UK banking system for years to come. In the final article we complete the story of Northern Rock's demise as the UK government is finally forced to nationalise the business.

The second example of bank failure added to this topic examines the failure and subsequent bailout of the Citigroup. In the analysis of this article we will see how the US government came together with other parties to rescue a bank that was one of the hardest hit by the ongoing credit crisis. It was a perfect example of a bank that floated high in the atmosphere of euphoria and unrestrained growth prevalent in the first few years of this millennium and then crashed to the ground as economies faltered and financial markets crashed.

The following six articles are analysed in this section:

Article 33
Fresh turmoil in equity markets
Financial Times, 11–12 August 2007

Article 34
Repo market little known but crucial to the system
Financial Times, 11–12 August 2007

Article 35
Growing sense of crisis over interbank deals
Financial Times, 5 September 2007

Article 36
Bank throws Northern Rock funding lifeline
Financial Times, 13 September 2007

Article 37
Brown saw no other option
Financial Times, 18 February 2008

Article 38
US government agrees to take biggest single stake in Citigroup
Financial Times, 28 February 2009

These articles address the following issues:

- the credit crisis;
- mortgage-backed securities;
- the sub-prime crisis;
- retail and wholesale deposits;
- the repurchase markets;
- the interbank markets;
- structured investment vehicles;
- lender of last resort facility;
- the role of the Bank of England, Financial Services Authority and the UK treasury;
- the nationalisation of Northern Rock;
- preferred shares;
- sovereign wealth funds.

Bank 1: Northern Rock: the road to nationalisation

At the start of 2007 if you had gone into the street and asked some random people to name a UK bank, you would have found that very few mentioned Northern Rock. Unless, that is, you carried out this survey on the streets of the north-east of England where it was based. However, just a few months later this bank's name became world famous almost overnight. It came close to being the first UK bank to fail in almost 141 years. The media revelled in capturing the daily drama as queues of worried savers waited patiently to remove all their money from their accounts. Their fear was that it was about to fail, and they were concerned that in such an event only the first £2000 of their savings would be fully protected by the Financial Services Compensation Scheme (plus 90 per cent of savings from £2000 to £35 000). Many of the savers had far more than this upper limit in their accounts.

There is little doubt that the resulting panic at one stage threatened to undermine confidence in the other banks and indeed the entire UK financial system looked at serious risk of meltdown. Against that background the government, the Bank of England and the Financial Services Authority were finally forced into action to shore up Northern Rock. On the 17 September 2007 at 6 p.m. the Chancellor, Alistair Darling, came on TV and announced that all savings at the bank would be 100 per cent protected. In the analysis of these five articles we will see how the crisis developed and how it ended up with the ultimate nationalisation of Northern Rock in February 2008.

Article 33

Financial Times, 11–12 August 2007 **FT**

Fresh turmoil in equity markets

Krishna Guha, Michael Mackenzie and Gillian Tett

Fresh turmoil gripped financial markets yesterday with shares in London and Europe suffering their worst one-day fall in four years and Japan also tumbling sharply as the US Federal Reserve and other central banks scrambled to avert a liquidity crunch.

As worries spread over deepening troubles arising from credit markets, the Fed was forced to drop its 'business as usual' stance to inject $35 bn (£17 bn) into the financial system to stem the risk of crisis.

The Fed also promised to provide whatever funding was needed to ensure the banks were able to continue lending to each other at normal rates.

The moves marked the most radical action taken by the US central bank to calm markets since the aftermath of 9/11 and followed similar emergency moves by the European Central Bank and the Japanese central bank in the past two days.

In another sign of its concern about the situation in the markets, the Fed started accepting high-quality mortgage-backed securities as collateral for the entirety of these funds – something it rarely deems acceptable.

These moves were apparently triggered by signs of faltering confidence in banks worldwide, with financial stocks tumbling and interbank borrowing rates surging as institutions became more nervous of extending credit lines to each other. Bank stocks sold off sharply, amid intense speculation over the extent of credit markets troubles.

In London, the FTSE-100 suffered its worst fall in more than four years. After losing 1.9 per cent in the previous session, the index slumped a further 232.9 points – 3.7 per cent – to 6038.3. The FTSE-100 has been the only major stock index so far to officially 'correct' – having fallen more than 10 per cent from its June peak.

Northern Rock, the bank, fell 9.6 per cent to 713.5p while hedge fund manager Man Group tumbled 9.1 per cent to 479p.

The FTSE Euro first also suffered its worst day in four years, falling 3.04 per cent. In Asia, the Nikkei 225 Average relinquished its gains for the year, falling 2.4 per cent.

On Wall Street, the Dow Jones Industrial Average and the S&P 500 tumbled sharply on opening trade but were both set to close virtually flat.

The radical Fed action yesterday calmed the mood in the US interbank market. At midday, the effective Fed funds rate was trading near its target level of 5.25 per cent, after surging earlier to 6 per cent.

■ The analysis

How did the crisis in the credit markets start?

The downside of the increased internationalisation of financial markets is that an economic event in one country can now have major consequences for financial markets and institutions that are based in other countries. In this case the crisis at Northern Rock can be traced to the United States. In the aftermath of the terrorist attacks in New York on 11 September 2001 the Federal Reserve Bank embarked on a series of interest rate cuts that culminated in their main short-term interest rate, the Federal funds rate, hitting a low of just 1 per cent in June 2004. The result of this easing in monetary policy was that the economy boomed, fuelled by the availability of cheap credit. The housing market benefited from these conditions with homeowners seeing sharp rises in house prices throughout the country. Not surprisingly, this began to encourage more and more people into the housing market in the search for capital growth. Some of these were lower-income borrowers and the US banks were all too willing to lend to these groups that in the past might have been considered to be too risky. This was the birth of the 'sub-prime lending market' in the US. However, this boom soon gave way to bust as the Fed's policy went into reverse with a significant tightening in monetary policy and the resulting increase in mortgage rates causing many homeowners to be forced into defaults on their loans. In the wake of record repossessions the housing market crashed and the 'sub-prime crisis' was born.

During summer of 2007 this new phenomenon started to hit the headlines across the world as the problems in the US started to impact on other countries. The problem was that these mortgages had been pooled together and sold as 'mortgage-backed securities' to international banks across the globe. This meant that it was not clear which of them had the greatest exposure to the risks associated with the sub-prime crisis. In June Bear Stearns, the US investment bank, were forced to admit that it had made $1.6 bn losses in its hedge funds which owned vast amounts of these sub-prime mortgage debts. In August the French bank, BNP Paribas, had to suspend some of their investment funds that were also exposed to these debts. Other large banks began to calculate their financial exposure to this problem. Soon speculation mounted as the search was on for the banks at greatest risk. Stock market investors were quick to liquidate their holdings in banking shares. In the first article taken from August 2007 we see quite clearly the impact that this was having on financial markets as the 'liquidity crisis' began to bite. As a result 'the Federal Reserve was forced 'to inject $35 bn (£17 bn) into the financial system to stem the risk of a crisis'.

How did this crisis impact on Northern Rock?

In the wake of these developments international banks started to become concerned about lending money to each other. Suddenly the interbank market, which is normally seen to be an almost risk-free prospect, was perceived to be potentially highly risky. If one bank lent a large amount of funds to another bank and that bank ran into severe difficulties because of its exposure to the 'sub-prime crisis', there could be a significant risk of default on these loans. The Federal Reserve attempted to calm fears in the interbank market by promising to inject enough liquidity as was necessary 'to ensure that the banks were able to continue lending to each other at normal rates'. In addition, it began to accept mortgage-backed securities as collateral for its short-term money market operations (called 'repurchase' operations). These actions did have the desired result in calming the mood in the money markets with the effective Federal funds rate falling from 6 per cent back to 5 per cent close to the Fed's target level. However, in the equity markets there were clear signs of nervousness with the FT-SE 100 index falling sharply to close at a little over 6000. And there was a clear sign of things to come as one Bank's share in particular was hit. The shares in Northern Rock fell by 9.6 per cent to 713.5 p. The crisis at Northern Rock was beginning.

| Article 34 | *Financial Times*, 11–12 August 2007 **FT** |

Repo market little known but crucial to the system

Michael Mackenzie

The repurchase, or repo, market is a little-known part of the financial system but it acts as a crucial safety valve in times of stress. It enables the flow of cash between central banks and financial institutions, providing the plumbing that keeps markets functioning smoothly.

This week, as financiers faced higher overnight borrowing costs in the money markets, central banks came to the rescue and flooded the financial system with cash. This was done to keep in line with one another the actual and target overnight borrowing rates, such as the US Federal Reserve's Fed funds rate.

The Fed injects cash into the money market on a daily basis so that the effective rate stays near its present target level of 5.25 per cent. Early yesterday the effective funds rate traded at 6 per cent as banks demanded higher rates to lend to each other, and then fell towards 5.375 per cent after the Fed injected $35 bn (€26 bn, £17 bn) in two separate operations.

This week, money market rates for eurodollar deposits and commercial paper rose well above normal levels. That meant banks, companies, insurers and hedge funds that rely on using short-term funding faced higher costs.

That pressure pushed the Fed funds rate higher, which, if sustained, could imperil the economy.

In the Fed's repo operation, dealers posted mortgage securities as collateral and received cash in return from the Fed. Next week, the dealers and the Fed will reverse the trade. Usually, the Fed does not accept mortgages as collateral for repo transactions but the move signals an attempt by the central bank to alleviate financing fears.

Wall Street dealers are seeking the sanctuary of government bonds and are selling their holdings of riskier assets such as mortgages.

Traders said that if the financing problems continued and the effective funds rate remained above its target level, the Fed was likely to repeat repo operations until the market settled down.

'Central banks can ultimately fix a liquidity crunch by shipping in boatloads of cash and they are effectively doing that', said Alan Ruskin of RBS Greenwich Capital.

'There is very little doubt that they will come through in the end.'

Article 35

Financial Times, 5 September 2007 **FT**

Growing sense of crisis over interbank deals

Gillian Tett

As bankers have returned to their desks this week after the summer break, they have been searching frantically for signs that the markets are gaining a semblance of calm after the August turmoil.

However, the money markets are notably failing to offer any reassurance. While the tone of equity markets has calmed, the sense of crisis in the interbank markets actually appears to be growing – especially in London.

In particular, the cost of borrowing funds in the three-month money markets – as illustrated by measures such as sterling Libor or Euribor – is continuing to rise, suggesting a frantic scramble for liquidity among financial groups.

This trend is deeply unnerving for policymakers and investors alike, not least because it is occurring even though the European Central Bank and the US Federal Reserve have taken repeated steps in recent weeks to calm down the money markets.

'What is happening right now suggests that the moves by the Fed and ECB just haven't worked as we hoped', admits one senior international policymaker.

Or as UniCredit analysts say: 'The interbank lending business has broken down almost completely ... it is a global phenomenon and not restricted to just the euro and dollar markets.'

If this situation continues, it could potentially have very serious implications.

→

One of the most important functions of the money markets is to channel liquidity in the banking system to where it is most needed.

If these markets seize up for any lengthy period, there is a risk that individual institutions may discover they no longer have access to the funds they need.

This danger has already materialised for vehicles that depend on the asset-backed commercial paper sector – short-term notes backed by collateral such as mortgages.

In recent weeks, investors have increasingly refused to re-invest in this paper.

As Axel Weber, a member of the ECB council, admitted this weekend: 'The institutions most affected currently are conduits and structured investment vehicles ... Their ability to roll these short-term commercial papers is impaired by the events in the sub-prime segment of the US housing market.'

This problem is affecting the wider banking system because these vehicles are now tapping other sources of finance – mainly liquidity lines from banks.

It appears that the prospect of receiving new liquidity demands has prompted banks to rush to raise funds – and, above all, hoard any liquidity they hold.

The high demand from banks to secure liquidity for the next three months, coupled with their desire not to lend out what liquidity they have, has made it virtually impossible to execute trades – even at the official prices quoted for such borrowing.

That has created some extraordinary dislocations such as the fact that the cost of borrowing three-month money in the sterling Libor markets is now higher than borrowing six-month or 12-month money. 'The system has just completely frozen up – everyone is hoarding', says one bank treasurer. 'The published Libor rates are a fiction.'

This situation could become increasingly dangerous in part because many other markets, such as swaps, are priced off the three-month Libor and Euribor rates. So the interbank freeze could have knock-on effects throughout the financial system.

A more pressing problem is the large volume of asset-backed commercial paper due to expire in coming weeks, which is set to increase the scramble for cash by the banks. 'Money market stability needs to return as soon as possible', says William Sels, of Dresdner Kleinwort. Jan Loeys, of JPMorgan, notes: 'The longer it lasts, the greater the risk that the current liquidity crisis will worsen.'

The crucial uncertainty is what, if anything, policymakers can do to combat the sense of panic. Some observers hope the problems in the sterling market, at least, may dissipate when the current maintenance period at the Bank of England comes to an end.

Others, such as Mr Weber, have suggested that banks themselves need to raise more funds in the capital markets to meet liquidity calls. However, many private sector bankers, for their part, say that radical steps from the central bankers are needed to remove the sense of panic.

Whether the central bankers are willing or able to really help – in the UK or anywhere else – remains the great question.

■ The analysis

What role did the repo and the interbank markets play?

The repo, or to give it its full name the repurchase market, lies at the heart of the banking system in most countries. The clearing banks are involved in a great deal of financial activity each day that results in large amounts of cash flowing in and out of their accounts. For example, if a large number of customers withdraw cash to spend in the shops through their cashpoint cards, this will result in that bank seeing a significant reduction in liquidity. At the same time another bank might see an exceptional number of customers making cash deposits, which results in an increase in their liquidity. These daily cash imbalances are not a serious problem and they are largely alleviated through the commercial banks lending cash to each other to meet their short-term needs. This is done through the key money market which is the London Interbank Offered Rate (Libor). There are times, however, when the entire banking system requires a cash injection from outside. This is where the repo market comes into centre stage. As Article 34 says 'the repurchase, or repo, market is a little known part of the financial system but it acts as a crucial safety valve in times of stress'.

So how does a repo work?

Stage 1

The Central Bank
It has spare liquidity that it is willing to inject into the money markets

The Commercial Bank
It needs to make up a liquidity shortage by borrowing money.
It has plenty of collateral available in the form of high-quality government bonds.

Stage 2

The Central Bank
Announces the availability of a 14-day repo facility at a fixed interest rate.
This means that it will make a short-term (14-day) purchase of high-quality government bonds from a commercial bank.

The Commercial Bank
It makes a short-term (14-day) sale of £500 m of government bonds to the central bank.

Stage 3 (in 14 days' time)

Central Bank
It sells back the £500 m of government bonds to the commercial bank at the same price that it paid for them plus an additional amount equal to the repo rate on the 14-day loan.

The Commercial Bank
It is obliged to repurchase the £500 m of government bonds from the central bank and in addition pay an extra amount equal to the repo rate for the 14-day loan.

One key function of these repo operations is to ensure that money market rates stay close to the central bank's desired target level. As Article 34 says: 'The Fed injects cash into the money market on a daily basis so that the effective [Fed fund] rate stays near its present target level of 5.25 per cent'. However, the impact of the credit crisis began to spread into the interbank markets with the effective Fed funds rate hitting 6 per cent as the banks became increasingly reluctant to lend to each other. Effectively for a period in late August and early September 2007 the interbank markets stopped functioning. This is clear from Article 35 which reports that 'the cost of borrowing funds in the three-month money markets – as illustrated by measures such as sterling Libor or Euribor – is continuing to rise, suggesting a frantic scramble for liquidity among financial groups'. There was particular unease about these developments as the problems were continuing in the interbank markets despite strong measures being taken by the Fed and the European Central Bank in an effort to restore normal trading in these markets.

This had very serious implications because of the number of financial institutions and markets that were dependent on this form of short-term funding. The world economy faced the risk of a sudden collapse into recession if the liquidity in the money markets continued to drain away. As Article 35 notes, there were serious concerns especially in the markets for commercial paper, short-term asset-backed securities, as investors become reluctant to re-invest in these instruments. Liquidity in the banking system was virtually non-existent with banks unwilling to lend funds, while at the same time they were desperately searching for additional three-month borrowing themselves. As a result, even the published interbank interest rates were largely irrelevant as traders could not execute deals at these levels.

The key question facing financial markets at this time was whether the central banks would be able to inject enough liquidity to restore normal trading in the money markets. As Article 35 puts it: 'Whether the central bankers are willing or able to really help – in the UK or anywhere else–remains the great question'. This would soon be answered.

Article 36

Financial Times, 13 September 2007 **FT**

Bank throws Northern Rock funding lifeline

Peter Thal Larsen and Neil Hume

The Bank of England will on Friday throw a lifeline to Northern Rock by providing emergency funding to the beleaguered mortgage lender that has fallen victim to the liquidity squeeze in the banking sector.

In an unprecedented move, the Bank, working with the Financial Services Authority and the Treasury, will step in to bail out Northern Rock by providing it with a short-term credit line that will allow it to carry on operating. The rescue, approved by the Chancellor of the Exchequer, is the most dramatic illustration to date of how the British banking sector is being hit by the wave of turmoil that has paralysed the money markets.

It will lift the uncertainty that has been hanging over Northern Rock's future for much of the past month because it could not access the wholesale funding upon which it is heavily dependent. The Bank is also expected to reassure thousands of Northern Rock's customers that their deposits are secure.

Northern Rock is the first institution to be propped up since the Bank, in 1998, revised the rules under which it will act as a lender of last resort to banks in financial difficulty. The Bank is expected to say on Friday that a similar facility is available to any other institution facing short-term difficulties. However, it is understood that no other banks have asked for financial support.

The Bank is understood to be confident about the quality of Northern Rock's mortgage book, which has no exposure to sub-prime borrowers and which will provide collateral for the emergency facility. But the bank, one of the UK's largest mortgage lenders, has proved particularly vulnerable to the liquidity squeeze because it has a smaller deposit base than other lenders.

Northern Rock approached the Bank at the end of last week to discuss using the facility, people familiar with the situation said. The bank made its decision because it faced pressure to refinance obligations, including mortgage-backed securities that will mature in the next couple of weeks.

Northern Rock executives are expected to say on Friday that it will try to trade through its difficulties with the help of the Bank of England facility.

However, the move is likely to make it harder for Northern Rock to remain independent.

The bail-out is a devastating blow for the bank, which grew from its roots as a building society in the north-east of England to become the most efficient mortgage lender in the UK, winning wide praise for its business model and its ability to take advantage of the innovations in the capital markets.

The bank is set to issue a trading update on Friday describing the impact of the recent market turmoil on its business.

Northern Rock, the Bank of England, the FSA and the Treasury all declined to comment.

Since hitting their peak in February, shares in Northern Rock have lost half their value amid concerns that the rising cost of wholesale funding would squeeze margins and limit the bank's growth. On Thursday, the shares closed down 33 p, or 4.9 per cent, at 639 p.

The turmoil will fuel speculation that Northern Rock could end up being taken over by a bank with a larger retail funding base. The bank, which derives almost all its revenues from the UK market, would be an attractive takeover target for several UK lenders or European banks seeking to establish a foothold in the UK. However, any buyer is likely to take a careful look at Northern Rock's balance sheet before making an offer.

About a quarter of Northern Rock's balance sheet is funded by retail deposits, with the rest coming from various sources of wholesale funding.

It raised £10.8 bn in mortgage-backed securities in the first half of the year. But any further securitisation is thought to be on hold until market conditions improve.

Note: additional reporting by Neil Hume.

12

BANK FAILURES FEATURING NORTHERN ROCK AND CITIGROUP

■ The analysis

How did the government and the Bank of England act to save Northern Rock?

The growing crisis in the world's financial markets increasingly focused on one UK bank in particular. That bank was Northern Rock, which had enjoyed a rapid rise since its stock market flotation in October 1997. The obvious question is: why did it impact on that bank especially? The answer is that they had a particularly aggressive business model. Unlike other banks that get most of their funds from their savers, Northern Rock had raised its finance largely from the financial markets. As the *Financial Times* article says, 'About a quarter of Northern Rock's balance sheet is funded by retail deposits, with the rest coming from various sources of wholesale funding'. In the first half of 2007 this amounted to some £10.8 bn in mortgage-backed securities. This is where large amounts of mortgages are pooled together and then sold on in the form of financial market securities. They made up any short-term funding needs by accessing the wholesale money markets. In the wake of the credit crisis both these avenues of funding were effectively shut down. Northern Rock had run out of cash and it was heading into a financial meltdown.

The story was finally broken by Robert Peston, the BBC's business correspondent, on 13 September on the BBC's *News 24* service. The next day queues started to form outside all their branches as worried customers tried to remove their cash deposits. The fourth *Financial Times* article in this case study reports that 'The Bank of England will on Friday throw a lifeline to Northern Rock by providing emergency funding to the beleaguered mortgage lender that has fallen victim to the liquidity squeeze in the banking sector'. The article discloses that in a unique operation the Bank would be combining with the Financial Services Authority and the Treasury in an attempt to reassure investors and to stop any further casualties among the UK banking industry.

The Bank's lending to Northern Rock comes under its key function as 'the lender of last resort'. This means that if a bank is in financial difficulty it can always go to the central bank to obtain emergency funding. Despite this intervention by the Bank of England the queues continued to grow each day. Finally on the 17 September at 6 p.m. in the evening the Chancellor used the opportunity of a televised press conference with the US Trade Secretary, Henry Paulson, to make an announcement that the government had agreed to guarantee all the deposits held at Northern Rock. This action effectively ended the run on the bank and the queues outside their branches gradually disappeared. In a twin move a few days later the Bank of England announced that it would inject £10 bn into the UK money markets to try to reduce the cost of interbank borrowing. It also allowed, for the first time, banks to use a wider group of assets to act as collateral for these loans, including mortgages. In the immediate term these actions calmed savers and rebuilt some confidence in financial markets. However, there were longer-term worries that the actions of the UK authorities in bailing out Northern Rock might have encouraged other banks to attempt to adopt a similarly risky business model. This is termed 'moral hazard' and it is quite possible that this had been injected into the financial system, but in reality the government and the Bank of England had little choice but to act. The risk of a major UK bank going bust was simply too great for any government to take.

Brown saw no other option

George Parker and Peter Thal Larsen

Gordon Brown took the agonising decision to nationalise Northern Rock at around 2 p.m. in Downing Street yesterday after he and Alistair Darling concluded there was no other option, write George Parker and Peter Thal Larsen.

Mr Brown's verdict came even as one of the bidders, the bank's management team, was still answering questions about its proposal on Sunday morning. The management group and Sir Richard Branson's Virgin consortium had sent in final bids on Friday night, having had earlier offers rejected.

Goldman Sachs, the government's advisers, realised the bids still failed to offer good value for money for the taxpayer. Virgin came closest to matching the Treasury benchmark.

The Treasury negotiating team, led by one of its top officials, John Kingman, went back for more. Virgin was told it would have to give the taxpayer a greater share of any upturn in fortunes and pay more in return for a government-backed bond issue. Sir Richard could not offer more.

Even if Virgin met Treasury conditions, it might have had to tweak its plan to reflect changes required by state aid authorities in Brussels.

There may have been other concerns. According to people close to the negotiations, the prime minister was reluctant to nationalise Northern Rock but feared the Virgin bid would amount to delayed nationalisation because shareholders would reject it. Whitehall officials dispute this.

Mr Kingman decided late on Saturday that the private sale option had run its course. 'Goldman Sachs came to the same conclusion', said a government insider. Virgin was told not to bother supplying any new information.

Ron Sandler, lined up to run the nationalised bank, only learned he had got the job on Sunday afternoon.

■ The analysis

The final stage: nationalising Northern Rock

Following the bailout of Northern Rock their chief executive, Adam Applegarth, resigned from his position on the 16 November 2007. At this stage the clear aim of the government was to identify another private-sector group that was willing to pay a high price for the business and also to offer a speedy plan for the government's loans to the beleaguered bank to be repaid. The two initial bidders to emerge were the Olivant group, led by former Abbey boss Luqman Arnold, and the Virgin Group, headed by Sir Richard Branson. A little later there was also a proposal from the existing managers of Northern Rock to rescue the bank. Sadly for the government the financial value of the various bids was considered to be simply too low. Selling out at the offered prices meant there was a risk that the business might be bought out and re-structured and then sold on, giving one of the bidders a substantial profit during the lifetime of the current government. This would have been quite an embarrassment for the Prime Minister and his Chancellor if either of the prospective buyers had been able to make such a spectacular return on their investment. Imagine the headlines in the press if the Virgin Group had pocketed a £1.5 bn profit 'at the expense of the poor old British taxpayer'. This could have done irrevocable damage to the Labour government's reputation.

So in the end the government's advisers, Goldman Sachs, decided that 'the private sale option had run its course' and on the 17 February 2008 the bank was nationalised, with Ron Sandler confirmed as the new executive chairman. The clear losers in this whole business were the shareholders of Northern Rock. In the wake of the announcement trading in their shares was immediately suspended. It was left to an independent firm to assess their monetary value on the day of the nationalisation. This resulted in the shareholders taking legal action alleging that the government's compensation scheme left the value of the shares at virtually zero compared to the book value of Northern Rock before the nationalisation which amounted to some £4 per share.

So should we feel sorry for the shareholders? In one sense it is hard to ignore the massive financial loss that many of them suffered through no fault of their own. However, if this outcome reinforced the reality that investment in shares is a risky business this could be a useful warning for future investors.

Bank 2: Back in the USA, the government acts to save Citigroup

As we have seen earlier in this Topic the credit crisis was firmly 'born in the USA' and in this final article we examine the remarkable collapse of the US bank, Citigroup. If one bank personified the excesses of the banking world in the heady days of 2006 it was Citigroup. This was a bank that had built its ambitious growth model on a high-risk investment strategy. It was one of the market leaders in the new markets of mortgage-backed securities and collaterised debt obligations. The bank's senior managers seem to have encouraged a culture that involved taking ever greater risks in order to grow the business and to reap substantial financial rewards. Traders at Citigroup specialised in creating billions of dollars worth of the now infamous 'mortgage-backed securities'. In the good times this model worked, and the bank made billions of dollars from consumer borrowing (credit cards), housing debt (mortgages), corporate borrowing (company loans), merger advice (investment banking fees) and the activities of their investment banking teams (trading profits). Sadly, there was insufficient attention paid to the key area of providing independent risk management for all these activities.

In particular, nobody bothered to ask the key question: what happens if the economy slows and house prices start to fall?

Article 38   *Financial Times*, 28 February 2009   FT

US government agrees to take biggest single stake in Citigroup

Francesco Guerrera and Alan Beattie

The US government agreed to become the biggest single shareholder in Citigroup yesterday, in the latest attempt to save the ailing financial group and to shore up the country's banking system.

The partial nationalisation will give the government a stake of up to 36 per cent in the troubled lender, capping a spectacular fall from grace for what was one of the world's largest financial institutions.

At yesterday's share price, the market value of Citi – which has some $1600 bn (£1117 bn) in assets and operations in 130 countries – was less than $9 bn. The latest plan, the third time in four months that the authorities have had to rescue Citi,

marks the first time the government has had to take a big stake in a bank with this scale and geographical reach.

The government's stake in Citi will bolster its depleted capital base but will also increase the authorities' sway over the company and Vikram Pandit, its chief executive. Mr Pandit said the deal would not change Citi's 'strategy, operations or governance'. But the government has already told Citi to revamp its board by appointing new independent directors and is likely to further constrain its activities in risky areas.

The rescue has been closely watched by investors as a possible model for others.

Under the plan, first reported by the *Financial Times* last week, the Treasury will not provide fresh funds but convert up to $25 bn of its $45 bn-worth of preferred stock into common equity at $3.25 per share – a 30 per cent premium to Citi's closing price on Thursday.

Other preferred shareholders, including Government of Singapore Investment Corporation and Saudi Arabia's Prince Alwaleed, will convert up to $27.5 bn of their holdings at the same price.

The deal would result in a huge dilution for the bank's common shareholders. Shares were down 35 per cent at $1.58 in early afternoon in New York.

Analysts said the structure of the deal made it virtually impossible for common or preferred shareholders not to approve it, as failure to convert the shares or ratify the deal would end Citi's life as a public company.

■ The analysis

When the credit crisis appeared with a vengeance in the summer of 2007 the problems at Citigroup quickly began to surface. By the early autumn the bank was forced to write off $1.3 bn worth of sub-prime, mortgage-related assets. A slow death of Citigroup had begun and its share price went into an almost permanent slide, reducing the company's stock market value from a high of nearly $240 bn to a little over $20 bn in just two years. By the autumn of 2008 Citigroup was forced to go to the US government for urgent financial assistance. After emergency talks with the US Treasury, the New York reserve bank and Citigroup's shareholders a rescue deal was put in place to head off a further sell-off of their shares. In a further move the bank ran full-page adverts in newspapers to reassure investors and customers that the bank would survive the crisis. The US government agreed to provide emergency support by injecting $45 bn in return for taking preference shares in the bank. These shares were far from free money for the bank as they agreed to pay a 5 per cent rate of dividend on them.

Despite this cash injection the problems at Citigroup remained severe and, as the *FT* article included here shows, in early 2009 the US government was forced once again to step in to save Citigroup. They feared that the bankruptcy of Citigroup could easily have risked the collapse of the country's entire banking system. There is little doubt that among the US authorities who were firmly committed to the 'free-market' model there was a strong antipathy towards the government taking an equity stake in any privately owned bank. This was the chief reason for them allowing both Lehman Brothers and Bear Stearns to fail at an earlier stage in the credit crisis. However, by the time that Citigroup was in serious trouble the US government had little choice but to act. It was a case of step in and partly nationalise the bank or face the unthinkable prospect of allowing it to go under as well. In the event Citigroup reached a deal which left the US government owning 36 per cent of the struggling bank. This new rescue plan was built on the earlier programme of assistance for the bank. It would see the conversion of up to $25 bn of the preference shares into ordinary shares at a price of $3.25/share. The advantage to Citigroup was that the dividend on these shares would only be a nominal amount. In addition, it would now not have to pay the 5 per cent dividend on the remaining preference shares.

This swapping of preference shares for ordinary shares was also adopted by the other holders of Citigroup shares including various sovereign wealth funds (SWFs) such as the Government of Singapore Investment Corporation as well as such extremely wealthy private investors as Saudi Arabia's Prince Alwaleed Bin Talal. Before the banking crisis a number of the SWFs had been viewed with deep suspicion. The concern had been that their acquisition of large stakes in Western-owned companies might allow some countries to extend their influence and possibly to use this power in a detrimental way. However, when the banks ran out of cash, many larger governments across the world were forced to put such concerns on the back burner in the desperate search for cash for their beleaguered banks.

Against a background of the slightly more stable economic background that existed in early June 2009 Citigroup were able to report their first quarterly net profits for almost two years. The bank actually made a profit of some $1.6 bn compared to losses of over $5 bn in the same period a year before. However, allowing for the dividend payments to preferred shareholders, this profit turned into a $1 bn loss. Despite this, the results were still better than expected, resulting in a temporary bounce in the share price to $3.65 per share. The damage suffered by its longstanding shareholders can be shown by comparing this figure to the peak level of the share price which was close to $60/share in 2006 before the credit crisis was born.

It should be clear from these examples from both sides of the Atlantic that, when the banks got into trouble, the big losers were their shareholders and their many employees who lost their jobs. We can but hope that the banks learnt lessons and that their mistakes would not be repeated in the future.

■ Key terms

Federal Reserve The Federal Reserve is the central bank of the United States. The key part of the Fed is the Federal Open Market Committee (FOMC) that decides on changes in US monetary policy. It is made up of 12 individuals. The core seven come from the Central Federal Reserve Bank (based in Washington) and the other five represent the various Federal District Reserve Banks. One of these, New York, has a permanent place on the FOMC. The other 11 banks share the remainder of the votes on a complex rotation system. The FOMC reviews the outlook for the economy before deciding on the next move in interest rates.

Credit crunch This refers to the cost and availability of credit. It might be a government borrowing (in the government bond market), a company borrowing (in the corporate bond market), a house owner (with a mortgage) or a consumer (with a credit card). We have a 'credit crunch' when the cost of borrowing is considered to be prohibitively expensive by historic standards or it is simply very difficult for more risky borrowers to obtain finance at all.

Mortgage-backed securities This is where a large amount of mortgage debt is pooled together and then sold to a different set of investors in the form of a securitised financial market instrument.

Collateral This refers to any property or other assets that can be given as security on a loan. If the borrower fails to make timely interest payments or return the principal, these assets can be seized.

FTSE 100 We start with the FTSE 100, which is the most is widely quoted UK stock market index. It is based on the value of the 100 largest UK companies in terms of their market capitalisation. It started with a base level of 1000 in January 1984. This index is now quoted in real time on the various news information systems that serve the city traders.

Hedge funds This refers to a particular type of investment management where the fund manager will employ a range of different investment tools in an attempt to maximise the returns or try to make gains even in a falling market. The fund will rely on large amounts of borrowing and will use derivative markets and short selling to achieve these aims.

FTSE Eurofirst (300) This is one of the *FT*'s more recently created stock market indices. It attempts to track the performance of the leading European stock markets. It is shown on the Front of the *FT* each day in the World Markets Data section.

Nikkei 225 This is the most closely followed index of Japanese share prices. The index is quite broad as it is based on Japan's top 225 blue-chip companies quoted on the Tokyo Stock Exchange.

Dow Jones Industrial Average The DJIA is the main US stock market index. It is based on the market movements of 30 of the largest blue-chip industrial companies that trade on the New York Stock Exchange. The selection of these companies is revised regularly. It includes companies like American Express, Boeing, Disney, General Electric, Honeywell, Intel, JP Morgan Bank, Procter and Gamble.

Fed funds (effective) This is the most important short-term interest rate in the United States. It refers to the overnight interbank lending that takes place in the United States money markets. The money that one bank lends to another comes from any excess reserves held at the Fed. A target level for the official Fed funds rate is set by the Federal Open Market Committee.

Repurchase market The term 'repo' is a shortened version of the term 'repurchase' agreement that is used with this instrument. A commercial bank that is short of liquidity can obtain some cash by selling high-quality financial market securities (normally bonds) to the central bank, usually for a period of just 14 days. At the end of these 14 days the bank must repurchase the securities from the central bank at the same price. However, it also has to pay an additional amount which is determined by the current level of the repo rate.

Eurodollar deposits These are simply deposits of US dollars that are held outside the US. Despite their name, Eurodollars do not have to be held in Europe.

Commercial paper This is a form of very short-term financing instrument used by companies. The normal maturity of commercial paper is 270 days.

Interbank markets This refers to activities that take place in the money markets. There will be some banks that have too much money and other banks with a lack of funds. This leads to a very active interbank market where the banks borrow and lend short-term funds between themselves. The key financial market instrument traded here is the London Interbank Offered Rate (Libor).

Sterling Libor or Euribor This is the rate used for loans made to low risk banks in the London money markets. You can get a Libor rate for a wide range of money market maturities. It starts with overnight money and then goes to one month, three months, six months and one year.

The Euribor rate is the equivalent interbank rate but now for borrowing and lending Euros in the money markets.

ECB Council This is the key part of the European Central Bank system. It is made up of a President of the ECB plus five other members who are responsible for the ECB's day-to-day activities including determining the daily money market operations.

Structured investment vehicle (SIVs) These are large programmes created by investment banks who seek to take advantage of the differences that exist between the cost of borrowing short-term funds and the cost of borrowing long-term funds. SIVs will typically raise their cash in the short-term commercial paper markets and then invest the proceeds in much longer-dated securities such as bonds and mortgage debt. SIVs came to prominence during the 'sub-prime crisis' as many of them invested heavily in large amounts of collaterised debt obligations (CDOs). These CDOs are packages of debt with various degrees of risk. Some CDOs invested heavily in the sub-prime mortgage debt. As a result of the default of some of these mortgages there are large numbers of CDOs that will be worth much less than they are currently perceived to be. The investment banks that own the CDOs were forced to write off a significant part of the value of these SIVs.

Bank of England The UK's central bank. It was made independent from the UK government in 1997. Since then it has been in charge of setting short-term interest rates in the UK money markets. The main official interest rate in the UK is called the 'repo rate'. The target for this rate is set by the Bank of England's Monetary Policy Committee. At the time of the Northern Rock crisis, the Bank of England's Governor was Mervyn King.

Financial Services Authority This is an independent non-governmental body that has a key role in regulating the performance of financial services institutions. It is made up of a FSA board with a chairman, a chief executive officer, three managing directors and nine non-executive directors. The FSA has its statutory powers granted under the Financial Services and Markets Act of 2000. At the time of the Northern Rock crisis the FSA's chief executive was Hector Sands, a former investment banker at Union Bank of Switzerland (UBS).

The Treasury This is the part of the government that is in charge of official spending and revenue decisions. In addition, it plays a key role in the regulation of the financial services industry. The Treasury is overseen by the Chancellor of the Exchequer. At the time of the Northern Rock crisis the Chancellor was Alistair Darling.

Lender of last resort The central bank has a key function in being the lender of last resort. This means that if a bank has nowhere else to go to in order to get funds, it can always go to the central bank to borrow some money to clear a cash imbalance. Without this faculty the banks would be at risk of running out of cash and then facing a complete loss of confidence among their depositors.

Retail deposits This refers to the bank deposits held by ordinary customers. In contrast, wholesale deposits are held by companies and other financial institutions.

Securitisation The process of breaking down a very large financial asset into smaller units that can be sold to investors. A good example might be mortgage-backed securities where the mortgage debt is pooled together and then sold in smaller units.

Sovereign wealth funds (SWF) These are a form of investment vehicle used by countries to build up financial assets with the funding coming largely from their reserves. The primary aim of these funds is to make investments that will benefit the country's economy and citizens over the long term. The countries with a proliferation of SWFs will normally be those with significant budget and trade surpluses which have allowed them to build up a pool of reserves that can then be invested. In addition, the SWFs are also common among countries rich in raw materials including the oil states.

■ What do you think?

1. Is it correct to blame the crisis at Northern Rock entirely on developments in the international financial markets?

2. In the context of the US mortgage market explain the term 'sub-prime' lending.

3. Explain how complex financial instruments like CDOs and SIVs were a key part of the 'credit-crisis'.

4. Why was Northern Rock unable to access funds from the repo market or the UK money markets?

5. In what ways was the business model employed by Northern Rock very different from that used by other UK banks?

6. To what extent did conflicts between the Treasury, the Financial Services Authority and the Bank of England contribute to the failure to deal with crisis effectively in the early days?

7. Discuss the long-term impact of the Northern Rock crisis on:

    a. The UK government (especially the Treasury).

    b. The Bank of England.

    c. The UK's reputation in international financial markets.

    d. The UK banking system.

    e. UK savers and borrowers.

8. It has been claimed that in bailing out Northern Rock the UK authorities ran the risk of injecting moral hazard into the financial services industry. What is meant by this term and do you agree that this is a serious risk?

9. 'The biggest losers in the Northern Rock crisis were the shareholders. They saw a sharp fall in the value of their shares and had a planned dividend cancelled on the 25 September 2007'. Do you agree with this statement?

10. Why did the UK government finally decide to nationalise Northern Rock?

11. Explain how the US government used 'preferred stock' in the rescue of Citigroup.

12. What are sovereign wealth funds? What role did they play in the bail-out of Citigroup?

13. Explain how the swapping of preferred stock for common equity was used to alleviate the problems at Citigroup in early 2009.

■ Investigate FT data

You will need the Companies and Markets section of the *Financial Times*. Go to the Market Data section – this is normally about six pages in from the back page.

Find the section on Interest Rates (right-hand side of page – halfway down). Now go to Market Rates. You will see:

US$Libor
EuroLibor
£ Libor, etc.

Focus *only* on £ Libor:

1. What is the overnight £ Libor rate?

2. What is the one-month £ Libor rate?

3. What is the three-month £ Libor rate?

4. What is the one-year £ Libor rate?

Using this information, describe the current state of the UK money markets. Are there any signs of a continued premium rate for banks to borrow funds for three months plus?

■ Go to the web

Go to the Bank of England website at www.bankofengland.co.uk.

Now go to the Markets Section (see top of page). Now go to Sterling Money Market Operations Section (see sections on left-hand side).

You are required to explain fully the Bank of England's 'four specific objectives' for their operations in the sterling money markets. Make sure you do this in your own words.

■ Research

Brummer, A. (2008) *The Crunch: The Scandal of Northern Rock and the Escalating Credit Crisis*, London: Random House.

Turner, G. (2008) *The Credit Crunch: Housing Bubbles, Globalisation and the Worldwide Economic Crisis*, London: Pluto Press.

Walters, B. (2008) *The Fall of Northern Rock. An Insider's Story of Britain's Biggest Banking Disaster*, Petersfield, UK: Harriman House.

You can also learn a great deal about the role of the Treasury, central banks and the Financial Services Authority from their official websites. They are all fantastic learning resources with a great deal of material on their activities.

For reference you will find these at:

www.federalreserve.gov

www.ecb.int/home/html/index.en.html

www.bankofengland.co.uk

www.fsa.gov.uk

www.hm-treasury.gov.uk

It is also essential to read the *Financial Times* just after the major meetings of these official bodies.

Go to **www.pearsoned.co.uk/boakes** to access Kevin's blog for additional analysis of recent topical news articles and to post your comments. Download podcasts containing short audio summaries of the main issues relating to each article and check your understanding of in-text questions with the handy hints provided.

Glossary

AAA-rated This is the highest credit-rating that a bond issue can receive. See Bond CREDIT RATING for more details.

Activist hedge funds Activist hedge fund managers target companies that are seen to be underperforming compared to their rivals. They will then build up a stake in the business and use that power to demand significant changes in the way the business is being run. This might include an attempt to oust the existing managers or close down loss-making activities. (page 188)

Activist shareholders Shareholders range from private investors with small stakes in the business right up to the large financial institutions that often own a significant percentage of the equity of a business. It is normally among these larger shareholders that we find the activist shareholders. These are the shareholders who believe that the managers are not doing a good job and as a result they will attempt to alter company policy and even possibly seek to replace existing senior managers with new people who they think will do a better job. (page 12)

Annual general meeting (AGM) All public companies must invite their shareholders to an AGM to vote on a number of important issues. This will include the approval of the annual report and accounts, the re-election of the directors and the dividend level. This is the key forum allowing the shareholders to express their views to the managers of the company. For example, in recent years it has allowed some pressure groups to exert pressure on companies involved in the arms industry or other so-called unethical sectors. (page 170)

Arbitrage This is a very common practice among financial market traders. They will simultaneously sell (or buy) a financial instrument (for example a share or a bond) and at the same time take an equal and opposite position in a similar instrument. This transaction will give them a financial profit. An arbitrage is possible where there is a clear price anomaly that has been identified between the markets involved. In theory such arbitrage trading is considered risk free. This makes it particularly attractive. (page 73)

Auctions (bonds) Most new government bond issues are sold through a system of auctions. Normally the country's Treasury is in charge of new issues. They will give an early warning of the maturity of the issue. And then a week or so before it will firm up details of the size of the issue, the total amount being raised, the maturity and the bond's annual coupon. (page 65)

Bank of England The UK's central bank. It was made independent from the UK government in 1997. Since then it has been in charge of setting short-term interest rates in the UK money markets. The main official interest rate in the UK is called the repo rate. The target for this rate is set by the Bank of England's Monetary Policy Committee. (page 209)

Banks analyst This is the person employed at an investment bank whose job it is to advise the bank's clients on the major financial institutions operating within the financial services industry. The analyst will be required to value these businesses and offer comparisons between his/her own and the market's valuations as reflected in the current share prices. (page 77)

Benchmark 10-year Treasury note The United States has the world's largest government bond market. The Treasury market is backed by the US government and, as a result, is seen as having no default risk. It sets the standard for all other dollar-denominated bonds. As a result, other dollar issues will see their yields set in relation to the equivalent US Treasury issue. (pages 29, 52)

Benign credit conditions See CREDIT CONDITIONS

Bond A bond is a security issued by a government or a corporation which represents a debt that must be repaid normally at a set date in the future. Most bonds pay a set interest rate each year called the bond's coupon. The other key characteristic of a bond is its maturity. This is the date that the bond will be redeemed. (page 76)

Bond auction process See AUCTION (bonds)

Bond credit rating New bond issuers are normally assigned credit ratings by the various companies that are involved in this activity. They include Standard and Poor's and Moody's. The highest credit rating allocated by Moody's is a AAA. For example, this is awarded to the German government's bond issues. (pages 66, 82)

Bond yields See YIELDS

Bond yield spreads This refers to the yield on a particular bond issue minus the yield on the nearest comparable government bond issue. The spread is determined by a combination of the bond's credit rating, liquidity and the market's perception of its risk relative to the other bond. (page 66)

Book runner This is the lead manager who is in charge of the whole process in a new bond issue. They will be jointly responsible with the issuer for inviting other banks to work on the new issue in activities such as syndication and underwriting. (page 73)

Break-even A company achieves break-even when its sales revenue equals total costs. These costs will include some fixed costs as well as the variable costs that will be dependent on the level of sales. (page 96)

Brokerage commissions If you wish to use the services of a stockbroker in order to buy or sell shares, you must pay the broker's fees. This 'brokerage commission' is normally a set percentage of the total transaction or some kind of flat-rate charge. (page 129)

Budget deficit A country's budget deficit refers to the difference between its spending and its revenue. It is normal for any government to spend more money on health services, education, defence etc. than it can raise revenue from income taxes, sales taxes, etc. The result is a fiscal deficit or a budget deficit. We normally like to compare a country's budget deficit by expressing it as a percentage of the country's gross domestic product or income. (page 66)

Bulldog bonds These are sterling-denominated bonds issued by a foreign borrower in the UK domestic market. (page 76)

Bunds These are simply German government bonds. These are used to fund the difference between federal government spending and revenue. As normal, the benchmark long-term government bond is the 10-year maturity. (pages 58, 83)

Business risk This refers to the general risk that can impact on a company's cash flow or profitability. It could be caused by general economic conditions (consumer spending, level of interest rates, etc.) as well as more specific company factors (changes in key staff, strike action by employees, etc.). (page 96)

Capital calls This can be defined as any additional money that equity holders will be required to provide to meet a company's financial deficit. (page 144)

Capital expenditure This is where a company spends money on various types of fixed assets such as property and plant and equipment. These assets cannot easily be turned into cash and are generally viewed as long-term investments. (pages 17, 154)

Capital structure This refers to the long-term finance that a business needs in order to trade. This is made up of debt and equity finance. The debt finance will normally be in the form of a bond that carries fixed interest payments and a set date when it will be redeemed. In contrast, there are no guarantees of any financial returns to the providers of equity (the shareholders). If a company does well and is highly profitable it is likely that there will be significant dividends paid to the shareholders. However, if the company runs into financial difficulties, the dividends will be cut back and they might disappear altogether. It should be clear that in terms of capital structure the shareholders take a greater risk than the debt holders. As a result, it is reasonable for the shareholders to expect a higher level of financial returns to compensate for this higher risk. (page 92)

CBI surveys The Confederation of British Industry (CBI) is widely described as the employers' organisation. It is voluntary group made up of around 1500 UK-based manufacturing companies. It carries out a wide range of surveys to gauge its members' views on the current state of economic activity. It provides a useful overview of the state of manufacturing industry. The surveys are sent out at the end of each quarter and the results are published about three weeks later. (page 181)

Chief executive officer (CEO) This is the top person in the company who will have the main responsibility for implementing the policies of the board of directors on a daily basis. Put simply, he or she runs the business. (page 12)

Collateral This refers to any property or other assets that can be given as security on a loan. If the borrower fails to make timely interest payments or return the principal these assets can be seized. (page 207)

Commercial paper This is a form of very short-term financing instrument used by companies. The normal maturity of commercial paper is 270 days. (pages 62, 208)

Companies' cost of capital This refers to the financial return that is expected by an investor in a company's debt or equity issues. The cost of capital is seen as the annual percentage return that an investor would expect if they were buying shares or bonds issued by a company. (page 101).

Convergence This refers to the process that took place in the late 1990s whereby all the prospective eurozone countries saw their government bond yields fall to the level of the lowest yield that existed at this time. The view was that if the bonds were now issued in the same currency they should enjoy the same level of risk and therefore identical yields. (page 82)

Conversion premium This term refers to the difference between the current market share price and the set conversion price. You will normally see this expressed as a percentage of the current market share price. (page 56)

Conversion price It is the price that has to be paid per share when the bond holder decides to convert their bond into shares. (page 56)

Conversion ratio This is the number of shares that a convertible bond can be converted into. For example, if the conversion ratio is set at 40 then an investor will be able to convert every £100 nominal value of the bond issue into 40 shares in the issuing company. (page 56)

Conversion value of the bond This is the value of a convertible bond if it were converted into shares at the current market share price. (page 56)

Convertible bond These are bonds which provide the holders with the right to convert their bonds into shares in the issuing company. This conversion option will be at an agreed price at a set date in the future. Initially this will not be a worthwhile transaction as the conversion share price will be set well above the current market share price. However, as the market share price rises in value over time so the conversion will soon be a valuable option for the bond holder. (pages 62, 73, 92)

Corporate brokers These are important financial institutions that will make a market in a company's shares. This means that they must be willing to quote both buy and sell prices, enabling investors to deal in the shares. They could also act as an adviser to a company that was organising a new share issue. (page 101).

Corporate governance This is a general term used to describe the relationship between the owners of a business (the shareholders) and the managers of the business. It covers the various mechanisms by which the shareholders can try to make sure that the managers act in their interest. This should ensure that the managers are open, fair and fully accountable for all their actions. (page 7)

Coupon This is the interest rate that is set for a bond when it is first issued. In practice, the coupon is normally paid in two equal instalments. (page 72)

Credit conditions This simply refers to the cost of borrowing money. It might be a government borrowing (in the government bond market), a company borrowing (in the corporate bond market), a house owner (with a mortgage) or a consumer (with a credit card). We have 'benign credit conditions' when the cost of borrowing is considered to be low by historical standards. We have 'tight credit conditions' when the cost of borrowing is considered to be high by historical standards. (page 57)

Credit crunch This refers to the cost and availability of credit. It might be a government borrowing (in the government bond market), a company borrowing (in the corporate bond market), a house owner (with a mortgage) or a consumer (with a credit card). We have a 'credit crunch' when the cost of borrowing is considered to be prohibitively expensive by historical standards or it is simply very difficult for more risky borrowers to obtain finance at all. (page 207)

Credit default swaps (CDS) This is a financial market instrument that is designed to offer a bond investor complete protection against the risk of default. Essentially, the seller of the swap takes over the risk of default on the bond issuer for a one-off payment. In the event of any default the seller of the swap will be fully liable to pay the par value of the bond and any due interest payments to the credit swap buyer. (page 83)

Credit risk premium This is the higher return that a bond investor will require to compensate for the possible financial loss due to the bond issuer being unable to make timely payments of interest or the principal. (page 83)

Currency risk See ECONOMIC RISK, TRANSACTION RISK and TRANSLATION RISK.

DAX index The DAX index is the most important German stock market index. It is considered to be the standard benchmark for shares quoted on the Frankfurt Stock Exchange. It started in 1984 with an initial value of 1000. This is referred to as the Xetra DAX index on the front of the *Financial Times* in the World Markets data. (page 57)

Debt capital See CAPITAL STRUCTURE.

Debenture This is the most secure form of bond issue that a company can offer. The holder of the bond will be entitled to receive various assets owned by the company if there is any default on the terms of the issue.

Default This where a borrower takes out a loan but fails to keep to the original agreed schedule of interest payments and final capital repayments. A bond issued by the governments of the United States or United Kingdom is generally regarded to be free of default risk. In contrast a bond issued by a company might well have significant risk of default. For example, a company might not be able to keep up with the interest payments on the loan as a result of a downturn in its profitability. (pages 13, 38)

Delisting This is simply when a company is removed from a stock exchange. This might be done by a company that decides that it has simply become too onerous to meet all the rules and regulations set out by the stock exchange. Such companies are not necessarily bankrupt and it is quite possible that the shares will still trade in the over-the-counter-market where buyers and sellers will be brought together. (page 7)

Diluted (shareholdings) This is when a company issues additional share capital resulting in existing shareholders seeing a diminished value in terms of their voting power and their value. (page 102)

Discounted cash flow valuation Put very simply, this is where we take the future cash flows which will be earned by a company and multiply them by an appropriate discount factor to get their present value. This is a widely used technique to place a value on the share price of a particular company. (page 116)

Dividends A normal dividend is simply the payment made each year to all shareholders in the company. The exact level is set by the company's board of directors. This payment will be made to all shareholders who are registered on a particular date. In most cases these dividends are paid in cash. (page 156)

Domestic bond This is where the issuer launches a bond in its local currency and home country. For example, a UK company might launch a new £500 m bond issue in London. (page 61)

Dovish See HAWKISH.

Dow Jones Industrial Average (DJIA) The DJIA is the main US stock market index. It is based on the market movements of 30 of the largest blue-chip industrial companies that trade on the New York Stock Exchange. The selection of these companies is revised regularly. It includes companies like American Express, Boeing, Disney, General Electric, Honeywell, Intel, JP Morgan Bank, Procter and Gamble. (pages 52, 208)

ECB Council This is the key part of the European Central Bank system. It is made up of a President of the ECB plus five other members. They are responsible for the ECB's day-to-day activities including determining the daily money market operations. (page 209)

Economic risk Type of currency risk that is caused by exchange rate movements impacting on the competitiveness of a company. Put simply, if a company's home currency appreciates, this will make the company less competitive as its goods and services become more expensive in overseas markets. It is normal to see economic risk described as being a much more general risk than either transaction or translation risk. (page 181)

Efficient market This refers to the way that share prices react to new information. A stock market is efficient if it reacts quickly and accurately to a new market-sensitive announcement. So if a company announces a surprise increase in dividends, its share price should rise immediately. If instead it reacts very slowly or indeed even falls in price, the market will be highly inefficient. (pages 81, 116)

Emerging markets This refers to the financial markets of developing nations. In general, these markets have not been trading for long and as a result they are seen as being more risky than traditional financial markets. (page 116)

Equity capital See CAPITAL STRUCTURE.

Equity fund-raising This simply refers to the company raising additional finance through the issue of extra share capital. (page 102)

Euribor This is the interbank rate that applies to all short-loans money market made in the euro. The rate that applies to these loans will generally be close to the European Central Bank's repo rate.

Eurobond This is where the issue takes place outside of the country of the currency that the bond is denominated in. For example, a German company might launch a new $500 m bond issue in France. This type of bond is called a Eurobond because the issue is in US dollars and it takes place outside of the United States. You should be aware the term Eurobond does not mean that the issue has to take place within the European financial markets. (page 61)

Eurodollar deposits These are simply deposits of US dollars that are held outside of the US. Despite their name Eurodollars do not have to held in Europe. (page 208)

European Central Bank (ECB) This is the eurozone's central bank. It sets the level of short-term interest rates for all the countries that have adopted the euro. The main policy objective of the ECB is to maintain price stability in the medium term. This is defined as a 0–2 per cent target range for consumer price inflation. The key part of the ECB is the Governing Council that meets every fortnight on a Thursday. (page 58)

Eurozone The countries that use the euro as their common currency. (page 82)

Exchange Rate Mechanism (ERM) In the days before the existence of a single European currency, there was a very complex system set up to control exchange rate fluctuations between participating currencies. For a very brief time the UK became part of this system and this caused severe problems for the UK economy which was then in recession. The government had to keep interest rates very high in the middle of this downturn in a vain attempt to defend the pound's value. This policy came to a dramatic end on Black Wednesday in September 1992. The pound crashed out of the ERM and interest rates fell sharply. (page 180)

Exotic products This is a term to cover new innovative financial markets products. The use of the terw 'exotic' denotes that these are different from the normal version of this product. You will see it used in several contexts such as exotic bonds, exotic swaps, exotic options. (page 73)

Federal Reserve (and the Federal Open Market Committee) The Federal Reserve is the central bank of the United States. The key part of the Fed is the Federal Open Market Committee (FOMC) that decides on changes in US monetary policy. It is made up of 12 individuals. The core seven come from the Central Federal Reserve Bank (based in Washington) and the other five represent the various Federal District Reserve Banks. One of these, New York, has a permanent place on the FOMC. The other eleven banks share the remainder of the votes on a complex rotation system. The FOMC reviews the outlook for the economy before deciding on the next move in interest rates. (pages 27, 207)

Fed funds rate (effective) This is the most important short-term interest rate in the United States. It refers to the overnight interbank lending that takes places in the United States money markets. The money that one bank lends to another comes from any excess reserves held at the Fed. A target level for the official Fed funds rate is set by the Federal Open Market Committee. (pages 26, 208)

Fed watching This refers to the various economists who spend their time studying every market movement or speech from a key official of the Federal Reserve Bank in order to try to predict the next move in US interest rates. Getting these predictions right is worth a great deal to the large investment banks as their traders can use these forecasts to make massive profits in their bond, share and money market trading operations. (page 26)

Financial Services Authority (FSA) This is an independent non-governmental body that has a key role in regulating the performance of financial services institutions. It is made up of an FSA Board with a chairman, a chief executive officer, three managing directors and nine non-executive directors. The FSA has its statutory powers granted under the Financial Services and Markets Act 2000. (page 209)

Flat yield curve A flat yield curve shows the level of yields being broadly similar across the maturity spectrum. (pages 27, 65)

Foreign bond This is where an issuer goes to another country to issue a bond in a foreign currency. For example, a German company might launch a new $500 m bond issue in the United States. This type of foreign bond issue is called a Yankee bond. (page 61)

FTSE Eurofirst (300) This is one of the FT's more recently created stock market Indices. It attempts to track the performance of the leading European stock markets. It is shown on the front of the FT each day in the World Markets data section. (page 208)

FTSE indices We start with the FTSE-100 index which is the most widely quoted UK stock market index. It is based on the value of the 100 largest UK companies in terms of their market capitalisation. It started with a base level of 1000 in January 1984. This index is now quoted in real time on the various news information systems that serve the City traders. Next we have the FTSE-250 index which is simply an index of the next 250 companies in terms of their market capitalisation. Next we have the FTSE-350 index which simply combines the FTSE-100 and the FTSE-250 indices. Lastly, there is the FTSE All-Share UK index, which, as the title suggests, is the broadest of the UK stock market indices. It covers over 800 companies which together account for about 98 per cent of the total market capitalisation. (pages 144, 181, 208)

Fund managers The fund manager's main role is to build a successful investment strategy enabling them to optimise the value of the investment portfolio. He or she will have to monitor financial markets and constantly assess market risks. In addition, the fund manager will have to communicate their objectives to their clients. (page 188)

Futures markets In the money markets there is a well established futures market that allows banks to deal at a set interest rate for a transaction on a specified future date. For example, a bank could arrange to lend £10 m to another bank at a set interest rate on a specific date in the future. The attraction of this deal is that both parties know now what the interest rate is going to be. There is no uncertainty as this transaction will not be affected by any subsequent rise or fall in money market interest rates. (pages 43, 83)

Gainsay This means to deny or contradict something or somebody. In this context the *FT* article suggests that the need to get shareholder approval for a new share issue prevents companies from acting against the interests of their shareholders by going to 'more management-friendly' investors to fund a new share issue. (page 102)

Gearing This refers to the proportion of debt in the company's capital structure. A company is termed highly geared if it has a large amount of debt finance and only a small amount of equity finance. In contrast, a low geared company will be largely financed by equity finance. (page 96)

German DAX index See DAX INDEX.

Global credit crisis This refers to the crisis that affected financial markets in the summer of 2007, which stemmed from the subprime crisis that started in the US. As a result, banks became very reluctant to lend to each other and the interbank markets saw their liquidity dry up. (page 82)

Government debt These are bonds issued by governments to fund the difference between their spending and revenue. (page 82)

Greenmailer This refers to a very unusual situation in corporate takeover bids. It is where one company (the takeover company) deliberately builds up a large stake in another business (the target company) and then appears to launch an unfriendly takeover. This whole process is designed to force the target company to repurchase the stock at a substantial premium to prevent a takeover bid. (page 170)

Growth capital deals This refers to the provision of finance to those companies that seem to offer the prospect of particularly high rates of growth. This might be because of the type of service or goods that they provide. For example, a high-technology company might be viewed as being higher growth than a utility like an electricity supplier. (page 144)

Growth strategy This refers to the strategy employed by a company aimed at increasing its market share. It is possible that in the short term a company might set out to chase additional sales even at the cost of reducing short-term earnings. (page 17)

Growth/mature company A growth company is one that has a rate of growth that is significantly higher than is the norm. They will generally be characterised by heavy investment programmes and low dividend payments to their shareholders. In contrast, a mature company has already done its growing and it has now reached the stage where future expansion plans are limited by the size of their market. These companies will be characterised by much less ambitious business investments but rather more generous dividend payments to shareholders.

Group of seven This refers to some of the most influential economies in the world including the United States, Germany, Japan, France, UK, Canada and Italy. They meet regularly to discuss economic policy. These days their meetings often involve Russia (so it is really a G-8 now). (page 44)

Hawkish (and dovish) In the context of central banks, commentators often use the terms hawkish and dovish to describe members of the central bank committees that set interest rates. For example, a hawkish member of the FOMC tends to be very concerned about maintaining a clear anti-inflation policy and so is more likely to vote for an increase in interest rates. In contrast, a dovish member of the FOMC tends to be more relaxed about the inflation outlook and as a consequence is less likely to vote for any increase in interest rates. (page 30)

Hedge fund This refers to a particular type of investment management where the fund manager will employ a range of different investment tools in an attempt to maximise the returns or try to make gains even in a falling market. The fund will rely on large amounts of borrowing and will use derivative markets and short selling to achieve these aims. (pages 38, 73, 131, 143, 188)

Hedging This term is widely used in financial markets to indicate that an investment in a financial market product is being made to minimise the risk of any unfavourable movement in the price of a particular financial asset. In the context of the foreign exchange market, hedging refers to the process of a company attempting to protect itself against an adverse movement in the foreign exchange market. The most commonly used hedging technique in this context is the forward foreign exchange market. (page 181)

Infrastructure This is defined as investment projects that will focus on a nation's basic network of assets such as roads, railways, communications systems, etc. (page 144)

Initial public offer (IPO) An IPO refers to the situation where a company first sells its shares by listing on the stock exchange. This gives it a much wider access to increase its shareholder base. In addition, it provides much great liquidity in terms of the trading of the shares in the company. Companies considering a new IPO will appoint an investment bank to manage the process. They will meet the company and be heavily involved in valuing the shares, preparing a prospectus and getting investors interested in the new issue. The investment bank will be very well rewarded for this work with substantial fees often being paid to ensure a successful IPO. (pages 38, 111)

Institutional investors These are the large pension funds and insurance companies that are the key investors in financial markets. They look to invest in long-term assets to match their long-term liabilities (paying out pensions). These investors have flourished in recent years due to the greater wealth of the private sector. In contrast, the private clients refer to the individuals who invest on their own behalf. (page 112)

Interbank markets This refers to activities that take place in the money markets. There will be some banks that have too much money and other banks with a lack of funds. This leads to a very active interbank market where the banks borrow and lend short-term funds between themselves. The key financial market instrument traded here is the London Interbank Offered Rate (Libor). (page 208)

Intermediaries These are financial institutions that act as a middleman between those cash surplus units in the economy (the lenders) and the cash deficit units in the economy (the borrowers). Put simply, they enable people with money to meet people who need money. (page 129)

Internal rate of return The internal rate of return (IRR) is a widely used method for companies to decide if a new business investment is worthwhile in financial terms. The IRR of a project is the discount rate that equates the present value of the expected future cash outlays with the present value of the expected cash inflows. As a result, the project's net present value is zero. (page 139)

Investment banks An investment bank acts as an intermediary between the issuers of capital (governments and companies) and the investors in capital (pension funds and insurance companies). The staff employed in an investment bank will work either in the investment banking division (IBD) which deals with the new issues of debt and equity capital or the markets division which deals with the investors in new bond and equity deals. (pages 37, 101)

Investor protection This refers to the defence of shareholders' rights including in this case the first opportunity to buy any new shares issued by the company. (page 102)

Investor relations A key aspect of good corporate governance is the requirement that the senior managers of a company are expected to keep a constant dialogue with the shareholders. This includes the necessity to make sure they are in touch with their opinions on a range of important issues. This should be done through such things as the annual general meeting, the sending of regular news updates and the provision of a company website. Most of these websites now include a section covering investor relations. (page 7)

Japanese government bonds (JGBs) This is the world's second largest government bond market. There has been a massive increase in the size of the JGB market in recent years. This is due to a long-standing recession that has led to the government's efforts to boost economic growth through massive tax cuts and large government spending increases. (page 76)

Leases See SALE AND LEASE BACK.

Lender of last resort The central bank has a key function in being the lender of last resort. This means that if a bank has no where else to go to in order to get funds it can always go the central bank to borrow some money to clear a cash imbalance. Without this faculty the banks would be at risk of running out of cash and then facing a complete loss of confidence from their depositors. (page 209)

Leveraged This refers to the capital structure of the new company being formed. The term leveraged suggests that the company will be financed largely by borrowed money. (page 139)

Leveraged buyout This term is used in the context of management buyouts and it suggests that the new company will be financed largely with debt capital. (page 139)

Liquid yield option notes (lyons) These are zero-coupon bonds that are issued below their par value. This guarantees the holder a return despite the zero coupon. (page 74)

Liquidity In financial markets this normally refers to how easily an asset can be converted into cash. Therefore, notes and coins are the most liquid financial asset. In general, the more liquid an asset, the lower is its return. (page 65)

Liquidity premium This term refers to how easily an asset can be converted into cash (notes and coins). In general, the more liquid an asset, the lower is its return. Investors will pay a higher price in order to secure a liquid financial asset. This is what is known as the liquidity premium. (page 83)

List This refers to the companies whose shares are quoted on the Main List of the UK Exchange. Companies who want to be listed must meet the very exacting criteria which are contained in the Stock Exchange's 'Yellow Book'. These criteria include the amount of shares that have to be in the public's hands ahead of trading in the shares, the company's trading and financial history and the suitability of the board of directors. (page 111)

London Interbank Offered Rate (Libor) This is the rate used for loans made to low-risk banks in the London money markets. You can get a Libor rate for a wide range of money market maturities. It starts with overnight money and then goes to one month, three months, six months and one year. (page 43)

London Stock Exchange (LSE) This is the main stock exchange in the UK where companies raise new equity finance through their initial public offer (IPO) and subsequent share issues (rights issues). (page 102)

Long-term finance In most companies this is the key finance that underpins business activities. It is made up of a combination of equity finance (provided by the shareholders) and debt finance normally issued in the form of new bond issues. This long-term finance will allow the company to make new investments and it could also fund mergers and acquisitions. (page 12)

Margins This is the difference between the company's average selling price for its goods or services and the costs that are required to produce them. (page 116)

Market buyouts This term is normally associated with the provision of finance to help the existing managers of a business take control of their company. The private equity firm will help them fund the buyout in the hope of generating a significant return for their shareholders. (page 144)

Market capitalisation This gives the current overall stock market value of the company. It can be easily calculated by multiplying the numbers of shares in issue by their current market share price. In some cases companies will have more than one class of shares. In this case it is necessary to add together the different classes of shares to get the total value of the company. (page 156)

Matilda bonds Australian dollar-denominated bonds issued by a foreign borrower in the Australian domestic market. (page 76)

Mergers This is where two companies decide that it would be to their joint benefit to come together to form a new business entity. With a merger the process is normally friendly with the full consent of both sets of shareholders. (page 165)

Monetary Policy Committee The Bank of England's Monetary Policy Committee (MPC) is in charge of setting UK interest rates. It is made up of nine members: the Governor of the Bank of England, two Deputy-Governors, two Bank of England Executive Directors and four independent members. The MPC is required by the government to ensure that the UK economy enjoys price stability. This is defined by the government's set inflation target of 2 per cent. (page 42)

Monetary policy When you see the term monetary policy in the context of central banks it refers to interest rate policy. A central bank tightens monetary policy when it raises interest rates. (page 30)

Money laundering Money laundering is the process of trying to conceal the source of funds generated by some illegal activity. This money might have come from a range of activities including drug smuggling, illegal gambling, etc. The aim of the operation is to make it seem as though the money that has been illegally earned actually comes from a perfectly legal activity.

Monopolies and Mergers Commission The Competition Commission actually took the place of the Monopolies and Mergers Commission in 1999. In simple terms, the MMC had the task of ensuring that the market in the provision of various goods and services remains competitive. (page 102)

Mortgage-backed securities This is where a large amount of mortgage debt is pooled together and then sold to a different set of investors in the form of a securitised financial market instrument. (pages 38, 207)

NASDAQ composite This is a rival stock market exchange based in the United States. It is run by the National Association of Securities Dealers and its automated quotation system gives us the NASDAQ index, which began in 1971 with a value of 100. It now includes nearly 5000 companies with each one assigned to one of the eight sub-indices – Banks, Biotechnology, Computer, Industrial, Insurance, Other Finance, Telecom and Transportation. In general, the NASDAQ index is seen to focus on newer and emerging companies. (page 52)

Nikkei 225 index This is the most closely followed index of Japanese share prices. The index is quite broad as it is based on Japan's top 225 blue-chip companies quoted on the Tokyo Stock Exchange. (page 208)

Nominal share price This is merely a value given to a company's share which is only used for accounting purposes. Unlike the par value of a bond it has no direct link to the market price. (pages 120, 129)

Nonagenarian This refers to a person who is aged between 90 and 99 years old. (page 129)

Non-executive chairman and **non-executive director (NED)** This is supposed to be a person who is independent of the core management team. He or she will normally be employed on a part-time basis and will chair the main board of directors. In addition, the CEO can look to the non-executive chairman for advice and guidance. You will also see the term NED, which stands for non-executive director. Most public companies will employ a number of part-time NEDs to give independent advice on the running of the company's operations. (pages 13, 17)

Non-voting preference shares In many ways, preference shares can be seen to be very similar to bond finance. They normally pay dividends at a set percentage very much like the coupon on a bond issue. And, in addition, they will normally have a set redemption date. However, unlike bonds, the dividends on a preference share are paid at the discretion of the board of directors of a company. Most preference shares are non-voting which means that the holders will not have the right to vote on corporate policy at the annual general meeting. (page 92)

Pension fund deficit This refers to the crisis that affected companies in the wake of the financial market weakness of 2008, which led to many companies having inadequate financial provision in order to cover the liabilities to their employees in terms of future pension payments. (page 120)

Plain vanilla This denotes the simplest version of any type of financial market instrument. It alludes to ice cream varieties. A plain vanilla ice cream is the simplest type you can buy. It has no chocolate flake or any sauces! (page 74)

Poison pill When a company is subject to an unwanted takeover bid there a number of measures that it can take to try to defend itself. One such technique is called a poison pill. This is where a company introduces some measure that will seriously damage the interests of the company making the takeover bid. This might, for example, be an issue of a new bond which following a takeover bid would give the bond holders the option to redeem their bond immediately at a significant premium to its par value. This will act to deter any bidder. (page 170)

Pre-emption rights This refers to one of the very longstanding principles of corporate law. It gives all shareholders the first right to buy any additional shares being sold by companies. The new shares would be offered to existing holders in direct proportion to their existing holdings. So that if you owned 10 per cent of the existing shares in a company you would be given the right to buy 10 per cent of the new shares being sold via a rights issue. These additional shares are normally sold at a significant discount to the existing market share price to ensure a successful completion of the transaction. (page 101)

Price–earnings ratio The PE ratio is calculated by taking the market share price and dividing it by company's earnings per share. This ratio is often used to compare the current stock market value of a company. (pages 112, 157)

Primary and secondary markets The IBD will work with companies with their initial issue of new shares. This is called the primary market. The markets division will then work in the secondary market, which is where new buyers can purchase these shares from existing holders. This is normally a standard marketplace like the stock exchange's official list. (page 38)

Private banking This refers to banks that manage the financial affairs for 'high net worth' individuals. (page 77)

Private equity This term is used to describe the activities of a group of companies that invest in businesses that are already privately owned or ones that the buyers intend to remove from the stock market as soon as possible. Once they are removed from a quoted stock market, the private equity firms can then set about making a series of significant changes designed to increase their ultimate market value. The term private equity is also used also to cover other areas such as venture capital where new start-up businesses receive finance in their early stages of development. Strictly speaking, private equity is different from venture capital as the deal size tends to be much larger and the investment is in more established companies. (pages 115, 139, 143)

Profits warning Companies are required to keep shareholders well informed in terms of the performance of the company. As a result, if a company knows that its future profits will be significantly less than the stock market currently believes, it is required to warn the market. The result of such a warning is normally a sharp fall in the share price. (page 7)

Property assets Accountants like to distinguish between current assets (these are very short term and will last less than a year) and fixed assets (longer term and will last more than a year). For example, the key fixed asset for a company such as a large supermarket chain will be its vast property portfolio. This will include many high street stores as well as distribution warehouses. (page 115)

Proprietary trading This is where the investment bank uses its own capital to fund trading strategies that are designed to earn them significant profits. (page 38)

Real estate group This is a key division within an investment bank that deals with any aspects of commercial property deals. (page 38)

Redeemable 'B' shares This refers to a type of share capital which has reduced or zero voting rights. These shares are generally redeemable which means that they have a fixed life, unlike most ordinary shares which have an infinite life. In recent years a number of companies have given their shareholders redeemable 'B' shares instead of cash dividends. (page 154)

Repurchase rate (repo rate) The term repo is a shortened version of the term 'repurchase' agreement that is used with this instrument. A commercial bank that is short of liquidity can obtain some cash by selling high quality financial market securities (normally bonds) to the central bank usually for a period of just 14 days. At the end of these 14 days the bank must repurchase the securities from the central bank at the same price. However, it also has to pay an additional amount which is determined by the current level of the repo rate. (pages 42, 208)

Retail deposits This refers to the bank deposits held by ordinary customers. In contrast, wholesale deposits are held by companies and other financial institutions. (page 209)

Retail Price Index/Consumer Price Index Until 2003, the UK government's target for inflation was set in terms of the percentage annual increase in the average prices of goods and services as measured by the Retail Price Index (RPI). There was some controversy in 2003 when the relevant inflation measure was changed to the Consumer Price Index (CPI), which excludes certain important costs such as council tax and mortgage interest payments. (page 43)

Rights issue This is where a company issues some additional shares on a pro rata basis to existing shareholders. The new shares are normally sold at a discount to the current market price. These issues provide no access to new shareholders. Normal rights issues are popular because they can be made at the discretion of the board of directors. The shareholders like the discounts available and they leave the balance of voting rights unchanged. (page 170)

Risk aversion Most rational people will always prefer to buy investments that carry the lowest possible risk. So, if faced with the choice of a perfectly safe government bond (AAA–rated) or a bond issue from another country with a poor credit history, the rational person will always select the low-risk option. (page 84)

Risk premium This is simply the extra financial reward that will be required to convince an investor to hold an asset that has a risk of returning a capital sum that is less than the original amount paid for it. (page 83)

Rival bid This is where there is a corporate takeover in progress and a new bidder emerges to challenge the current company that is looking to buy a business. (page 120)

Sale and lease back This is a very common transaction used by companies that want to extract the value of any significant assets. A company can sell its property and then lease it right back from the buyer (normally a financial institution) in the same transaction. This enables the owner to get the cash from the sale but at the same time the owner can still use the property to carry out its business. The financial institution that buys the property is guaranteed a long-term income from the lease on the property. (pages 116, 120)

Samurai bonds Yen-denominated bonds issued by a foreign borrower in the domestic Japanese market. (page 76)

Securitisation The process of breaking down a very large financial asset into smaller units that can be sold to investors. A good example might be mortgage-backed securities where the mortgage debt is pooled together and then sold in smaller units. (page 209)

Secured and unsecured debt Companies will normally have a range of different types of debt capital. The lowest risk form of debt capital will be secured debt. This means that the debt is secured on various assets owned by the business including property or plant and machinery. If the business goes into liquidation, the secured bond holders will have a claim on these assets so that their investment will be protected. In contrast, the unsecured debt holders do not enjoy this form of protection. They accept a higher degree of risk which must be compensated for by a higher level of return. (pages 61, 92)

Severance package This refers to the pay and benefits that an employee receives when their employment contract is terminated. It will normally be partly additional salary as well as some contribution to their pension fund. (page 144)

Share buyback This is an increasingly common method for companies to return cash to their shareholders. The process is relatively simple. The normal technique is for companies to make a 'tender offer' to all shareholders inviting them to sell their shares back to the company at a set price. Second, a company might offer to buy from a particular group of shareholders and lastly, the company could make a stock market purchase of its shares. (pages 153, 156)

Shareholders In most companies the shareholders provide the bulk of the long-term finance. This makes them the key stakeholders in the business. They are the owners of the business and the managers must always remember that they are merely acting as agents working on behalf of the shareholders who are the principals. We normally assume that the primary objective of a company is to maximise the wealth of its shareholders. In practice this is simplified to maximising the company's share price. The shareholders range from private investors with small stakes in the business right up to the large financial institutions that often own a significant percentage of the equity of a business. (pages 12, 101)

Shareholders' funds This is a measure of the total value of the shareholders' stake in the company. It is made up of the total share capital plus any reserves. (page 102)

Shorting shares This is used to refer to traders who sell a financial market security that they do not yet own. In other words, they have not yet made an offsetting purchase. This is a very risky activity as if the price of the financial market security rises the trader will have to pay an ever higher price to secure the stock. The reverse process is when a trader goes long. This means that they have bought some financial market securities which they have not yet sold. (page 73)

Sovereign entities This simply refers to a country or a supranational body like the World Bank or the European Bank for Reconstruction and Development, which are both regular issuers of bonds. (page 83)

Sovereign Wealth Funds (SWF) These are a form of investment vehicle used by countries to build up financial assets with the funding coming largely from their reserves. The primary aim of these funds is to make investments that will benefit the country's economy and citizens over the long term. The countries with a proliferation of SWFs will normally be those with significant budget and trade surpluses which have allowed them to build up a pool of reserves that can then be invested. In addition, the SWFs are also common among countries rich in raw materials including the oil states. (page 210)

Special dividend This refers to the situation where a company decides to return any surplus cash to shareholders through a one-off payment. This should be seen as an additional payment on top of any expected normal dividend. The significance of labelling this dividend as 'special' is that it is a signal from the company that it will not be able to maintain annual dividends at this higher level. It is a one-off benefit that shareholders should not see as becoming the norm. (page 156)

Spreads This is a measure of the relative cost of issuing more risky bonds. It is best seen with an example. Let us assume that the United States government has close to zero risk of default. As a result a 10-year US Treasury bond might have a yield of 4.5 per cent. In contrast, a 10-year issue from Ford Motor Company which has significantly more risk of default might have a yield of 6.5 per cent. This gives us a credit yield spread of 6.5 per cent minus 4.5 per cent = 200 basis points difference. If investors now start to buy lots of the higher yielding (more risky) bonds, this could result in 'tighter credit spreads' as the relative cost of these bonds falls. In this case the yield on the 10-year issue from Ford might fall back to 5.5 per cent. This would reduce the yield spread to just 100 basis points. This would be a 'tighter credit spread'. (pages 76, 82, 129)

Stakeholders This refers to the various parties who have a share or an interest in a company. This will include the shareholders, managers, employees, suppliers, government and the members of the local community. (page 165)

Standard and Poor's (S&P) 500 The S&P composite index is based on the market movements of 500 companies that are listed on the New York Stock Exchange. This index is one of the most widely used measures of US equity performance. (page 52)

Sterling Libor or Euribor This is the rate used for loans made to low-risk banks in the London money markets. You can get a Libor rate for a wide range of money market maturities. It starts with overnight money and then goes to one month, three months, six months and one year. The Euribor rate is the equivalent interbank rate but now for borrowing and lending euros in the money markets. (page 208)

Stock dividends This is an alternative to an ordinary cash dividend. In this case the dividend is paid in the form of extra shares. For example, a 5 per cent stock dividend means that each shareholder gets an extra five shares for every 100 he or she owns. (pages 129, 156)

Stock split If a company is concerned that their share price has become too expensive they can divide the shares into smaller units. For example, if a company's market share price hits £14 this can be split into two £7 shares. The aim is to enhance the liquidity of the shares and therefore make it easier for smaller shareholders to buy their shares.

Structured investment vehicles (SIVs) These are large programmes created by investment banks who seek to take advantage of the differences that exist between the cost of borrowing short-term funds and the cost of borrowing long-term funds. SIVs will typically raise their cash in the short-term commercial paper markets and then invest the proceeds in much longer-dated securities such as bonds and mortgage debt. SIVs came to prominence during the sub-prime crisis as many of them invested heavily in large amounts of collaterised debt obligations (CDOs). These CDOs are packages of debt with various degrees of risk. Some CDOs invested heavily in the sub-prime mortgage debt. As a result of the default of some of these mortgages there are large numbers of CDOs that will be worth much less than they are currently perceived to be worth. The investment banks that own the CDOs were forced to write off a significant part of the value of these SIVs. (page 209)

Takeover This is the purchase of one company's ordinary shares by another company. In this process one company is seen to dominate the other. (page 165)

Tax relief on interest The tax treatment of long-term debt finance is very different from that of equity finance. The interest on long-term debt finance can be charged against pre-tax profits, which effectively means that the taxpayer subsidises the cost of debt finance. In contrast, dividends are merely an appropriation of after-tax profits. As a result, any interest paid is an allowable deduction from profits chargeable to tax. The existence of this tax relief on interest payments has the effect of subsidising any highly leveraged deal. (page 139)

Tender offer This is simply where the takeover bid is made through a public offer which is open to all shareholders allowing them to sell their shares at a price that is usually well above the current market price. (page 170)

10-year bunds See Bunds.

10-year Treasury notes See Benchmark 10-year Treasury note.

The Treasury This is the part of the government that is in charge of official spending and revenue decisions. In addition it plays a key role in the regulation of the financial services industry. The Treasury is overseen by the Chancellor of the Exchequer. (page 209)

Tick size In most financial markets if you ask a market maker for a price, he/she will quote both an ask price (buying price) and a bid price (selling price). The market maker makes a profit by setting the ask price above the bid price. This means that the market maker can sell the security for a higher price than he or she buys it for. We call the difference between the ask and bid price the spread. Suppose the ask price for a particular share is £14 and the bid price is £14.20 p then the 'bid–ask spread' is 20 p. This can also be called the 'tick' size. (page 129)

Tight credit spreads See SPREADS.

Tightening monetary policy See MONETARY POLICY.

Tranches This term is derived from the French word 'tranche', which means a slice. In this context a tranche simply refers to the individual parts of a new bond issue. You might also see the term 'tap' or 'mini-taplet' used. (page 77)

Transaction risk Type of currency risk that is associated with a particular financial commitment entered into by a company that will involve a currency transfer. For example, if a UK company borrows money in the US dollar and it is committed to make interest payments in dollars, thecompany is exposed to transaction risk. So that each $1000 interest payment will cost £500 at an exchange rate of £1 = $2. However, if the pound falls sharply in value so that £1 = $1, the $1000 interest payment will now cost £1000. (page 181)

Translation risk Type of currency risk that applies to multinational companies which see their consolidated financial accounts being affected by exchange rate movements. This might occur when a company has various overseas subsidiaries and exchange rate volatility impacts on its consolidated accounts when the subsidiaries' figures are combined into the group's overall financial results. (page 181)

Transparency This refers to the way that a central bank makes information available about the whole process of setting interest rates. At the end Article 6 there is a suggestion that the current policy of selecting internal (from within the Bank of England) and external (from outside the Bank of England) members of the MPC is non-transparent. This means that to any outsider the selection procedure and criteria are unclear. (pages 27, 43)

Treasury bills US Treasury issues with a maturity from three months to one year. (page 52)

Treasury bonds US Treasury issues with a maturity of 10 years plus. (pages 29, 52)

Treasury notes US Treasury issues with a maturity from 2–10 years. (pages 29, 52)

Unemployment and non-farm payroll employment release This economic release is made up of three parts. The first figure is the percentage rate of unemployment which is based on a random survey of people. The second part tells us the change in thousands each month in the number of people on companies' payrolls. It excludes various special categories such as the self-employed, unpaid family workers and the armed forces. The final measure looks at the current trends in employee wage costs. It can provide early evidence of any rising cost-push inflation. (page 51)

Unit trusts These are a very important form of collective investment. They allow private investors to get exposure to a range of different sectors including the standard equity funds, bond funds, money market funds and various property funds. The attraction of unit trusts is that they allow fairly small investors to spread their risk across a more diversified portfolio. (page 111)

Unsecured debt This is a much more risky form of debt instrument issued by companies. It will not be backed by specific assets owned by the business. This means that in the event of a default the holders are much less likely to receive their money back.

Upgrades Investment banks employ analysts who research the prospects for a company and then place a target value for their share price. When the prospects for a company improve, these analysts will raise their forecasts. This is called a profit upgrade. It might follow a new investment opportunity or a change in the company's business strategy. (page 116)

Valuation premium The correct valuation for the shares in a company is usually based on important factors like the company's future dividends or earning streams. It is normally the case that we place a higher or premium value on companies that are expected to achieve significantly higher growth rates than other companies in similar business sectors. (page 17)

Venture capital activity This is the form of finance that is normally provided to young start-up companies. The idea is to help them survive and then expand in their early years of trading. In return, the hope will be that they might provide an exceptionally high rate of return for the venture capital company. This is a classic form of high-risk but high-return investment. (page 144)

Warrant This is a derivative instrument that gives the holder the right to purchase financial market securities from the issuer at a set price within a certain time period. Warrants are commonly attached to certain new bond issues giving the holder the right to buy some shares in the issuing company. (pages 62, 170)

White knight This is where the company being chased will seek out an alternative, friendlier suitor that will form an alliance to act as a defence against the first bidder. (page 165)

Yankee bonds US dollar-denominated bonds issued by a foreign borrower in the American domestic market. (page 76)

Yield curves A yield curve is a graphic representation showing the structure of interest rates. It shows each bond yield plotted vertically with the maturity plotted horizontally. It is normal to refer to the shape of the yield curve as being either upward sloping as the level of yields increases in line with maturity. Or it might be downward sloping as the level of yields decreases in line with maturity. Or it might even be relatively flat with yields broadly similar across the maturity spectrum. (pages 27, 58)

Yields (and interest rates) When an individual or a company borrows money there is a cost that they have to pay in order to obtain the funds. If it is a short-term loan (up to one year) this is normally referred to as an interest rate. So we might take out a one-month bank loan with an annual interest rate of, say, 8.5 per cent. This is the interest rate, or the cost of obtaining the funds. If a company needs to borrow funds for a longer time period, this will normally be through the issue of a bond market security, which is usually repaid at a fixed rate of annual interest (this is called the coupon) until it is finally repaid on the date that it redeems or matures. The yield on the bond issue is the cost to the issuer or the return to investor who buys the bond. (pages 62, 82)

Zero-coupon bond This is a bond that does not have any interest payable but will instead be offered at a significant discount to the par value. This results in a large capital gain at redemption. (pages 62, 72)

Index